THE PRINTED WORD AND THE COMMON MAN

Popular Culture in Ulster 1700–1900

J. R. R. ADAMS

The Institute of Irish Studies
The Queen's University of Belfast

To Amber and Alexandra

Published by
The Institute of Irish Studies
The Queen's University of Belfast

© J. R. R. Adams, 1987
Published 1987

ISBN 0 85389 304 7

Printed by W. & G. Baird Ltd. at the Greystone Press, Antrim.

Acknowledgements

This book is based on my recent M.A. thesis presented to the Queen's University of Belfast, and I would like to thank my supervisor, Professor L. A. Clarkson, for his help and advice. Thanks are also due to the Trustees of the Ulster Folk and Transport Museum for their support.

The librarians and staffs of the following libraries were of great help to me, and I would like to record my gratitude: the Linen Hall Library, Belfast; Belfast Public Libraries; Dublin Public Libraries; the National Library of Ireland; Queen's University, Belfast; and the Southern Education and Library Board, Local Studies Department.

The frontispiece and plates I, II, IV, VI, VIII and IX are reproduced by permission of the Ulster Folk and Transport Museum. Plates III, V and VII are reproduced by permission of the Linen Hall Library.

Illustrations

Tables

Contents

Introduction

A recently published paper noted that 'literary and social historians are increasingly interested in the question of who was
reading what in past centuries, but sources for examining such
questions directly are notoriously inadequate or simply do not
exist.'[1] This book examines the reading habits of the ordinary
person in Ulster during two of those past centuries, and demon-
strates that for one part of the English-speaking world at least,
sources are not wanting. Why should one be interested in popular
reading habits? For the very simple reason that the texts read in
the past form some of the most important guides to past life and
thought. The printed matter which the common reader bought in
the eighteenth and nineteenth centuries reflects the preoccupations of the ordinary person of those times better than most
other surviving artifacts. A book is not just an object, capable of
being described bibliographically; it is the medium by which
people absorbed ideas and saw reflected their views and hopes.

Popular culture is a term that has spawned numerous definitions. Perhaps the best is that of Peter Burke, who has defined
'culture' as 'a system of shared meanings, attitudes, and values,
and the symbolic forms (performances, artifacts) in which they are
expressed or embodied' and 'popular culture' as 'the culture of the
non-elite';[2] the little tradition, in other words, as opposed to the
great tradition of those exposed to the latest developments in the
arts and sciences. It is a nonsense, however, to regard the two
cultures as being mutually exclusive. Both lived in the same world.

That world, however, was a changing one. In 1700, when the
present survey begins, the Williamite wars were only ten years in
the past, the very shape of the map of Ireland had only been
determined accurately a few decades before, and wolves were still
roaming in isolated parts. In 1900 the first motor cars were
puttering along the roads of Ulster, Einstein's theory of relativity

---

[1] Jan Fergus, 'Eighteenth-century readers in provincial England: the customers of
Samuel Clay's circulating library and bookshop in Warwick, 1770–72' in *Papers of the
Bibliographical Society of America*, xxviii (1984), p. 155.

[2] Peter Burke, *Popular culture in early modern Europe* (London, 1978), p. ix.

was only a few years away from publication, and the first world war was looming on the horizon. The period covered ranges from what has been called the era of 'traditional literacy',[3] when reading was valued more than any other literary skill by the masses and reading material consisted of a relatively small number of books which nevertheless circulated widely and sold steadily for long periods, to an era where widespread literacy was the rule and mass communications were becoming more and more all-pervasive.

This volume looks at the changes that occurred during those two hundred years in one part of the British Isles – the province of Ulster. The consequence of concentrating on one limited area over a long period is that a fairly exact picture can be drawn of real reading habits; studies at a national level tend either to be London-based or to iron out regional differences, picking examples from Birmingham, Glasgow, or Dublin to draw a picture that is not really representative of any one region and thus dimming our perceptions of the processes by which popular literature interacted with the population within which it circulated.

But no part of the English-speaking world is isolated from a wider context, and Ulster, especially in the eighteenth century, provides a particularly interesting example. The popular literature shows ties to England, to Scotland and to the rest of Ireland. Especially significant are the links across the Atlantic to America, where so many Ulster emigrants had gone in search of a better life. The culture of eighteenth-century Ulster possessed many similarities to that of the fledgling United States, and the chapmen of the north of Ireland carried round much the same material as the 'hawkers and walkers' of America.[4] One little volume, in particular, provides in microcosm an outline of Scotch-Irish cultural connections. It is an edition of Alexander Peden's *The Lord's trumpet sounding an alarm against Scotland*, consisting of prophetical sermons. The imprint reads: 'Printed at Newry. Reprinted at Newburyport by Angier March for Alexander Walker, 1798'. Here we have a Scottish covenanter, whose life and prophecies were constantly read in Ulster, being reprinted in the United States from an edition printed in an Ulster town.

The present work traces the history of elementary educational

[3] David Hall, 'The uses of literacy in New England, 1600–1850' in William L. Joyce and David D. Hall (ed.), *Printing and society in early America* (Worcester, 1983), p. 24.

[4] Richardson Wright, *Hawkers and walkers in early America* (New York, 1965), pp. 50–51.

institutions in Ulster from the era of the 'hedge school' to that of the national school, looking *en route* at both literacy and school-books. The latter are especially important in the nineteenth century, with first the little books produced by the Kildare Place Society and then the readers of the Commissioners of National Education becoming universally available in the countryside, the latter in particular paralleling the McGuffey readers of the United States[5] in both their all-pervasiveness and the extent to which they entered the popular consciousness.

Also traced are the various elements of the book trade, which formed the essential link between the producers and the con-sumers of popular literature, consumers becoming even more numerous with the spread of education. Printers, booksellers, newspapers, libraries are all examined, but for the eighteenth century one figure emerges as the most significant – the chapman. He it was who provided the most intimate link with the unsophisti-cated readers of the small towns and countryside, travelling from door to door and from market stall to market stall, selling many different items, which had only one thing in common: they were cheap. Books and other small printed items formed an essential part of the stock of these itinerant traders, sold to them wholesale by the shops of Belfast and the larger towns. One bookseller in particular is highlighted – James Magee of Belfast, who for a large part of the eighteenth century was one of the main suppliers of popular literature. He, alone of the booksellers, printed long advertisements aimed specifically at the chapmen, his customers, thus providing essential evidence about eighteenth-century read-ing habits, all the more valuable in that his judgments were based on purely commercial arguments.

As the early nineteenth century progressed, we find the chap-man becoming less and less important in the distribution of printed books as both communications and the nature of retail trade changed. New figures emerge as local producers of popular books, figures as important as Magee in the previous century – Joseph Smyth and the firm of Simms & M'Intyre, who like Magee before them became so involved in this part of the book trade that the books distributed by them form a valuable insight into popular taste. Finally we find the whole area, towards the end of the century, being swallowed up in the mass British market.

Throughout this long period genres of literature rise and fall in popularity, which is indeed what one might expect. But the printed word did not exist in isolation. The material sold by the

---

[5] Henry Ford, 'The McGuffey readers', in *Colophon*, new ser., i (1936), pp 587–603.

chapman or the village shop frequently bore some relationship to oral tradition; songs in particular come to mind as obvious examples. It is often no easy matter to decide whether a particular song has a genuine oral history or has at some point seen print, passing back again into oral channels. Even more complicated examples exist. The chapbook mummers' plays printed in the nineteenth century in Belfast bear many points of similarity to the popular book *The seven champions of Christendom*. This was first written in the late sixteenth century, based on older sources, printed and oral. Elements from it became incorporated in the mummers' plays, which were passed on within an oral tradition until at least one was printed in the very early nineteenth century. This and following editions would again have made a contribution to the oral record, and so the interaction between print and other methods of retaining text continued. Nowadays many, if not most of the mummers' plays performed are based on 'scholarly' texts collected from this later oral tradition, the text in this manner having yet again passed into printed form and out again to the people.

Popular printed matter at the lower end of the market (that is at the level of the 'chapbook' or small pamphlet) frequently derived from much longer printed texts as well. Chapbook versions exist of such popular novels as *Robinson Crusoe* and of longer traditional texts such as *Valentine and Orson*, reducing a full-length book to twelve or twenty-four pages. More surprising derivations, as well, exist. About 1850 the Glasgow firm of W. & R. Inglis produced a twenty-four page chapbook entitled *An account of the imprisonment and execution of poor Dennis an Irishman, who was hung for robbery, and afterwards restored to life by his friends, and is now living in America!!! With an account of a highwayman whom he employed to rob his master*. This turns out to be a reprint, with some cuts, of chapter 21 of John Gamble's *View of society and manners in the north of Ireland in the summer and autumn of 1812*, published in London in 1813, featuring a story set in County Antrim. At the level of this kind of text, the printer simply took what he wanted without acknowledgement, whether writing it for himself, copying from another chapbook exactly, taking it from oral sources, or abstracting it from another larger work. All was grist to his mill.

This book largely concerns itself with the printed matter read by the common reader in book form, though other forms of popular printed expression are not ignored. In order to arrive at an accurate assessment of the nature of this material, methods much wider than those of historical bibliography have been used. Thanks to the efforts of antiquarian bibliographers over the years, it is a fairly easy matter to scan virtually the entire surviving output of the Ulster presses, and pick out examples that one feels must have had popular appeal. This can, indeed, provide a few examples, but will only show a small part of the picture. For one thing, the number of books known only from unique copies shows how time and use have thinned the ranks, so that what we have today by no means represents the total number of titles produced, and, furthermore, the attrition rate has been heaviest, for obvious reasons, in the field of popular literature itself. In addition, the subjective judgments used to pick out popular literature can be severely flawed – the tendency will be, almost inevitably, to pick out quaint items, especially if they possess old-fashioned woodcuts. But the worst flaw in this method is the assumption that all local reading material was locally produced. Nothing could be further from the truth. Books were imported into Ulster from London, from Glasgow and from Dublin, and it was perfectly possible for a book to be in constant demand without a single edition being printed locally. C. A. Herrick, dealing with seventeenth-century America, noted the same thing as long ago as 1918. There historians assumed that the settlers in New England regaled themselves purely on sermons, theological works, and law books, because such were the surviving items from the local presses. But inventories told a different story.[6]

But inventories, and other similar sources such as library catalogues, are not of much help to the study of the readership of popular literature. By and large, they reveal reading habits at the level of the middle classes and above. Contemporary sources that shed light on the bottom end of the market are necessary. Such sources are used in this book. Different techniques have had to be used for different periods, as might be expected from the time span covered and the evolution of publishing and other aspects of the book trade. For the eighteenth century the main sources are the advertisements specifically aimed at his chapman customers by James Magee, and printed inside certain of the books he printed. Most of the books listed by him in these advertisements have no surviving local editions. This information is supplemented by other advertisements, newspaper sources, reminiscences, and so forth. The three surviving Magee catalogues, dated between 1750 and 1780, are reproduced as appendices II, III and IV. Appendix I consists of bibliographical details of some 167 books printed in Ulster between 1699 and 1800 which are either surviving editions

[6] C. A. Herrick, 'The early New Englanders: what did they read?' in *Library*, 3rd ser., ix (1918), pp 1–17.

of works mentioned in the text or certain advertisements for such works. They are arranged chronologically and numbered. A reference to this appendix will contain a list of these numbers; by their aid the books containing advertisements for a particular work can be identified, and the reader may, if he wishes, form a judgment as to the duration of that work's popularity.

For the nineteenth century, different criteria apply. Here the basic data is contained in the advertisements on the back paper covers of the little books produced during the first half of the century by the Belfast firms of Joseph Smyth and Simms & M'Intyre, supplemented by information from a wide variety of other sources. The validity of this methodology is shown by the clearly seen progression from the material discovered for the eighteenth century, where a classic pattern of innovation and survival can be perceived. In the second half of the nineteenth century the absorption of popular reading habits into the main- stream of Victorian publishing can be seen, and local production degenerated into the issuing of song sheets and the occasional humorous work.

A number of conclusions can be made. The first is central to this book. It is that popular reading habits, if accurately determined, can form a reliable mirror in which we can see the mind of past generations at work and play. The past may be a different country, but it *is* possible to travel there and meet, and understand, the natives.

As far as the specific subject matter of this work goes, one fact that clearly emerges is that at the level of extended text remark- ably little of the material is of Irish origin. This is by no means a drawback – if a work is current among the masses its importance rests on that fact, not the origin of the material; though that can be fascinating to trace, and in some cases can be traced back for millenia.

Finally, it is apparent that the culture was an amazingly shared one. With the exception of purely sectarian religious works, and one or two little books of popular history relating to the Williamite wars, it is impossible to assign material to a protestant or a catholic tradition. Political ballads exploiting some cause of the moment were different, of course, but even then, in the late eighteenth century the most famous radical songs were gathered together by a presbyterian clergyman. The folk play *The battle of Aughrim*, celebrating a protestant victory, was enjoyed on both sides of what is now called the sectarian divide. Henry Cooke, the presbyterian, remembered much the same material being avail- able as William Carleton, the catholic. The division between religious works and secular ones was similarly blurred, with such books as the *Confession of faith* containing advertisements for chivalric romances.

Popular literature was a very broad church indeed.

PLATE I
Insurrection in a hedge school
From William Carleton. *Traits and stories of the Irish peasantry* (4th. ed., Dublin, 1836), iv, p. 124

CHAPTER 1

Education and Literacy in the Eighteenth Century

The province of Ulster, by the beginning of the eighteenth century, was entering a period of political stability such as had not existed since the commencement of the plantation nearly a century before. The plantation itself, the events of 1641 and afterwards, and the Williamite war, together with the several floods of Scottish immigrants during that century, which gave a more and more Scottish flavour to the area, meant both political instability and a changing social climate; but by the early eighteenth century the violent political changes were past and Scottish immigration had largely ceased.

The population of Ulster at the beginning of the century numbered in the region of half a million,[1] of which about a third were presbyterians of Scottish descent. Of the remainder rather more than half were Roman Catholic and the rest episcopalian. However, although the presbyterian element was far from being in the majority, it had an influence out of all proportion to its size on the intellectual life of the province, at least that part of intellectual life which expressed itself through the medium of the printed word. In the fields of religion and poetry, especially, the influences predominating are respectively nonconformity and Scottish literature.

Scottish presbyterian culture had a traditional respect for education and reading, and one symptom of this was the constant efforts made by the ministers in the early eighteenth century to obtain reading matter. The lack of what they regarded as suitable reading material resulted, in 1715, in the following resolution of the General Assembly:

That they the ministers endeavour with the utmost industry to improve themselves in learning, particularly in the knowledge of the original lan-

---

[1] David Dickson, Cormac Ó Grada, and Stuart Daltrey, 'Hearth tax, household size, and Irish population change, 1672–1821' in *Proceedings of the Royal Irish Academy,* lxxxii, sect. C (1982), p. 155; R. J. Dickson, *Ulster emigration to colonial America, 1718–1775* (London, 1966), p. 3.

guages, of the most celebrated controversies in divinity, of ecclesiastical history, and that they carefully read the most valuable treatises, both ancient and modern; and, because generally we have but few books, it will be expedient for supplying that want that they keep a correspondence among 'emselves, and have frequent conferences on subjects of learning.[2]

At this time, as well, a system had grown up of mutual inspection of ministers' libraries. At the visitation of the congregation, two of the ministers present were appointed to inspect the books. Though many such references survive, for instance in the minutes of the Presbytery of Down,[3] no satisfactory picture of reading habits can be built up, as the ministers always used some kind of empty formula, such as 'a tolerable number of useful books'.

The presbyterian authorities themselves took a hand in the supply of literature of a religious nature. In 1715 a Mr Kirkpatrick made a complaint that though

he was desir'd by the interloq^r of the Gen: Synod to send to Holland for sixty copies of *Altare Damascenum*; that he procur'd them as cheap as possible; that he got a bill from a mercht. of Belfast; that the copies were in danger of being lost, he having noe accott. of 'em for a long time, was oblig'd to send express to Scotland to enquire for 'em; and he further says ye ministers neglecting to take the copies off his hand, he has not been able to pay off the same bill, but that it is still lying over his head bearing interest, and that ten or a dozen of 'em are yet unsold.[4]

The fact that presbyterians from the minister down were expected to be literate had an important bearing on education, but unfortunately very little can be discovered about popular education in the early part of the century. There were the academies, such as that kept by James McAlpine in Killyleagh between 1697 and 1714,[5] but these were not popular schools catering for mass education. It should not be forgotten that at this time presbyterian schools, like those of the catholics, were discouraged, leading the presbyterians to complain to Queen Anne

as a great grievance to us that education of our youth is extremely discouraged by our being deprived in many places of the liberty of entertaining common schoolmasters of our own persuasion . . . And even many of those who teach only to read and write in country parishes are prohibited and persecuted, to the great prejudice of children and discouragement of parents, who are conscientiously concerned for their education.[6]

[2] *Records of the general synod of Ulster* (3 vols, Belfast, 1890–98), i, 383.
[3] Minutes of the presbytery of Down (P.R.O.N.I., D1759. ID/16).
[4] *Records of the general synod of Ulster*, i, 371.
[5] John A. McIvor, *Popular education in the Irish presbyterian church* (Dublin, 1969), pp 26–8.
[6] Ibid., pp 31–2.

The session of the church was expected to keep an eye on the teacher where there was one, as in Aghadowey in 1706 when the local teacher, Samuel McCulloch, was ordered to remove himself out of Caheny for maintaining heretical doctrines. Session also helped occasionally with fees and books in deserving cases.[7] The presbyerian ideal was to have at least one school in each congregation, often taught by a person who hoped to go on to the ministry.[8]

The Church of Ireland had a general responsibility for secular education, and efforts were supposed to be made to ensure a school in every parish under the terms of the act 28 Henry VIII, c. 15,[9] though as the master was usually totally dependent on parental contributions the school collapsed if the local people did not have confidence in him. For this reason the schoolmaster was often the parish clerk or the curate.[10]

The Roman Catholics were in the worst straits, with the force of the law bearing on them socially and economically, most forcefully in the early part of the century. In 1731 the Church of Ireland bishop of Derry could write:

There are not any popish schools; sometimes a straggling schoolmaster sets up in some of ye mountainous parts of some parishes, but upon being threatened, as they constantly are, with a warrant, or a presentment by ye churchwardens, they generally think proper to withdraw.[11]

Worse still, the catholics were threatened by a system of proselytising education in the shape of the charter schools. These came into existence with the formation in 1733 of the Incorporated Society for Promoting English Protestant Schools in Ireland, which aimed to take poor catholic children and instruct them in English, Bible reading and protestantism, writing, and arithmetic, as well as instruction in such manual exercises as ditch-digging and spinning. Schools were dotted over the countryside, supported by private subscriptions and such other sources of funds as the licence fees paid by hawkers and pedlars, granted to the society in 1745.[12] However, the schools were never numerous, and most seem to have had only twenty or so children at a time. Reading material was provided, as well as the Bible, but all of a strictly

[7] Ibid., pp 52–3.
[8] Ibid., p. 43.
[9] *First report of the Commissioners on Education in Ireland*, H.C. 1825 (400), xii (hereafter cited as *First report of the commissioners*), p. 37; appendix, pp 13–15.
[10] Walter Alison Phillips, *History of the Church of Ireland* (Dublin, 1935), pp 233–4.
[11] Patrick J. Dowling, *The hedge schools of Ireland* (Dublin, 1935), pp 48–9.
[12] *First report of the commissioners*, p. 6.

improving kind, such as the 4,000 small tracts against popery which a Mr Rathbone of Dublin donated in 1734, the same year in which an anonymous lady of Dublin sent 'an 100 *New Testaments*, and an 100 of Mr C. Clutterbuck's *Plain vindication of the liturgy of the Church of England: by way of question and answer*'. In 1736 an unknown lady of London sent '90 *Bibles*, 90 *New Testaments*, and 90 *Whole duty's of man*'.[13] Indeed the Incorporated Society had a list of some twenty books lodged with the master of each school, and these were inevitably of the most edifying kind, such as *Worshipping the Host, prov'd to be idolatry* and *Short and plain directions for the spending one day well*.[14]

The charter schools were largely ineffective, and though the system lasted into the nineteenth century it did not create any significant amount of literacy, mainly because that was not the primary aim. Most catholics who did receive an elementary education got it at a hedge school, and some were taught by their parents, such as Patrick Cunningham of Lisburn.

I was born June 24, 1742, in the parish of Lisburn, in the county of Antrim. My father and mother were of the Roman Catholic persuasion, and were very strict observers of the rites of that church . . . My father had some taste for learning, and took great pains to give me instruction.[15]

Many if not most of the hedge schools were wretched enough affairs, but several men of eminence were educated at them. One was Henry Cooke (*c.*1788–1868), the 'presbyterian pope', who was educated at several schools in the Maghera area of County Londonderry. His first school was at Ballymacilcurr.

The house was a thatched cabin. The seats were black oak sticks from the neighbouring bog. A fire of peat blazed, or rather smoked, in the middle of the floor, and a hole in the roof served for a chimney. The teacher was a Mr Joseph Pollock, or Poak, as he was familiarly called – a tall Scotchman, distinguished by an enormous nose, a tow wig, a long coat of rusty black, leather tights, grey stockings, brogues, and a formidable hazel rod.[16]

Pollock seems to have been a typical hedge-schoolmaster. William Carleton, describing them as a class, mentioned two points which recommended them to the peasantry – an inordinate love of

[13] *Abstract of the proceedings of the Incorporated Society in Dublin, for Promoting English Protestant Schools in Ireland, from . . . 1733 to . . . 1737* (Dublin, 1737), p. 28.
[14] Ibid., pp 38–9.
[15] Patrick Cunningham, *Life of Patrick Cunningham* (Belfast, 1806), p. 3.
[16] J. L. Porter, *Life and times of Henry Cooke* (Belfast, 1875), p. 3.

whiskey and a slight touch of derangement.[17] That some had more than a touch of derangement is shown by the following advertisement from the *Belfast News-letter* of 1795.

MURDER!!!

Whereas on Thursday morning the 24th inst. William Donaldson, of Bally-harry, was *murdered* at Newtownards, with many circumstances of savage barbarity, by Pat. Beatty and Thomas M'Neight. Through the active and spirited exertions of the inhabitants of Newtownards, Beatty was taken but M'Neight has eluded their most diligent searches. M'Neight is about 30 years of age, about 5 feet 10 inches high, well made, has black woolly hair, and a wild unsettled look. He is nearly deprived of the use of the fingers and thumb of the right hand, which are shrivelled up and contracted from his having fallen into a furnace of boiling lye. He can, however, write tolerably with them and earned his livelihood by teaching school and as a day-labourer. He is a man of noted bad character, and has long been the pest and terror of this town and neighbourhood. . . .[18]

It says much for the parents' desire to see their children taught to read and write at least that they were willing to entrust them to the tender mercies of such a terrifying character. Carleton has tales of schoolmasters who, purely for amusement, would arrange the pupils in a circle with their bare legs pointing inwards, cut a large branch of thorn, and sweep this round and round until a circle of blood was visible on the ground.[19]

The income of the hedge-schoolmaster was small. Reliable evidence dates from the very early nineteenth century, but is applicable much earlier. In the parish of Dunaghy, County Antrim, the fees payable were 2s.6d. to 3s.4d. for reading, 4s. for writing and 5s. for arithmetic.[20] At the same time in Ballintoy the fees for reading and writing were 2s.8½d., and for arithmetic 5s.5d.[21] All these fees were payable quarterly. If the fees were small, the education was sometimes scanty. In Ballintoy, for instance, Rev. Robert Trail remarked that the 'education of almost the entire parish extends only to the acquirement of reading English, writing a miserable scrawl, with perhaps a little arithmetic'.[22] But by no means all hedge schools dispensed such poor education. Frank Glass, one of Henry Cooke's masters, had

[17] William Carleton, *Traits and stories of the Irish peasantry* (4th ed., 5 vols, Dublin, 1836), ii, 143.
[18] *Belfast News-letter*, 5 Oct. 1795.
[19] Carleton, op. cit., ii, 231–2.
[20] William Shaw Mason (ed.), *Statistical account, or parochial survey of Ireland* (3 vols, Dublin, 1814–19), i, 260.
[21] Ibid., i, 158.
[22] Ibid., i, 157.

an almost passionate love of classical literature, especially Horace, and while there Cooke learnt to appreciate not only that author but Virgil, Cicero, and Demosthenes.[23] A great number of hedge schools would have dispensed a perfectly adequate elementary education, though perhaps not as many as modern folklore suggests.

The physical condition of the school had little to do with the standard of the education dispensed. The building in which Frank Glass taught the glories of classical literature was described by Cooke:

We were compelled to remove five times in search of accommodation. We had flitted like fieldfares in the commencement of bad weather. The house we got at last had two window frames, but no glass. One was well secured against light by earthen sods; the other was open, for some light we must have, and it served to admit, in company with the light, a refreshing portion of rain and snow. We were furnished with one table, whereat our master sat for audience and judgment. Stones were the seats. I had myself the only stool in the house; but, the master being too tender to sit on a cold stone, I was robbed of the stool, 'to save him,' as he said, 'from the colic.'[24]

Many, perhaps most, of the schools existed in even worse conditions than this. In the parish of Maghera, County Londonderry, the school-houses in the early nineteenth century were

in general wretched huts, built of sods in the highway ditches, from which circumstance they are denominated hedge schools. They have neither door, window, nor chimney; a large hole in the roof serving to admit light, and let out the smoke, which issues from a fire in the middle of the house. A low narrow hole cut in the mud wall on the south side of the hut, affords ingress and egress to its inhabitants. These schools are fully attended in summer – half empty in spring and harvest, and from the cold and damp, utterly deserted in winter.[25]

The books used in these schools were of an extremely miscellaneous description. Cooke, in his evidence to the Commissioners on Education in Ireland in 1825, mentions only three school-books proper – Manson's *Primer* and *Spelling book* and Fenning's *Universal spelling book*, but gives a long list of other material:

I recollect one book being common in the schools, called the *Lilliputian Magazine*; another, the *Youth's instructor*, those were good books . . . I recollect reading a book, called the *Seven champions of Christendom and Destruction of Troy*; I

[23] Porter, op. cit., pp 5–6.
[24] Ibid., p. 4.
[25] Mason, op. cit., i, 598.

recollect reading *Hero and Leander, Gesta Romanorum,* and *Seven wise masters*; I recollect having read the *Chinese tales*; I recollect having read the romance called *Parismos and Parismenes,* and *Don Belianis of Greece*; another extravagant tale I recollect having read, the *History of Captain Freney,* a robber; I perfectly and distinctly recollect that. . . .*Valentine and Orson* . . . *Irish rogues and rapparees,* and a book, called the *History of Redmond O'Handlon*.[26]

Carleton gives a broadly similar list, adding the *Royal fairy tales,* the *Arabian nights entertainments, Dorastus and Fawnia,* the *History of Reynard the fox,* the *Chevalier Faublax,* the *Battle of Aughrim,* the *Siege of Londonderry* (this was Michelburne's *Ireland preserv'd*), the *History of the young Ascanius,* the *Forty thieves, Robin Hood's garland* and the *Garden of love and royal flower of fidelity,* 'along with others, the names of which shall not appear on these pages'.[27] As we shall see later, most of these titles were among the common reading material of the countryside at large.

Of course there were schools in the towns as well. Belfast had many urban versions of the hedge school – one writer commented in 1795 on the large number of day-schools, available to nearly all because of their low rates, which were found in nearly every street.[28] There were charity schools also, where deserving children were educated free of charge. Belfast had one such by 1770, supported by charity sermons and dances.[29] It was open to the children of poor labourers, weavers and bleachers who held cottages on the Earl of Donegall's estate. Twenty children were educated here in reading, writing and arithmetic, as well as the knowledge of the Christian religion, and were chosen by lot from the names put forward.[30] The reading material provided was spartan in the extreme: twelve Bibles, twelve prayer books, and twelve copies of the *Whole duty of man*[31] – remarkably like the fare provided in the charter schools.

During the last two decades of the eighteenth century a new type of school began to make its appearance – the Sunday school. One of the first in Ulster was in the parish of Kilmore, County Down, around 1780.[32] The Doagh Book Club started one in 1785,[33] there was one at Hillsborough in 1787,[34] and T. D. Lawrence

[26] *First report of the commissioners,* appendix, p. 820.
[27] Carleton, op. cit., ii, 235–6.
[28] *Belfast News-letter,* 27 Apr. 1795.
[29] Ibid., 30 Oct. 1770.
[30] Ibid., 10 Mar. 1775.
[31] Ibid., 28 Dec. 1775.
[32] William Cleland, *History of the Presbyterian Church in Ireland* (Toronto, 1890), p. 277.
[33] *Belfast Mercury,* 11 Nov. 1785.
[34] *Anthems &c as performed at Hillsborough Church* (Belfast, 1790), p. 7.

published a book of poems in aid of the Lawrencetown school in 1789.[35] The Sunday school at Derryloran, County Tyrone, where the children of poor parents were taught to spell and read, and carefully instructed in the Christian religion, was supported in 1795 by the proceeds of a ball.[36]

However, after an initial burst of enthusiasm, interest waned during the last decade of the century,[37] and when a member of the Cleland family tried to establish a Sunday school about 1790 in Bangor, he met, at least initially, with considerable discouragement and opposition.[38] At the same time it was noticed that the Belfast Sunday school was suffering a great decline.[39] It was not until the early years of the next century, with the formation of the Sunday School Society for Ireland, that Sunday schools began to play a significant part in mass education.

At this time as well, local reactionaries must have shared the worries expressed by Richard Twiss in 1775, when he observed some bare-legged boys near Dunleer learning to write: he thought it better that the lowest class of people should remain illiterate, as literacy would only excite desires that could not be satisfied, and therefore lead to unhappiness.[40] There were other, more serious reservations. If people could read, they could not only learn of new things to want in the material sense, they could imbibe new ideas; and in the late eighteenth century there were a number of new ideas in the air which the establishment would prefer to remain unknown. James Porter's Squire Firebrand certainly felt so.

O! how times are changed and all for the worse. Your catholic college – your catholic schools – your catholic emancipation – your Sunday schools – your charter schools – your book societies – your pamphlets, and your books, and your one h-ll or another are all turning the people's heads, and setting them a thinking about this, that and t'other.[41]

Squire Firebrand would have suffered apoplexy had he discovered how James Thomson, the father of Lord Kelvin, was taught to read. Thomson, who was born in 1786, was taught by his sisters, using for the purpose handkerchiefs on which were printed

---

[35] T. D. Lawrence, *Miscellaneous works . . . published for the benefit of the Sunday School at Laurence Town* (Dublin, 1789).

[36] *Belfast News-letter*, 17 Aug. 1790; 21 Dec. 1795.

[37] *Northern Star*, 10 Oct. 1792.

[38] *Northern Whig*, 19 Feb. 1846.

[39] *Belfast News-letter*, 8 Jan. 1790.

[40] Richard Twiss, *A tour in Ireland in 1775* (London, 1776), p. 74.

[41] *Northern Star*, 15 July 1796.

mottoes and verses composed by the United Irishmen.[42] This was certainly unusual, and most children would have been taught from the conventional textbooks available, though many, like the young Jemmy Hope (later a prominent United Irishman), would have been taught by such people as the farmers who hired them as servants.[43]

By the middle of the century the standard school-books in Ulster, as opposed to the more miscellaneous matter mentioned earlier, were those advertised in the catalogue of chapmen's books contained in Robert Russell's *Seven sermons* in 1750.[44] As they were specifically advertised as being for sale to the travelling chapmen, it follows that they were at that time the school-books for which there was the heaviest demand. Two were spelling books: Brown's *Spelling book* and Dyche's *Spelling book* (i.e. his *Spelling dictionary*). In view of the prominence of reading and spelling skills on the hedge school curriculum this is not surprising. There is one arithmetic, the famous *Arithmetic* of Edward Cocker, popular since the later seventeenth century. There is one other work advertised which fell into this category: John Hill's *The young secretary's guide*, which taught letter-writing and basic business documentation. This would have been intended for the more advanced pupils. Taken together, these four volumes satisfied all the requirements of the elementary schools at mid-century.

As the century wore on, the number of school-books increased. Of the spelling books such old favourites as Brown[45] and Dyche[46] continued to be distributed, but they were joined by others, such as Thomas Dilworth's *Spelling book* (i.e. *New guide to the English tongue*),[47] Fenning's *Universal spelling book*[48] – one of those recollected by Cooke as being used in the hedge schools of his youth – *The child's new play-thing*,[49] which was a spelling book intended to make learning to read a diversion instead of a task, and books by David Manson, the best-known educationalist in eighteenth-century Ulster: the *New primer*,[50] the *Spelling book*[51] and the *Pronouncing and*

[42] Elizabeth King, *Lord Kelvin's early home* (London, 1909), p. 1.
[43] W. T. Latimer, *Ulster biographies relating chiefly to the rebellion of 1798* (Belfast, 1897), pp 50–51.
[44] See appendix I. no. 34; appendix II.
[45] Ibid., nos 34, 105.
[46] Ibid., nos 34, 46, 61, 97, 98, 160.
[47] Ibid., nos 52, 53, 61, 86, 97, 98, 127, 160.
[48] Ibid., nos 97, 98, 160; also advertised in *Belfast News-letter*, 3 May 1765.
[49] Ibid., nos 52, 53, 61, 127.
[50] Ibid., nos 52, 53, 61, 127, 160.
[51] Ibid., nos 61, 74, 76, 97, 98, 100, 105, 107, 109, 132, 160.

spelling dictionary,[52] the first two of these being remembered by Cooke as being in general use in his childhood. Manson was born in the parish of Cairncastle, County Antrim, in 1726, and came to Belfast in 1752, not as a schoolteacher but as a brewer.[53] In fact, as late as 1782 he simultaneously advertised both his school and fine beer of his own manufacture.[54] It was not until 1755 that he opened his school, on principles that forbade the use of the rod and encouraged the gaining of knowledge by intermixing exercise with instruction. He rewarded merit with free rides on his 'flying chariot', and in addition earned an honest sixpence by charging the public that sum each time, provided that they observed decorum.[55] He published his *Spelling book* in 1760, and a decade later had introduced his 'literary cards' for teaching children to read, spell, and count. There were four packs, and any 'sensible person' could learn all the games of any one pack in an evening.[56] Manson spawned several imitators, such as Thomas Templeton, of Londonderry, who taught 'reading and spelling grammatically, without the use of the rod',[57] and James Conchy, of Ballymena, who was 'several years ago recommended by Mr Manson of Belfast', and who promoted emulation among his pupils, by 'rewarding and preferring those who behave well, and by disgracing those who are negligent'.[58] But his importance lies not so much in his educational methods as in the fact that his textbooks were almost universally used in Ulster for many years, and in various guises appeared well into the nineteenth century.

Other aids to literacy were Dr Lowth's *Short introduction to English grammar*;[59] Robert Dodsley's *Preceptor: or, lessons for reading, speaking, and writing letters*;[60] Watts' *Spelling book*;[61] the *Royal primer: or, an easy and pleasant guide to the art of reading*,[62] which, though it contained twenty-seven illustrations and was cheaply priced at 4*d.*, seems to have never been popular; George Fisher's *Instructor: or, young man's best companion*;[63] and John Hill's *The young secretary's*

[52] Ibid., nos 67, 89, 98, 11, 117, 160.
[53] J. J. Marshall, 'David Manson, schoolmaster in Belfast' in *Ulster Journal of Archaeology*, 2nd ser., xiv (1908), pp 59–72.
[54] *Belfast News-letter*, 12 Apr. 1782.
[55] Ibid., 19 Aug. 1760.
[56] Ibid., 2 Jan. 1770.
[57] Ibid., 2 Jan. 1770.
[58] Ibid., 13 Mar. 1770.
[59] See appendix I, nos 73, 120, 160.
[60] Ibid., nos 73, 160; also advertised in *Belfast News-letter*, 1760.
[61] Ibid., nos 52, 53, 61, 97, 98, 127, 160.
[62] Ibid., no. 46; also advertised in *Belfast News-letter*, 24 July 1752.
[63] Ibid., nos 46, 53, 97, 127.

guide,[64] available through the chapmen during most of the first
three-quarters of the century. Cooke, in his evidence to the
Commissioners on Education in Ireland, mentioned two books
that were popular as reading books in the hedge schools of his
youth – the *Lilliputian magazine* and the *Youth's instructor*. The
Lilliputian magazine[65] was one of the most popular children's books
of the eighteenth century. Subtitled *The young gentleman and lady's
golden library, being an attempt to mend the world*, it contained stories,
jests, riddles, and songs. It was first published in London about
1752, and in 1775 a Belfast edition appeared, omitting all illustrations, substituting a hymn for the original preface, and adding
hymns and prayers at the end.[66] The other volume mentioned by
Cooke as being common[67] was the *Youth's instructor*.[68] Local editions
of this were published in 1768, 1785, and 1794. It contained
stories, songs, accounts of foreign parts, fables, and prayers, and
was a fitting companion to the *Lilliputian magazine*.

In the field of arithmetic, though Cocker continued to be used,[69]
two books almost monopolised the market in the last half of the
century – George Fisher's *Arithmetic*[70] and John Gough's *Arithmetic*.[71] It is interesting to note that there was a strong local input into
mathematical textbooks towards the end of the century. Gough
was a schoolmaster from Lisburn, where he had moved in 1774,[72]
and Robert Telfair, who published locally a *Key to Gough*[73] and
revised three editions of the *Arithmetic*,[74] was a master in the Belfast
Academy.

An examination of the school textbooks contained in the lists of
works offered for sale to the travelling chapmen by the Belfast
bookseller James Magee in 1750, 1777, and 1780[75] is instructive.
The country schools supplied by these chapmen, or rather the
pupils supplied by them, did not form a market for anything but
the three Rs – there are no textbooks on foreign or classical
languages, none on geography, none on science, none on history.

---

[64] Ibid., nos 11, 15, 17, 20, 34, 65, 68, 86, 98.
[65] Ibid., nos 67, 74, 76, 95, 98, 107, 111, 116, 132, 160.
[66] J. E. Grey, 'The Lilliputian Magazine' in *Journal of Librarianship*, ii (1970), p. 108.
[67] *First report of the Commissioners*, appendix, p. 820.
[68] See appendix I, nos 52, 53, 56, 61, 127, 148, 160.
[69] Ibid., nos 50, 156; also advertised in *Belfast News-letter*, 15 Jan. 1760, 3 Jan. 1775.
[70] Ibid., nos 60, 67, 69, 74, 76, 79, 93, 97, 98, 105, 107, 109, 111, 114, 116, 132, 160.
[71] Ibid., nos 97, 98, 106, 107, 114, 132, 134, 143, 160, 161.
[72] *Dictionary of national biography* (66 vols, London, 1885–1900), xxii, 277.
[73] See appendix I, no. 147.
[74] Ibid., nos 134, 143, 161.
[75] Reproduced as appendices II, III and IV.

Evidently those schools that did teach the classics were too few and far between to attract the attention of the chapmen.

It is impossible to judge with any degree of accuracy the extent of literacy in eighteenth-century Ulster. It probably varied widely from area to area, with presbyterians the most likely to be literate in all areas. Such evidence as there is is highly fragmentary, and often anecdotal rather than objectively measured. For instance, there is the account of the experiences of Philip Skelton when he arrived to take up the living of Pettigo, County Fermanagh, in 1750. In this 'savage place, among mountains, rocks, and heath' the local population were a rough lot, addicted to fighting and illicit distillation. They 'seemed ignorant of the use of books, which they thought very few applied to but for some bad purpose'. When they saw Skelton working in his study they took him for a conjuror.[76] On the other hand Carleton, talking about the Clogher valley, County Tyrone, at the end of the century, says that of the local catholic families half could not read.[77]

Turning to a different kind of evidence, that provided by signatures to documents, we find that when in 1718 three hundred and nineteen prospective presbyterian emigrants from Macosquin, County Londonderry, sent a memorial to Governor Shute of Massachusetts, only thirteen signed with their marks.[78] Rather later, and from a rather different region, we find the eighty-nine inhabitants of the 'Town of Buncranagh, quarterlands of Ardaravin, Tollydush, Ballymacarry, Ballymagan, Monyworry, and Tullyarvill', in Inishowen, County Donegal, signing an advertisement expressing abhorrence at a recent outbreak of cattle-maiming on their landlords' properties.[79] Fifty-one signed with their marks.

The problem is that the ability to sign one's name cannot be taken as solid evidence pointing to any other ability. It was possible to read without being able to write, as reading was generally taught before writing in the hedge schools, and it was possible to write one's name without being able to read a connected narrative. All that can be said is that there were many hedge schools, which taught reading as the first literary skill, and that the evidence shows parents anxious to send their children to these schools. It follows that throughout the countryside there were numbers of people able to read a connected narrative, and, as

---

[76] Samuel Burdy, *Life of Philip Skelton* (Oxford, 1914), pp 60, 109, 111–12.

[77] William Carleton, *Life of William Carleton* (London, 1896), p. 77.

[78] John A. McIvor, *Popular education in the Irish presbyterian church* (Dublin, 1969), p. 32.

[79] *Londonderry journal*, 17 Aug. 1773.

will be demonstrated in later chapters, some of the material sold by the booksellers and chapmen clearly shows that there was a market for printed material that could not have appealed to any but an unsophisticated mind. It was this literate, but not learned, population, with a limited income, that formed the market. How was it supplied and with what?

PLATE II
James Magee, Belfast printer (1707–1797)
From F. J. Bigger. *The Magees of Belfast and Dublin, printers*
(Belfast, 1916), p. 7

CHAPTER 2

The Distribution of Printed Material
in the Eighteenth Century

The book trade that serviced the market for printed material
during this century was composed of three elements – the printers,
the booksellers, and the travelling chapmen. As the first stage in
the distribution of a book, after its composition by the author, is
the physical creation of the object to be marketed, the printers will
be dealt with first, though two points must be kept in mind. At this
period most, if not all, of the local printers were booksellers as well;
and seemingly most of the books sold were not locally printed at
all, to judge from the disparity between advertisements and the
number of surviving copies, but were imported from Glasgow,
London, and Dublin.

The first printing establishment in Ulster was begun in 1694,
when the sovereign of Belfast induced two printers, Patrick Neill
and James Blow, to settle in Belfast.[1] To set this in an Irish
context, Belfast was one of only four towns outside Dublin to
receive printing by the end of the seventeenth century; of the other
three, Waterford and Kilkenny produced nothing between the
initial short period of production, in the 1640s, and 1729 and 1759
respectively, and Cork only produced one, two, or three items
every five years between the 1640s and the 1690s.[2] Neill died about
1705, and left James Blow as the sole printer in the north, which
was galling to the orthodox presbyterians, as he sided with the
non-subscribers and published their works. They therefore
obtained Robert Gardner, who about 1713 became their printer,
and thus Belfast had at last two rival printing firms.[3] Various other
printers were active during the century in Belfast, but as far as the
supply of popular literature is concerned the most important was
James Magee, who was also a bookseller. In 1736 he was in

---

[1] George Benn, *History of the town of Belfast* (Belfast, 1877), p. 425.
[2] W. G. Wheeler, 'The spread of provincial printing in Ireland up to 1850' in *Irish Booklore*, iv (1978), pp 8–9.
[3] Benn, op. cit., pp 427–8, has 1720, but John Anderson, *Catalogue of early Belfast printed books* (Belfast, 1890), p. v., shows him working in 1713.

partnership with J. Potts and S. Wilson, and by 1744 was printing
on his own account in Bridge Street. He operated there until 1789,
when he went into partnership with William Magee. He retired in
1790, and died in 1797.[4]

In the first half of the century the printing trade was virtually
confined to Belfast, though a few items were printed at Armagh
and Londonderry before 1750.[5] By the end of the century about a
dozen towns had printing firms, but of these the only ones of any
importance were Newry, Londonderry, and Strabane. The earliest surviving book with a Newry title page is Thomas Stackhouse's
Life of our Lord and Saviour Jesus Christ (1761), which will be
examined below; and printing came a decade later to Strabane
with the commencement of the *Strabane Journal* in 1771.[6] But the
spread of printing did not happen as neatly as that, with a town
receiving in a particular year a printer who then worked indepen-
dently. The earliest Newry book is a case in point. *The life of our
Lord and Saviour Jesus Christ,* as befitted a large work being issued by
a printer just starting, was issued in fortnightly parts at 3*d.* each,
each of the seventeen numbers consisting of three sheets, making
twenty-four pages (number 17 has only fourteen). This resulted,
when bound, in a bulky quarto volume of 398 pages. There was a
list of subscribers totalling 230 names, some taking more than one
copy.

So far so good. But in 1763 another edition was published,
bearing the imprint 'Belfast: printed for William Stevenson, and
sold at his shop in London-Derry'. This would appear to show that
a Londonderry bookseller wished to sell a well known but large
book, and, feeling that it was too big a task for the local printers,
and being for some reason unable to import copies at an advantageous rate, decided to have it printed in Belfast. But a close
examination of the work shows that parts 7 to 17 are printed from
the same setting of type as the Newry 1761 edition, and parts 1 and
6 are printed from a different setting. How to account for this? The
most likely explanation is that by part 7 Carpenter had realised
that the Stackhouse volume had commercial possibilities outside
the Newry area, and increased the print run. There was another
bookseller in Newry at this time, George Stevenson, and if he was a
relative of William Stevenson in Londonderry, Carpenter could

[4] J. J. Marshall, 'Notes on old Belfast printers' in *Belfast Municipal Museum and Art
Gallery Quarterly Notes,* lii (1937), pp 15–18.

[5] E. R. McC. Dix, 'Ulster bibliography: Armagh' in *Ulster Journal of Archaeology,* 2nd
ser., vii (1901), p. 53; 'Ulster bibliography: Derry printing' in ibid., p. 133.

[6] A. A. Campbell, 'Early Strabane printing' (Linen Hall Library, Belfast, MSS 18,
19).

have persuaded him to get William to buy the extra copies. William Stevenson could then have got a Belfast printer to print parts 1 to 6 for him. This arrangement would provide a profit for everybody concerned. Daniel Carpenter would sell extra copies of parts 7 to 17; William Stevenson would buy these at a fairly cheap rate, since they were already set up in type by Carpenter for his own purposes, and thus no wages to compositors were involved for these extra copies; and the printer in Belfast would make a profit on the first six numbers. Even George Stevenson in Newry might have made something by the deal. If this was indeed what happened, it shows the complicated nature of the local printing trade, with small financial arrangements continually being made where the sale of a few extra copies of a 3*d.* number might mean success rather than insolvency. Something similar occurred in the next century, as will be seen.

Indeed, most of the printing done outside Belfast was on a fairly small scale, with the mainstay of the income coming not from printing books at all, but from printing newspapers, posters, forms of all kinds, and any kind of jobbing printing, together with selling books and other material not connected with the printed word. For instance, if we take a series of advertisements from George Stevenson of Newry between 1770 and 1774, we find him selling the following items, apart from books: Dr Norris's Medicine, lottery tickets, goose quills, paper, Dr James's Powders for Fevers, Maredant's Anti-Scorbutic Drops, Dr Anderson's Scotch Pills, liquorice, Mr James Inglish's medicines, maps, optical pillar machines for viewing prints, drawing books, music books, genuine Roman fiddle strings, violins, guitars, flutes, Barbary organs, pipe and tabors, guitar wires, the Carthusian Stomach Tincture, and similar goods.[7]

As stated above, most of the printers were also booksellers, and indeed at least one started as a bookseller – the same George Stevenson of Newry, who commenced printing in 1768 but was selling books as early as 1750.[8] The local history of the bookselling trade is rather more difficult to unravel than the printing trade, as it does not leave behind it a series of dated physical objects. What does emerge, from an examination of advertisements and the occasional illuminating imprint, is that the trade outside Belfast was divided into several layers, roughly comparable to the size of

---

[7] *Belfast News-letter*, 20 Feb., 10 Aug., 28 Sept. 1770; 21 May, 1 May 1771; 30 Apr. 1773; 8 Feb., 4 Mar. 1774.
[8] *Belfast News-letter*, 18 Sept. 1750; Philip Crossle, 'Newry printing' (typescript, Linen Hall Library, Belfast).

the particular town where the bookshop was. Bookshops proper, on the Belfast model, with a proprietor who styled himself 'bookseller' and a reasonable stock of books, though selling much different material, were largely confined to the larger towns such as Newry, Armagh, and Londonderry. The next layer consisted of those who styled themselves 'merchant' and regularly sold books, but whose stock in trade consisted overwhelmingly of other merchandise. These existed in such towns as Omagh and Enniskillen. Next came the village shops that sold a few cheap items of a popular nature and schoolbooks, many of them probably second-hand. Lastly there came the travelling chapmen and the ballad singers. All these different facets of the retail trade interacted with each other.

At least one writer stated that there were more booksellers in the north of the country than in the south. The anonymous author of *Letters between Henry and Francis*, published about 1774, noted: 'indeed they read more in the north than in the south. I have met with twenty booksellers' shops on this circuit, and there is not one from Dublin to Cork.'[9] To judge from contemporary advertisements, this was true to the extent that virtually every town had at least one shop that sold books on occasion. This is also brought out on examination of lists of subscribers. When a new work of any size was published locally, it was common for the person who was financing it to solicit subscriptions in advance, and those actually paying or promising to pay would have the privilege of seeing their names printed in the book. A number of subscribers' lists are available, but a very good one is in Thomas Stackhouse's three-volume *History of the New Testament,* printed and published by Henry and Robert Joy in 1750.

Outside Belfast, Newry is represented by two booksellers – Francis Boyd who took twenty-four sets and George Stevenson who took six. Armagh is represented by William Dickie, who took twelve sets. Londonderry is surprisingly absent, although a James Dawson, bookseller, was there in 1712,[10] and a John Louis, bookseller, in 1743.[11] Strabane has Thomas Young, bookseller, with seven sets, but he finds himself heavily outgunned by John Dening, merchant, with fifty sets. An almost exactly similar case exists in Coleraine, with Joseph Malcom, bookseller, taking six sets and James Adams, merchant, taking thirty. In Magherafelt

---

[9] Benn, op. cit., pp 440–41.

[10] Robert Craghead, *Walking with God explained* (Belfast, 1712), imprint.

[11] J. B. Bossuet, *An introduction concerning universal history* (Belfast, 1743), subscribers' list.

John Tomb, merchant, takes six sets; in Ballymena Richard Lendrick, merchant, takes eight sets; in Ballymoney Quanten Dick, merchant, takes three sets; in Newtownards Thomas Fisher, merchant, takes two sets; and in Limavady Hugh Shererd, merchant, takes fifteen sets. A number of 'gentlemen' take multiple copies, probably for distribution to the deserving or as school prizes, but perhaps to retail.

The above shows a fairly vigorous trade by mid-century, with most towns having at least one bookseller; but the significant examples of Strabane and Coleraine show that the bookseller's was by no means the most prosperous shop in the town, being liable to be overshadowed by a large local shopkeeper when a best-seller like Stackhouse came along, especially when the capital outlay was fairly large.

Soliciting subscriptions in advance was one way to get a book distributed round a network of small bookshops, but most books were not published in this way. It was quite common in the eighteenth century, when advertising a book in the Belfast press, to name a number of local bookshops where the book might be had. These lists were sometimes quite large. For instance, when James Magee and Robert Smith published *Letters of importance* by 'Pistophilos Philecclesia' in 1775, they advertised that it was sold by the following people: the booksellers in Belfast; R. Stevenson and D. Carpenter, Newry; Mrs Stevenson and James Blyth, Londonderry; Mrs Mitchell, Coleraine; Alexander Mitchell and William Crab, Ballymena; James Henderson, Hillsborough; John Martin, Dromore; Richard Haliday, Ballynahinch; and James Purce, Newtownards.[12]

Sometimes the local bookshops took part in the collection of advance subscriptions. When H. & R. Joy of Belfast were preparing to publish David Fordyce's *Dialogues concerning education* in 1752, they advertised a long list of shops that accepted subscriptions: Mrs Holmes, Antrim; Mr Lendrick, Ballymena; Mr Dick, Ballymoney; Mr Adams and Mr Malcom in Coleraine; Mr Shererd in Limavady; Mr Coulter in Londonderry; Mr Dening in Strabane; Mr Dickie in Armagh; Mr William Wilson in Lurgan; Mr Stevenson and Mr Boyd in Newry; Mr McGarry in Downpatrick; and Mr Wilson in Carrickfergus.[13] This list is very similar to the list of shops that subscribed to the same firm's edition of Stackhouse's *History of the New Testament*, two years previously.

When printers and booksellers outside Belfast issued a book,

[12] *Belfast News-letter*, 10 Mar. 1775.
[13] Ibid., 2 Oct. 1752.

they frequently specified sources from which it could be obtained. The following list is from J. M.'s *A mysterious doctrine unriddled,* printed by Daniel Carpenter and J. Gordon in Newry in 1775.[14] This book, which retailed at 6½d., could be bought from the two Newry people who were responsible for it; three Dublin booksellers; Hugh Gwyn, Castlewellan; Mrs McClinchy, Downpatrick; Robert Smith and Daniel Blow, Belfast; Mrs Mitchel, bookseller, Coleraine; Mrs Stevenson, bookseller, Londonderry; Andrew Gamble, merchant, Strabane; James Campbell, merchant, Omagh; John Burgess, merchant, Monaghan; James Reilly, bookseller, Armagh; James Fleming, Lurgan; William Gordon, Rathfriland; and John Fleming, bookseller, Drogheda. This list is not only interesting as showing the commercial contacts made by a small local issuer of books; it also shows that such contacts were not cast-iron long-term contacts. The Belfast booksellers mentioned by Carpenter and Gordon were Robert Smith and Daniel Blow, whereas, as we have seen, in the same year Carpenter was one of the two Newry booksellers listed by James Magee as selling his *Letters of importance.* However, some quite close alliances seem to have been entered into. Around 1782 James Magee's advertisements frequently mention the name of Margaret Hart, bookseller, Downpatrick, for no apparent reason.[15] The books concerned were not even of special Downpatrick interest – they included the *Annual register, The triumph of prudence over passion,* and *The adventures of a rupee.*

The naming of sources from which the book could be purchased often extended right down to very local publications indeed. When the *Ploughman's thoughts* was published in Strabane in 1787, it could be had from the following: John Alexander, John Bellew and James Anderson, Strabane; Moses Baird, Castlefin; Stephen McCreery, Killygordon; John Fraime, Raphoe; George Shiel, Convoy; James Moore, Letterkenny; William Hall, Ramelton; and Thomas McCobb, Manorcunningham.[16] In other words, the distribution of this book was expected to cover east Donegal. In the case of political literature, the same measures were sometimes taken to ensure distribution, but as in the case of the *List of the poll for the county of Antrim* (1790) the names were often not those of shopkeepers at all, but those of private individuals. The advertisement for this lists fifteen gentlemen in the county from whom the volume could be purchased.[17]

[14] J. M., *A mysterious doctrine unriddled* (Newry, 1775), p. 2.
[15] *Belfast News-letter,* 9 Apr., 21 May 1782.
[16] *Strabane Journal,* 23 Apr. 1787.
[17] *Belfast News-letter,* 2 July 1790.

To judge from the evidence of Henry Cooke, the shops that sold books in the smaller towns and villages were frequently grocers,[18] but in the larger towns the emphasis of the non-book stock was on patent medicines and music-related material. The examples of Stevenson of Newry has already been mentioned in connection with his printing interests, but he was only one of several. James Reilly of Armagh, in addition to the books in his stock in 1775, had such items as views, maps, music, harpsichord wires, guitar strings, Dr Earl's British Oil, Furlington's Balsam of Life, marking liquid for brown linen, leather and japanned ink pots, Keyser's Pills and so forth,[19] and in the same town in 1795 Mr Chichester owned a 'wholesale and retail cheap hardware, book, paper, stationery, buck, doe, lamb, and shamoy skin warehouse' which, apart from these items, sold muslins and ribbons to pedlars.[20]

The country booksellers were supplied from Belfast, or occasionally from another centre such as Newry, as we have seen, with a selection of new publications. But they also got their general stock of popular literature, schoolbooks, second-hand material, and what are now called remainders from the same source. In 1790 William Mitchell of Belfast was specifically aiming his advertisement at 'country booksellers' when he stated that he had recently purchased the stock of a Dublin bookseller, lately deceased, and could supply his customers at the lowest Dublin prices.[21] It is probable that, as well, the small country booksellers carried on a strictly local second-hand trade. But there was another very important element in the dissemination of printed literature through the Ulster countryside: the travelling chapman.

The chapman was essentially an itinerant small trader who travelled around the countryside, selling small, cheap articles from door to door or from a market stall. Chapman were by and large not specialised dealers. They carried round for sale such items as cloth, small items of clothing, combs, cheap books, and anything else that would bring in some profit.[22] William Carleton got the perusal of *Gil Blas* from a 'pedlar, who carried books about for sale, with a variety of other goods'.[23] Small books were an important part of the stock in trade of the chapman – Henry Cooke noted that in the country area where he grew up books were either obtained from grocers or from 'hawkers passing through the

[18] *First report of the Commissioners*, appendix, 820.
[19] *Belfast News-letter*, 12 Sept. 1775.
[20] Ibid., 2 Jan. 1795.
[21] Ibid., 21 Aug. 1790.
[22] Margaret Spufford, *The great reclothing of rural England* (London, 1984), pp 85–105.
[23] William Carleton, *The life of William Carleton* (2 vols, London, 1896), i, 125.

country generally',[24] and Andrew M'Kenzie, the poet, who was
born at Dunover, County Down, in 1780, laid out 'the small trifles
which he could command . . . in purchasing from travelling booksellers little tales and aught else which came up to his taste'.[25]
    Where did the chapmen get their stock? Basically from Belfast,
though probably any large shop would sell to a pedlar at wholesale
prices, especially if far removed from Belfast. For instance, the
imprint of a small song book printed at Monaghan about 1790
states that at the shop 'chapmen and dealers can be well assorted
with books, pamphlets, ballads, and coloured pictures, hardware,
&c. on moderate terms'.[26] But it was in Belfast that the trade was
concentrated. Local booksellers welcomed the trade of the chapman: in 1739 James Blow advertised that chapmen were 'kindly
used, and furnished with such books and stationery-ware as they
want, at reasonable rates',[27] and in 1750 James Magee, who for a
substantial part of the century was an important part of this trade,
had a special 'catalogue of chapmen's books sold by the printer
aforesaid'.[28]
    Advertisements specifically inviting chapmen to purchase are
legion in the Belfast press, mostly listing such items as fabrics,
stockings, handkerchiefs, knives, scissors, ribbons, pepper, and
what were called 'fountain pens',[29] but sometimes referring to
books. For instance, in 1739 we find John Potts (who we have
come across earlier in a brief partnership with the printer James
Magee) apparently deciding to give up the trade of bookseller
upon buying from John Brown, merchant, the stock of the late
Alexander Orr, woollen-draper. Designing to follow that trade, he
advertises a 'great variety of the most valuable books [and] . . .
will sell them to chapmen or others upon very easy terms'.[30]
    It is difficult to estimate the financial and social standing of the
chapmen with any accuracy, but neither was high, as a rule, This
was because it was the ambition of the chapman to own a proper
shop, and when enough finance was available he ceased to be a
chapman.[31] Because of the nature of the trade, the value of the
goods carried at any one time would not have been great. In 1750,

[24] *First report of the Commissioners*, appendix, p. 820.
[25] *Belfast Penny Journal*, i (1845), p. 353.
[26] *The manual exercise* (Monaghan, *c*.1790), p. 1.
[27] *Psalms* (Belfast, 1739), advertisement leaf.
[28] Robert Russell, *Seven sermons* (Belfast, 1750), advertisement leaf (reproduced as
appendix II).
[29] *Belfast News-letter*, 15 Aug. 1746.
[30] Ibid., 13 July 1739.
[31] Spufford, op. cit., pp 45–6.

for instance, a chapman came into Belfast to buy goods, and lost one light guinea and the greater part of his stock. He offered a crown reward to any person who returned it to James Magee or the printers of the *Belfast News-letter*.[32] It is likely that the stock that was lost consisted of books, as James Magee is specifically mentioned, though it may have contained some patent medicines as well. In any case the value cannot have been high, as the reward offered was only a crown. On the other hand it was worth while for the executors of the late Archibald McNeill, travelling chapman, to advertise the fact that any persons who were indebted to him should pay them within three months.[33] William Murdoch, chapman, of Belfast, had enough capital to get two evangelical pamphlets printed specially for him, with his name proudly in the imprints,[34] and between 1727 and 1730 four chapmen were admitted freemen of Belfast.[35]

Chapmen were, not unnaturally, regarded with some suspicion, given the itinerant nature of their calling, and when objects went missing the eye of authority fell on them. In 1754 a piece of fine linen was stolen from the bleach yard of David Lyons of Oldpark, near Belfast. Gentlemen in the linen trade, and others, were desired to keep a watchful eye on any person having fine cloth to sell 'and particularly on chapmen, as it's supposed it will be cut into small pieces, and put into their hands to sell'.[36] At the very bottom end of the market came such characters as William Scott, alias Tantra Barbus. Born near Ballynahinch about 1778, he became well known throughout the countryside for his eccentricity and his habit of making off with pewter from other people's dressers and brass knockers from their doors in order to exchange them for drink, in which he indulged to an alarming extent. He sold confectionery, pictures (i.e. cheap prints), toys, and hardware (not all honestly obtained) and varied this with begging, speech-crying (selling last dying speeches of criminals), and any other way of making money except hard work. He died in his sixtieth year in a 'fit of inebriety'. His life, with a suitable sub-Burnsian elegy, was printed in 1833, most suitably 'for the hawkers'.[37]

The chapmen were to be found manning stalls at every fair and

[32] *Belfast News-letter*, 19 Jan. 1750.

[33] Ibid., 24 July 1750.

[34] Walter Smith, *A directory: or, rules and directions for fellowship meetings* (Belfast, 1753); John Brown, *A vindication of fellowship meetings* (Belfast, 1753).

[35] R. M. Young (ed.), *Town book of the corporation of Belfast, 1613–1816* (Belfast, 1892), pp 290–92.

[36] *Belfast News-letter*, 23 Aug. 1754.

[37] *Life of William Scott, alias Tantra Barbus* (Belfast, 1833).

market, and there are numerous advertisements mentioning this fact, mostly in connection with the theft of goods from the said stalls. For instance, in 1750 Roger McKnight, chapman, advertised the theft of cambric from his stall at Lisburn market, and promised two guineas reward, payable by John Carson, merchant, at Lisburn, Joseph Malcolmson, merchant, at Lurgan or Samuel Jameyson, merchant, at Belfast.[38] In the same year the same thing happened to Peter McMullan, chapman, at Comber fair, and he offered five guineas reward, to be paid, interestingly enough, by the same two merchants in Lisburn and Lurgan and James Thomson in Belfast.[39] It would seem that there were certain traders who had a specially close relationship with chapmen, rather as James Magee had with those who carried books.

The printed material carried by the chapmen was of various types, neatly summarised in an advertisement placed by Thomas Stewart, bookseller of Newry, who sold 'all kinds of chapmen's books, with pamphlets, sheet-books and ballads'.[40] To take the 'chapmen's books' first, these were the sort of books listed in the 1750 James Magee catalogue (appendix II) and in his 1777 and 1780 catalogues (appendices III and IV). These were all full length-books, but printed on poor paper with crude illustrations if any at all. Printed matter cost in the region of 1d. a sheet – for instance, Samuel Chandler's *Short and plain catechism* was a duodecimo of twenty-four pages printed in Newry in 1767. This would have contained one sheet of paper, and was priced at 1d., including a blue paper wrapper.[41] Allowing a retail price of about 1d. a sheet, 6d. would have bought a duodecimo of 144 pages, and this is in fact about the size of most of the surviving examples. Daniel Blow, a rival printer to Magee, advertised a number of popular books in 1760.[42] These are mostly unpriced, but *Robinson Crusoe* is priced at 6½d., leading one to suppose to be a duodecimo of 144 pages in a cheap paper or sheepskin binding. The books themselves, as can be seen from the Magee catalogues, consist mainly of religious, traditional, and entertaining material.

The next category advertised by Stewart is 'pamphlets'. This included political pamphlets, such as those advertised in 1754 at prices ranging, in the main, from 2d. to 6½d.,[43] and topical

---

[38] *Belfast News-letter,* 14 Sept. 1750.
[39] Ibid., 12 Oct. 1750.
[40] Ibid., 18 Feb. 1755.
[41] Ibid., 1 Jan. 1768.
[42] Ibid., 14 Nov. 1760.
[43] Ibid., 17 Sept. 1754.

sermons. These were sometimes specially noted as being obtainable from the chapmen, as in the case of John Semple's *The survey impartially examined by sacred scripture and sound reason,* published in Belfast in 1754 by James Magee 'and sold by the booksellers, and by the hawkers'.[44]

Stewart then specifies 'sheet-books'. This signifies what are now known as chapbooks, that is small booklets consisting of a single sheet of paper folded to give sixteen or thirty-two pages, and selling at 1*d*. One specialised type of chapbook was the 'garland', which contained a number of songs instead of some sort of narrative. The term 'chapbook' is nowadays used somewhat loosely, to include any kind of popular printed material – for instance, Harry B. Weiss defines the term 'chapbook' as including

anything from a broadside to a good-sized book – anything printed – that was carried for sale by a chapman into villages, hamlets, towns. Although they varied in size, the small ones, as a rule, being intended for children, the majority were about 5½ by 3½ inches in size and contained from four to twenty-four pages, but there was really nothing fixed about their size or about the number of their pages. Selling for amounts ranging from a few farthings to a shilling, they were distributed by thousands.[45]

While there is some merit in this very broad definition, I feel that it is important to distinguish between the short one-sheet chapbooks and the dearer works containing some sort of extended narrative or argument. The distinctions seen by the Newry bookseller Stewart in the eighteenth century form a valid basis for definitions. His first two categories can be used as they are – 'chapmen's books' being larger works, containing more than one sheet of paper, usually in some sort of paper or sheep binding and usually priced at around 6*d*., and 'pamphlets' being political pamphlets or sermons. His category of 'sheet-books' can be rendered as 'chapbooks', and in fact most people when they visualise a chapbook think of a small booklet of one sheet of paper, issued folded, and priced at 1*d*. The term 'popular literature' or 'popular book' can be used to signify the whole field covered. These definitions not only clearly distinguish between various types of popular book, but are based on distinctions visualised in the eighteenth century.

The final category sold by Stewart is 'ballads', and this needs little explanation. These were single songs sold on a slip of paper, as distinct from 'garlands', containing a number of songs, which would have been included by Stewart in his category of 'sheet-

---

[44] Ibid., 11 June 1754.
[45] Harry B. Weiss, *A book about chapbooks* (Hatboro, 1969), p. 1.

books'. Ballads were by and large sold for a very small sum, such as a farthing or a halfpenny. Not a single locally printed ballad appears to survive from the eighteenth century, but a number of the chapbooks and garlands do, in the Linen Hall Library, Belfast, and in Harvard College Library.[46] Some forty-eight survive in these two libraries, nearly all printed in Belfast by James Magee in the 1760s. Insofar as they can be roughly classified twenty-four are garlands, ten have a religious theme, eight contain riddles, jokes, or humorous tales, three contain social satire and humorous remarks on courtship and marriage, two contain criminal biography, and one is a fortune book. Because the survivals are so rare, and contemporary references non-existent, the printed material to be discussed in the following chapters will largely fall into the category of 'chapmen's book', but it is important to remember that for every chapmen's book sold there were probably dozens of chapbooks and hundreds of ballads sold.

Only one description of the selling methods of any distributor of popular material in the eighteenth century survives, and that is a reminiscence set down in the middle of the nineteenth century. Aynsworth Pilson, describing life in late eighteenth-century Downpatrick, goes into some detail about the ballad singers.

Ballads were in much request, and were purchased and read by the younger people. They were printed by Daniel Carpenter, of Sugar Island, Newry, and were put into circulation by professional ballad singers, who traversed the street with thick folds of them over their left arm, whilst the right hand extended to the purchaser the literary condiments, receiving at the same time the half-penny, which was dropped into a capacious purse, placed in front of the performer. The proper tune appended to the ballad was sung by the professor, and thus the public were immediately in possession of the matter and the air at the same time. These ballads were sometimes of a plaintive character, but more frequently exhibited humour, wit and sarcasm.[47]

During the eighteenth century a new type of printed material arrived in Ulster – the newspaper. Newspapers had existed in Dublin since the late seventeenth century, but the first to be published in Ulster was the *Belfast News-letter*, begun in 1737 by Francis Joy.[48] At first merely a single folio sheet printed on both sides, it soon possessed four pages, a form that it would retain for

---

[46] W. C. Lane (ed.), *Catalogue of English and American chapbooks and broadside ballads in Harvard College Library* (Cambridge, Mass., 1905).
[47] A. Pilson, 'Miscellaneous essays chiefly relating to Downpatrick (middle and latter end of the eighteenth century)', transcribed by R. W. H. Blackwood (1937), pp 24–5; typescript in Linen Hall Library, Belfast.
[48] Benn, op. cit., p. 437.

over a century. It had a brief rival in the *Belfast Courant,* published for a short time in the middle 1740s,[49] but thereafter held the fort alone until the arrival in 1783 of the *Belfast Mercury,* the organ of the Volunteers, printed by John Tisdall, bookseller and printer.[50] The *Belfast Mercury* ceased in 1786, but was continued until about the end of 1787 as the *Belfast Evening Post.*[51] The only other eighteenth-century newspaper in Belfast was the *Northern Star,* the organ of the United Irishmen, which was founded in 1792 and ended its days in 1797 when the office was wrecked by a party of the Monaghan Militia. This act of politically motivated vandalism resulted in the whole nature of cheap publishing in the English-speaking world being revolutionised in the middle of the next century, for the remains were purchased by two journeymen, Messrs Doherty and Simms, who commenced a printing and bookselling business.[52] Simms later separated from Doherty and joined up with a Mr M'Intyre to form the firm of Simms & M'Intyre, whose career will be summarised in chapter 8.

During the second half of the century newspapers spread to the main centres of printing outside Belfast. *Carpenter's Newry Journal* was founded about 1761, *Jones's Newry Journal* about 1770, *Stevenson's Newry Journal* about 1774, and *Gordon's Newry Chronicle* in 1777.[53] From about 1788 on, however, the only survivor appears to have been *Gordon's Newry Chronicle,* which just saw the new century in. Strabane had two rival newspapers during the century: the *Strabane Journal,* which ran from 1771 until about 1801, and the *Strabane Newsletter,* which ran from about 1788 until about 1810. Londonderry, perhaps surprisingly, had only one, the *Londonderry Journal,* which began in 1772.[54]

Despite the apparently large number of newspapers, during the course of this century the newspaper press did not have a mass readership such as existed during the latter part of the nineteenth century. They were produced in very small numbers: if evidence from the next century can be taken as typical of this, sometimes only about a hundred copies were produced. Their price meant that only a fairly well-off person could regularly buy a newspaper – in 1750 the *Belfast News-letter* cost 4s.4d. a year if bought in Belfast,

---

[49] J. R. R. Adams, *Northern Ireland newspapers: checklist with locations* (Belfast, 1979), p. 7.
[50] Benn, op. cit., p. 441.
[51] Adams, op. cit., pp 8, 9.
[52] Benn, op cit., pp 442–3.
[53] Adams, op. cit., pp 20, 29.
[54] Ibid., pp 25, 35.

6s.7d. in Ballymoney and Coleraine.[55] In 1776 *Stevenson's Newry Journal* cost 13s. a year,[56] and by 1795 the *Belfast News-letter* cost 2½d. an issue. A rise in the cost of papers towards the end of the century was made inevitable by the stamp duties that were imposed. Although newspapers were first taxed in England in 1712, it was not until 1774 that the relevant duty became payable in Ireland. This commenced with a halfpenny stamp, increased to 1d. in 1785 and 2d. in 1798.[57] There was also advertisement duty, which commenced in Ireland at 2d. in 1774, and rose to one shilling in 1785.[58] Despite this, the *Belfast News-letter* claimed (admittedly in an advertisement for the sale of the paper) to print about 3,000 copies in 1795,[59] and the *Northern Star* claimed to sell about 4,000 copies in 1797.[60] There would thus appear to be a sharp division between the circulations of the Belfast papers and the provincial ones.

Of course, newspapers were read by more than one person. The *Belfast News-letter* reckoned that each copy was read by six persons;[61] and very early in the next century, at the time of the peninsular war, several people would club together to buy a newspaper or be given one by a well-off neighbour, and would then repair to a house where one of the party would read aloud to the others.[62] By this means, and by passing from hand to hand until it fell to pieces, a newspaper probably had a much larger readership than the *Belfast News-letter* stated, though it is probable that the editor only took gentlemen into account.

If poor people could not buy a newspaper on a regular basis, still less could they buy a book dearer than those the chapman sold. But a number of tradesmen did buy some relatively expensive books, as can be seen by examining a number of lists of subscribers. Three are extant from the first half of the century which show a large number of names covering a wide social spectrum. They are all Belfast-published: John Campbell's *Lives of the admirals* (1743), Robert Campbell's *Life of John, duke of Argyll* (1745), and Thomas Stackhouse's *History of the New Testament*

---

[55] *Belfast News-letter*, 22 May 1750.
[56] Ibid., 1 Oct. 1776.
[57] C. P. O'Neill, *Newspaper stamps of Ireland* (Enniskillen, 1978), pp 5, 19, 21.
[58] W. G. Wheeler, 'The spread of provincial printing in Ireland up to 1850' in *Irish Booklore*, iv (1978), p. 10.
[59] *Belfast News-letter*, 2 Jan. 1795.
[60] Benn, op. cit., p. 444.
[61] *Belfast News-letter*, 2 Jan. 1795.
[62] C. M'Alester, *Sketch of the life and literary labours of the late Robert Sullivan* (Belfast, 1870), pp 6–7.

(1750), the first two printed by Francis Joy and the last by H. & R. Joy, his sons. These volumes were relatively expensive, the *Lives of the admirals* costing 6s.6d. An analysis of the three subcribers' lists reveals the names of thirty-three tradesmen and craftsmen. In addition, of course, many small shopkeepers may have inflated their position to that of merchant – only one actually describes himself as a shopkeeper. There are three carpenters, one subscribing to two of the works. Three innkeepers are mentioned, and three watchmakers or clockmakers. There are two each of gaugers, bookbinders, bakers, tailors, cabinet-makers, and glaziers, and one each of a wide variety of trades such as cutler, turner, painter, shoemaker, gardener, stonecutter, coppersmith, and peruke-maker. Topographically there is a fairly wide spread, with roughly the same numbers coming from Belfast and the country towns, though none come from the countryside proper.

But these were relatively prosperous. People much further down the social scale collected books, after a fashion, other than the chapmen's wares. The folk poet Hugh Tynan of Donaghadee wrote a poem about a box 'where I usually kept my books' in 1796.

> Within this box my treasure lies,
> And with these books I feast mine eyes,
> Whilst I improve my mind:
> Within this little library
> Pleasures serene I clearly see,
> And joys unburthen'd find.
>
> Altho' their number be but small,
> (And yet it doth contain my all,
> And what I hold most dear)
> Yet I repine not at my lot,
> For worldly wealth I value not
> Nor want's stern aspect fear.[63]

Yet while Tynan was building up his 'little library', other libraries were being built up at the same time which were not the private preserve of some rich man but were open to a number of people, albeit at a price. There were two types towards the end of the century. The first was the commercial circulating library, the earliest in Ulster being probably that of Hugh Warren of Belfast, opened in the early 1770s.[64] By 1780 there was a catalogue, price 2d., of the more than one thousand volumes of history, novels,

---

[63] Hugh Tynan, *Poems* (Belfast, 1803), pp 1–2.
[64] *Northern Star*, 4 Jan. 1792, states that it was nearly twenty years established.

travels, voyages, lives, memoirs, and plays,[65] and in 1782 an appendix was published, also priced at 2*d*. There is no indication of the subscription, but the advertisement does state that single books could be read, if cash was paid at the time of borrowing,[66] so that it was possible for someone who was eager to read a particular book to do so at a cost much less than the cost of purchase. This may seem a small point, but prior to this there was no alternative to buying a copy or persuading a rich neighbour to lend it, if one could be found who possessed it. Though Warren does not state the subscription, an early rival does. This was John Hay, junior, who opened the Belfast Circulating Library in 1775.[67] His terms were 13*s*. a year, 4*s*.4*d*. a quarter, and 1*s*.7½*d*. a month. While it was out of the question for a working man to belong to such an institution permanently, it would have been possible for him to join for a month or so if he was eager to borrow a particular book or books.

By 1786 John Bellew had opened a circulating library at Strabane, and his prices were dearer – 16*s*.3*d*. a year, 5*s*.5*d*. a quarter – but there was a weekly rate of 6½*d*.,[68] which enabled a working man to get a sight of a book if he was determined to do so. Newry also had circulating libraries by 1777,[69] though the terms are unknown. There were doubtless more in other towns, such as Londonderry.

But another type of library was becoming prevalent towards the end of the century, one that sprang from the desire of the people to read and did not originate with the desire for commercial profit. This was the reading society. One of the first was the Doagh Book Club in County Antrim, formed in 1770 by William Galt, the local schoolmaster, with thirty members. By 1780 it was in a position to build a schoolhouse, which in addition housed the library. It had rather chequered fortunes, however, being wrecked by the yeomanry in 1798 and managing to recover thereafter.[70] Others in County Antrim were the Lowtown Book Club, formed in 1790, and the Roughfort Book Club, formed in 1796. These were merged into the Four Towns Book Club early in the next century.[71] The Belfast Reading Society was established in 1788, and this still

[65] *Belfast News-letter*, 4 Jan. 1780.
[66] Ibid., 26 Nov. 1782.
[67] Ibid., 12 Sept. 1775.
[68] *Strabane Journal*, 18 Dec. 1786.
[69] *Walker's Hibernian Magazine* (1777), p. 254.
[70] *Larne Literary and Agricultural Journal*, 1 Nov. 1838.
[71] *Uladh*, i, no. 2 (1905), pp 26–8.

survives in the form of the Linen Hall Library, the only remnant of the movement.[72]

In County Down the Newry Book Society was established in 1786,[73] and in 1797 there was another, the Newry Literary Society,[74] which, like its sister organisation in Doagh, was broken up by the military in 1798.[75] The Portaferry Literary Society was established in 1786,[76] and the Newtownards Society for Acquiring Knowledge about 1789.[77] According to one local historian, there was another reading society in Newtownards called the Shan Van Vocht Club, which was raided by the military in 1797.[78] The Ballynahinch Reading Club was founded in 1790, and by 1797 had gathered together a fair-sized library. One of their rules was 'that each member shall drink 3*d.* and no more, at their monthly meeting'.[79] This rule was doubtless suggested by bitter experience of the sort described in the poem 'The country book-club'.

> Thus, meeting to dispute, to fight, to plead,
> To smoke, to drink – do anything but read –
> The club – with stagg'ring steps, yet light of heart,
> Their taste for learning shewn, and *punch* – depart.[80]

The Banbridge Reading Society, founded in 1795, had similar alcoholic tastes, one of its chief glories during the eighteenth century being a punch jug, or jugs, inspiring the rather weak joke that its members dealt rather in quartos than in folios.[81] Other reading societies were at Dromore,[82] Downpatrick,[83] Purdysburn,[84] and Hillsborough, where the Marquis of Downshire, 'judging that reading would naturally produce information, and might have set the good people of Hillsborough to think', ordered the local book club to break up in 1796.[85]

---

[72] John Anderson, *History of . . . the Linen Hall Library* (Belfast, 1888).
[73] Drennan correspondence (P.R.O.N.I. D553/49–51).
[74] John Corry, *Odes and elegies* (Newry, 1797), p. 32.
[75] *Newry Magazine*, i (1815), p. 20.
[76] *Newtownards Chronicle*, 28 Nov. 1896, quoting *Belfast Commercial Chronicle*, 1818 (no longer extant).
[77] *Northern Whig*, 19 Feb. 1829.
[78] *Irish News*, 2 Oct. 1956.
[79] *Walker's Hibernian Magazine* (1797), p. 262.
[80] Charles Shillito, *The country book-club: a poem* (Dublin,1790), p. 32.
[81] Richard Linn, *History of Banbridge* (Banbridge, 1935), pp 6–7, 248.
[82] *Northern Star*, 11 Jan. 1796.
[83] Bookplate, Linen Hall Library, Belfast.
[84] Corry, op. cit., p. xi.
[85] *Northern Star*, 21 Nov. 1796.

It is notable that many of these societies were regarded with suspicion by the authorities, to the extent that several were broken up. It is true that many of them were inspired by the events occurring in America and France – many Ulster presbyterians had relatives who had taken the American side in the war of independence. But in the long run their importance is not so much in their political influence as in the fact that they made books available to a public that desperately wanted them. Some were beyond the reach of the lower orders – the Downpatrick Literary Society had an annual subscription of £1[86] – but others were being organised on a more democratic basis. Even the larger ones sometimes allowed free access to their shelves, as the Rathfriland Book Society did to the poet Hugh Porter in 1811.[87] The reading society movement involved the first faint stirrings of the feeling that books ought to be available to those who wanted to read them, an ideal that was still not fully realised in Ulster at the beginning of the twentieth century.

In the eighteenth century the main supplier of popular reading material was still the wandering chapman and ballad-singer. It is impossible now to judge the disposable income available to purchase his goods. Purchased they were, otherwise the trade could not have existed. Prices of printed matter varied from around a halfpenny to around 6*d*. This can be compared with the retail value of, say a stone of potatoes, gathered from market reports between 1773 and 1790. The lowest price recorded is 3*d*., and the highest 4½*d*.[88] Thus the price of cheap printed material compares very favourably with the price of a staple food, given the quantity of potatoes consumed at a sitting. Disposable income can really only be measured if accurate information about wages and prices is available, but its existence can be recognised if people are found indulging in luxuries. Thus Arthur Young noticed that many weavers around Waringstown had tea with the family breakfast in the late 1770s,[89] at a time when the price varied from 8*s*. to 11*s*.4½*d*. a pound.[90] Similarly Young noted that the little farmers on the Ards peninsula generally had meat once a week in summer, and salted in winter,[91] at a time when the price of beef varied from

[86] Down Literary Society, *Catalogue . . . with the laws* (Downpatrick, 1801), p. 1.

[87] Hugh Porter, *Poetical attempts* (Belfast, 1813), pp 154–63.

[88] *Londonderry Journal*, 11 June 1773; *Strabane Journal*, 12 Feb. 1787; *Belfast News-letter*, 28 Sept. 1790, 23 Nov. 1790.

[89] Arthur Young, *A tour in Ireland* (2nd. ed., 2 vols, London, 1780), i, 149.

[90] John Stevenson, *Two centuries of life in Down* (Belfast, 1920), p. 442; *Down Recorder*, 4 Feb. 1860.

[91] Young, op. cit., 156.

2*d*. to 3½*d*. a pound,[92] and mutton was somewhat similarly priced. Even the very poor sometimes had disposable incomes – Young found that in Lurgan, 'when provisions are very cheap, the poor spend much of their time in whiskey-houses. All the drapers wish that oatmeal was never under 1*d*. a pound.'[93] Given that the sort of spirit sold to these people would not have been very expensive, nevertheless, especially in times of cheap food, money was available. Moreover, the assumption should not be made that all books and other material passed from hand to hand at the original price – as it got older and more tattered, a book originally costing 6*d*., or even more, could end up selling for 1*d*. or less.

As we have seen, there were many links between the common reader and printed matter. But one of these links was preeminent during the course of the eighteenth century – the itinerant trader or chapman. Whether going from door to door, or from market to market, the chapman was the channel between the producers and the consumers of low-priced goods. The literature handled by him was the common literature of the countryside, reflecting the preoccupations of the population at large. Book distribution in the next century will be described in chapter 7; but for now it is time to examine the chapman's pack.

[92] *Strabane Journal*, 12 Feb. 1787; Young, op. cit., i, 149; *Londonderry Journal*, 11 June 1773; *Downpatrick Recorder*, 4 Feb. 1860; *Belfast News-letter*, 23 Nov. 1790.
[93] Young, op. cit., i, 142.

PLATE III
Orson and the Green Knight
From *The History of Valentine and Orson* (Belfast, 1783), p. 41

CHAPTER 3

Religious and Traditional Secular Material in the Eighteenth Century

It will come as no surprise to find that religious material formed an important part of the chapman's pack, as can be seen from the advertisements aimed at the chapmen by Magee. Bibles, psalm-books, catechisms, and such material formed the basic items, of course, but the field was much larger than this, and towards the end of the century evolving as well. For most of the century, the popular 'steady sellers' were the devotional and meditative works by nonconformist divines, largely seventeenth-century and roughly two-thirds English and one-third Scottish. It was an age when people, especially dissenters, were accustomed to reading and pondering on such material, and while it would be extremely simplistic to talk of an age of 'simple piety' nevertheless religion permeated a great deal of the social fabric.

Such material was not controversial – it encouraged faith and provided a focus for religious thought. Other, more controversial, material did emanate from the local presses – sermons and similar material attacking different points of view, for instance. This material, though being issued constantly, and occasionally in such quantities as to amount to a pamphlet war, never became cottage classics. It is doubtful whether they were much purchased by the common people at all – they seem to survive in greater numbers, bound in pamphlet volumes by their middle-class purchasers, than the nonconformist steady sellers, doomed to be read to bits, the true fate of the popular book.

But the common reader in eighteenth-century Ulster, and indeed throughout the English-speaking world, had a taste for material mostly much older than that produced by late seventeenth-century divines. This ranged from classical material such as Aesop's *Fables* to works produced in the seventeenth century, but the favourites were undoubtedly the chivalric and neo-chivalric romances dating from the medieval to Elizabethan periods. These gripped the popular imagination until well into the nineteenth century, having already been popular, with unsophisticated readers at least, from the middle of the seventeenth. Their function was escapism – they were the science fiction or fantasy of the period. With their aid the common reader could travel to magic cities, joust with strange knights, court veiled ladies, and vanquish monsters. The attractions of another place and another time, away from present worries, have always had an appeal for mankind; perhaps in a way devotional literature performed the same function. One particular book certainly belonged to both camps – John Bunyan's *Pilgrim's progress*. The *Pilgrim's progress* was advertised throughout the eighteenth century,[1] and of course remained popular long afterwards. It was closely followed by the same author's *Sighs from hell*,[2] though in the latter part of the century this, in common with other works by Bunyan and his contemporaries, fell by the wayside. His *Solomon's temple spiritualised*, by way of contrast, though not occurring in the first half of the century at all, made a dramatic comeback in the second half. As this has to do with freemasonry it will be dealt with later.

Other English nonconformist authors popular were Joseph Alleine, whose *Alarm to unconverted sinners*[3] was continually popular but whose *Explanation of the Assembly's shorter catechism*[4] did not sell in the second half of the century; Thomas Doolittle, represented by *A treatise concerning the Lord's supper;*[5] William Dyer, represented by *Christ's famous titles;*[6] John Flavel, represented by *A saint indeed*[7] and *A token for mourners*;[8] Benjamin Keach, represented by *War with the devil*,[9] mainly confined to the first half of the century, and *The travels of True Godliness*,[10] widely advertised in the second half; Matthew Mead, represented by *The almost Christian discovered;*[11] Edward Pearse, represented by *The great concern*[12] and Thomas Vincent, represented by *An explication of the Assembly's shorter catechism*[13] and *Christ's certain and sudden appearance to judgment.*[14]

Three Scottish authors are especially popular in the first half of

[1] See appendix I, nos 3, 4, 11, 15, 17, 20, 34, 68, 86, 105, 127, 155.
[2] Ibid., nos 4, 6, 15, 17, 20, 34, 105.
[3] Ibid., nos 11, 15, 17, 20, 34, 40, 99, 105, 107, 111, 117, 155.
[4] Ibid., nos 3, 4, 11, 15, 17, 20, 34.
[5] Ibid., nos 3, 4, 11, 15, 17, 20, 34, 40, 105, 111, 132, 155.
[6] Ibid., nos 3, 4, 11, 15, 17, 20, 34, 40, 68, 105, 111, 117, 155.
[7] Ibid., nos 4, 6, 11, 15, 17, 20, 26, 34, 37, 40, 43, 49, 67, 68, 74, 79, 105.
[8] Ibid., nos 11, 15, 17, 20, 105, 111, 117, 132, 155.
[9] Ibid., nos 4, 6, 11, 15, 17, 105, 127.
[10] Ibid., nos 37, 43, 49, 67, 69, 74, 107, 111, 132.
[11] Ibid., nos 6, 11, 17, 20, 34, 68, 105.
[12] Ibid., nos 4, 6, 11, 15, 17, 20, 34, 68, 105.
[13] Ibid., nos 11, 17, 34, 105.
[14] Ibid., nos 3, 4, 11, 15, 17, 20, 34, 105.

the century: Daniel Campbell, represented by *Sacramental meditations*;[15] William Guthrie, represented by *The Christian's great interest*,[16] which 'gained a circulation almost unparalleled among that class of people for whom it was perhaps chiefly intended, the intelligent Scottish peasantry'[17] and Henry Scougall, represented by *The Life of God in the soul of man*,[18] a classic held in high esteem both by presbyterians and by episcopalians, which has even gained a minor place in the history of printing, as a stereotype edition was printed by William Ged in Newcastle in 1742,[19] a proceeding that led to unrest among compositors, who managed to delay progress on this technical front until the next century.[20]

There was very little local input, excluding sermons and controversial works, which, though they were constantly being printed and disseminated through the countryside, did not assume any lasting individual importance. Robert Craghead, a local presbyterian minister, did produce two books which were advertised over a period of twenty years or more: *Advice for assurance of salvation*[21] and *Advice to communicants*.[22]

One episcopalian writer who managed to get on a list of chapmen's books is Lewis Bayly, bishop of Bangor (d. 1631). His *Practise of piety*[23] was a very influential work, so popular with puritan readers that some tried to disprove his authorship on the grounds that it could not possibly have been written by a bishop.[24] It was a doctrinal work combining meditations and prayers, and contained notable examples of God's judgment against sinners. A series of fires at Tiverton, in Devon, served as one example, and so influential was the work that the inhabitants were moved to protest against being thus held up.[25]

Though the literature of the first half of the century surveyed here was an overwhelmingly nonconformist one, some of the books would not just have been read by presbyterians – the *Pilgrim's progress* for instance. Overtly episcopalian works, such as the classic *Whole duty of man*, never struck deep roots in Ulster, though

[15] Ibid., nos 3, 4, 10, 11, 15, 17, 20, 34, 40, 68, 105.

[16] Ibid., nos 2, 3, 11, 15, 17, 20, 34, 68, 105.

[17] Robert Chambers, *Biographical dictionary of famous Scotsmen* (Hildesheim, 1971), pp 184–6.

[18] See appendix I, nos 22, 23, 24, 29, 34, 74, 79, 105, 107, 111, 117, 155.

[19] *Dictionary of national biography*, li, 120–21.

[20] H. R. Plomer, *Short history of English printing* (London, 1915), pp 195–6.

[21] See appendix I, nos 9, 11, 17, 20.

[22] Ibid., nos 11, 15, 17, 20; *Belfast News-letter*, 3 Jan. 1775.

[23] Ibid., nos 15, 17, 34.

[24] *Dictionary of national biography*, iii, 448–9.

[25] L. B. Wright, *Middle-class culture in Elizabethan England* (Chapel Hill, 1935), p. 261.

it was occasionally advertised and at least one edition was printed.[26] It was used by the established church as an organ of proselytism – copies were given to various charity schools, as seen earlier. Oddly enough, it was advertised in the 1729 edition of the *Confession of faith*,[27] along with psalters (with the addition of morning and evening prayer), and Common Prayer books. The 1750 and 1780 catalogues of chapmen's books also list Common Prayer books. One nonconformist divine of the seventeenth century whose works were strangely neglected in Ulster was Richard Baxter. He wrote two classics, *The saints' everlasting rest* and *A call to the unconverted*, but the first was totally neglected, and the second had only a brief vogue, in the usual 6½d. popular format, in the 1740s and 1750s.[28]

In the second half of the century, many of the older authors still retained popularity, but with a noticeable slackening off towards the end of the century. A number of new popular religious authors appeared for the first time, and the three most prominent were all Scottish – Ebenezer and Ralph Erskine and John Willison. Ebenezer Erskine was the founder of the Scottish Secession Church in 1733, and was a singularly contumacious man. As early as 1736 applications for ministerial supply had been sent to the Secession Synod from Ulster, and the seceders played a large part in restoring to presbyterianism its evangelical character. The church split in 1747 into the burghers and anti-burghers, and though the split had little to do with Ireland it spread here. Ebenezer, with his brother Ralph, took the side of the burghers.[29] Ebenezer was responsible for a number of popular works, such as *A lamp ordained for God's anointed*,[30] *The plant of renown*,[31] *The rainbow of the covenant*,[32] and *The stone rejected by the builder*,[33] while his brother Ralph produced a number of others.

John Willison was the complete opposite. During the controversy that ended in Ebenezer Erskine setting up the Secession Synod Willison tried to prevent a schism, and was grieved when Erskine spurned his conciliatory gestures. He tried by concessions to bring the seceders back into the fold, but failed.[34] A number of

[26] See appendix I, nos 15, 17, 87, 127.
[27] Ibid., no. 15.
[28] Ibid., nos 21, 23, 26, 29, 34, 37, 40, 43, 49.
[29] *Dictionary of national biography*, xviii, 404–7.
[30] See appendix I, nos 34, 37, 43, 49, 107, 109, 114, 124, 132.
[31] Ibid., nos 29, 34, 37, 43, 49, 74, 97, 107, 109, 114, 124, 132.
[32] Ibid., nos 29, 34, 37, 43, 49, 74, 97, 107, 109, 114, 124, 132.
[33] Ibid., nos 37, 43, 49, 124.
[34] *Dictonary of national biography*, xvii, 404–7.

his best-known works are listed in the 1780 chapmen's catalogue and widely advertised elsewhere: *The afflicted man's companion*,[35] *Balm from Gilead*,[36] *A treatise concerning the sanctifying the Lord's day*,[37] and *Sacramental meditations and advices*,[38] as well as others equally popular.

Two other popular newcomers were John MacGowan's *The life of Joseph the son of Israel*,[39] intended for the perusal of youth, and Samuel Palmer's *Protestant dissenter's catechism*,[40] a supplement to the *Shorter catechism* giving grounds for dissent.

Roman Catholic readers were apparently not supplied from Belfast, but from one of the Dublin booksellers who specialised in the production of popular religious matter, such as Patrick Wogan.[41] Only one book of a catholic nature seems to have been printed in Belfast – *The virgin's nosegay*. Printed in 1744 by Francis Joy, this was not a work on Mary, but a manual of advice on the proper education of girls, dedicated to the niece of the Duke of Norfolk. Though it is found on catholic booksellers' lists, naturally enough,[42] it was not of such a nature as to offend protestants.

A number of small chapbooks were also on religious themes. As we have already seen, William Murdoch, chapman, of Belfast, had two religious pamphlets printed specially for him, but during the later eighteenth century many chapbooks proper were printed, mainly by James Magee. These have rather charming titles, such as *Some directions how to improve losses, crosses and afflictions*, printed by Magee in 1766, *The door of salvation opened: or, a loud and shrill voice from heaven to unregenerate sinners on earth*, printed by Magee without date, *The glorious bridegroom's appearance: or, the midnight cry. To alarm drowsie and secure sinners*, printed by Magee in 1765, and *The history of the travels, persecution and cruel martyrdom of our blessed Lord and Saviour Jesus Christ, likewise the holy life, travels, and martyrdom of the twelve apostles . . . with the life and cruel martyrdom of St Mark the evangelist, and St John Baptist, the fore-runner of Christ . . . very fit for all Christian families*, printed in Belfast in 1765 by an unknown printer, probably Magee. The miracle of condensation achieved by this little work will be realised when it is revealed that it is only eight pages long.

---

[35] See appendix I, nos 29, 34, 37, 40, 43, 49, 67, 69, 74, 79, 97, 105, 107, 132, 155.
[36] Ibid., nos 105, 110, 111, 155.
[37] Ibid., nos 40, 105, 155.
[38] Ibid., nos 97, 105, 111, 132, 155.
[39] Ibid., nos 97, 98, 105, 107, 111, 128, 132, 155.
[40] Ibid., nos 91, 105, 107, 111, 117.
[41] Thomas Wall, *The sign of Doctor Hay's head* (Dublin, 1958), pp 71–90.
[42] Ibid., p. 87.

This is like the equal miracle of condensation achieved earlier by *The Bible the best New Year's gift*,[43] printed in Belfast in 1699 and advertised until 1714. This was a version of John Taylor's *Verbum sempiternum*, first published in 1614. The Book of Zephaniah, which in the original consists of three chapters, is rendered thus:

> He fills the good with hope, the bad with fear,
> And tells the *Jews* their thraldom draweth near.[44]

Of course most homes, especially presbyterian ones, had a full-sized Bible.

The little works described above were issued by the printer with exactly the same aims as he issued any other chapbook or other publication – to make money. If the populace did not buy such material, Magee, or any other printer, would simply not have bothered to print it. But by the end of the century a new sort of small religious work was being distributed: the religious tracts, differing from the above in that they were aimed at the poor and others by their betters in order to improve them, and largely distributed free or at a very low price by the said betters. By the middle of the century some tracts were already being issued, and Peter Wilson, a Dublin bookseller, included in his 1760 catalogue a 'collection of small tracts and pieces, proper to be distributed, by such charitable persons, as, having at heart the eternal welfare of their poor and uninstructed neighbours and servants, are disposed to give them away'.[45] Prices varied from 12s. a dozen to 10d. a dozen, and the list included, as well as anti-catholic material and established church works, the *Assembly's ABC, or shorter catechism*.

However, it was not until the 1790s that the tract idea really took root. In Ireland the prime mover was the Association for Discountenancing Vice and Promoting the Knowledge and Practice of the Christian Religion. This body was involved in educational matters in the early nineteenth century, but from its foundation in 1792 until the early 1800s concentrated on the distribution of cheap religious literature and tracts.[46] The association's report for 1795–6, attached to a sermon preached before its members, is very illuminating on the subject of tracts.

The pernicious tendency of most of the cheap publications, commonly entitled story books and ballads, which formerly constituted almost the whole

[43] See appendix I, nos 1, 3, 4, 11.
[44] *The Bible the best New Year's gift* (Belfast, 1699), p. 49.
[45] Peter Wilson, *Catalogue of books with their prices* (Dublin, 1760), pp 15–16.
[46] *First report of the Commissioners*, pp 30–31.

of the literary entertainment of the lower classes, suggested to a most worthy and respectable member of the association the idea of an attempt to destroy this source of corruption, and to substitute in its place such small tracts as might at once amuse and entertain the lower class of readers, and at the same time insensibly instil into their hitherto untutored minds moral instruction, by representing, under the garb of fable, the happy effects which naturally flow from the observation of the laws of Christian morality, and the destructive consequences of their violation.

This idea was zealously adopted by the association, and directed to be carried into immediate operation by a monthly publication of one or more tracts, of which twenty-four have already been published. Five thousand of each tract is printed, which, including a second impression of several of them, amounts to 150,000 tracts, of which number 120,000 have been actually dispersed and received by the readers for whom they are calculated with uncommon avidity.

. . . The advantages of this measure, by disposing the lower classes of society to honesty, sobriety, industry, cleanliness and submission to the laws, instead of the contrary vices to which they were accustomed to be stimulated by their former course of reading, are truly incalculable.

One of the principal obstructions which has hitherto occurred to the progress of the measure, has been the difficulty of procuring agents for the dispersion of the tracts, through the kingdom. This difficulty can no way be so easily removed, as by the co-operation of the gentry and clergy, by supplying shopkeepers, hawkers, and pedlars, in their respective vicinities, with an assortment of these tracts for sale . . .[47]

The report goes on to notice the work carried on in England by Mrs Hannah More, whose Cheap Repository Tracts were published between 1795 and 1798;[48] though it is careful not to give her too much credit, claiming that the idea was simultaneously arrived at in both England and Ireland. In fact the association's tracts were reprints of Mrs More's works, and William Watson, who was the printer to the association, was issuing them from 1795 onwards.[49]

Before leaving the subject of religious literature, it is as well to point out that the readers of even the rather more substantial and solemn of the works mentioned earlier were not inevitably exclusive readers of that material. John Flavel's *A token for mourners* and William Dyer's *Christ's famous titles* are both earnest religious works, published in Belfast in 1780 and 1782 respectively, yet they are also both bearers of advertisements for *Valentine and Orson* and

[47] William Magee, *A sermon preached before the Association for Discountenancing Vice* (Dublin, 1796), pp 71–2.
[48] G. H. Spinney, 'Cheap Repository Tracts. Hazard and Marshall editions' in *The Library*, 4th ser., xx (1940), p. 295.
[49] Ibid., p. 309

Richard Johnson's *Seven champions of Christendom*, and the latter, which contains a few slightly racy passages, was even advertised in the *Confession of faith*, printed in Belfast in 1729. On the other hand, the catalogue of chapmen's books found in the Belfast 1777 edition of Ovid's *Ars amandi: or, art of love* (reproduced in appendix III) lists only MacGowan's *Life of Joseph*, probably for its literary merits alone, and does not mention any of the other religious works at all. In effect there were those who would read only such material as the classic religious works, the Bible and such authors as the brothers Erskine, there were those who would read chapbooks, ballads, Ovid's *Art of love, Moll Flanders*, and that masterpiece of sexual misinformation 'Aristotle'[49a] without ever dreaming of lifting anything remotely religious, and there was a very wide band in the middle who read whatever came their way, whether it was Dyer or the *Seven champions of Christendom*.

This brings us to the secular material, and in particular to traditional material, by which is meant works of imagination popular for generations, sometimes for centuries, occasionally for millenia. Two of the works distributed originated in the classical period–Aesop's *Fables* and Ovid's *Art of love*. Aesop's *Fables*[50] need no introduction, having been popular in the English language ever since the first translation printed by Caxton in 1484.[51] If Aesop was perhaps mostly popular with children, the same could hardly be said of Ovid. The *Art of love*,[52] though advertised in a few religious books, was not seen as a very desirable work by the godly. This is shown by the nature of the books advertised in the Belfast 1777 edition. It contains, as we have seen, a catalogue of chapmen's books, but this is totally different in character from another such catalogue issued by the same bookseller, James Magee, only three years later, having virtually no religious content. Similarly, when Henry Cooke was being questioned by the Education Commissioners in 1825 about the books he knew of that were popular in the schools in the late eighteenth century, immediately after he had mentioned the *History of Captain Freney*, a highwayman, he was asked if he had ever read Ovid's *Art of love*, and on answering 'No' was asked if he had ever read Aristotle's *Masterpiece*[53] (a popular sexological work).

Another work with a long lineage is *The testament of the twelve*

[49a] Below, pp 81–3.
[50] See appendix I, nos 34, 98; *Belfast News-letter*, 12 Feb. 1765.
[51] F. J. Harvey Darton, *Children's books in England* (Cambridge, 1970), p. 10.
[52] See appendix I, nos 98, 107, 111, 117.
[53] *First report of the Commissioners*, appendix, p. 820.

patriarchs the sons of Jacob,[54] an edition of which was printed in Belfast by James Blow in 1720, adorned, if that is the right word, with a number of extremely crude woodcuts. This was an apocryphal book of the Old Testament, originally brought from the middle East in the early medieval period. The medieval period itself produced a number of tales still surprisingly active in the eighteenth century. One of the most interesting of these is *The famous history of the seven wise masters of Rome*,[55] believed to be of ancient Indian origin. The stories reached Europe in the middle ages, and were first printed in English in the early sixteenth century.[56] In these tales, the amorous wife of the emperor tries to get her stepson executed for refusing her advances, and tells her husband every night a story about a son dispossessing his father or about an emperor duped by his counsellors, while the boy's tutors – the 'wise masters' – tell the emperor stories about the treachery of women. Though the story is set in classical times the popular printed version has a medieval air – the emperor's second wife is a daughter of the king of Castille, and sons of the kings of Egypt, France and Spain feature among the barons and knights. The story is heavily symbolic:

> The emperor may signify the world, who having but one only son (who is man) him to bring well up is all his care. But man losing his own mother (who is Reason and Divine Grace) falling into the hands of the step mother (signifying sin) who is an empress of great bewitching, and one that commands the world; she works by all possible means the confusion of man, . . . he (Heaven) hath sent seven wise masters, which are seven liberal sciences, to give him wholesome instructions.[57]

From the Irish point of view this volume is especially interesting, as a version collected by Samuel Pepys in the late seventeenth century makes the following claim: '. . . of all histories of this nature, this exceeds, being held in such esteem in Ireland, that it is of the chiefest use in all the English schools for introducing children to the understanding of good letters.'[58] This may not be as improbable as it seems, as exactly this sort of material was to be found in schools in the next century.

A work mentioned by both Cooke[59] and Carleton[60] as being

---

[54] See appendix I, nos 13, 15, 17, 20, 68.

[55] Ibid., nos 15, 17, 76, 86, 98.

[56] George Ellis, *Specimens of early English metrical romances* (London, 1848), pp 405–11.

[57] *History of the seven wise masters* (Dublin, 1814), p. 1.

[58] Margaret Spufford, *Small books and pleasant histories* (London, 1981), p. 74.

[59] *First report of the Commissioners*, appendix, p. 820.

[60] William Carleton, *Traits and stories of the Irish peasantry* (4th ed., 5 vols, Dublin, 1836), ii, 235.

available in the hedge schools, but for some reason never advertised, is the *Gesta Romanorum*. It is a collection of short stories, compiled at the end of the thirteenth century or the beginning of the fourteenth, each with a moral attached, and appears to have been originally put together for the use of the preachers.[61] *The most pleasing and delightful history of Reynard the fox*[62] was another popular work with a long history. It can be traced well back into the medieval period, and is seen by one writer as a mock-epic.[63] It certainly had elements of this, but it claimed to be in the fable tradition.

In this small history, under the tables, or stories of birds and beasts, you will find things not only pleasant, but advantageous to the improvement of your understanding, to a degree that you may read men, as well as beasts, by their actions decypher'd in it. Here you may see policy, deceit, wisdom, power, strength, and many other things livelily set forth; and by the events or success, whether good or bad, judge according of those that use them, whether they tend to be honest, or evil purposes.

Here, as in a mirror, the politic statesman may see his counterfeit; the flattering parasite how to carry himself even, and sail with all winds; the powerful and mighty, how weak it is to rely wholly on strength, when they have a subtile enemy to deal with. And those that trust fawning friendship are here convinc'd, that in adversity but few will stand by them. And a number of other things is contained in it suiting the state and conditions of all sorts of people.[64]

Reynard is often very funny and sometimes rather coarse in a good old fashioned way. In one story King Lion has sent Sir Tybert the cat to fetch Reynard to the court. Reynard has tricked Tybert into a trap laid by a priest for the fox.

The cat all this while making a flouncing to and fro to get loose, awakened the parson, who supposing that it was the fox that had been taken, alarmed his whole family, and ordering Dame Jollock has wife to light up an offering candle, he leaped out of bed, and ran down stairs, being followed by Martinet, his son, and others, who laid so unmercifully on Tybert, that they not only woefully bruised him, but Martinet, thinking at one blow to deprive him of life, beat out one of his eyes, which the cat perceiving, and finding what danger he was in, taking a desperate leap between the naked priest's legs, with his claws and teeth caught hold of his genitals, and brought them clear

[61] *Gesta Romanorum* (Exeter, 1974); Ivor H. Evans, *Brewer's dictionary of phrase and fable* (2nd centenary ed., London, 1981), p. 476.
[62] See appendix I, nos 34, 65, 68, 86, 98; *Belfast News-letter*, 14 Nov. 1760.
[63] Margaret Schlauch, *Antecedents of the English novel* (London, 1963), pp 78–81.
[64] *The most pleasing and delightful history of Reynard the fox* (Belfast, 1814), pp 3–4.

away, which made him a perfect eunuch; this Dame Jollock seeing, cried out most piteously, and swore she would rather have lost ten years offerings, than one small morsel of those precious jewels, cursing her hard misfortune, and the time the gin was ever placed there, to occasion this loss and sorrow, saying to her son, see, Martinet, thy father's delight, and my jewel, taken away by the cursed cat, so that now it is quite spoiled, and though he may be recovered, and live long, yet he can never be recovered to my satisfaction, or be any ways useful to me, but it is spoiled to his shame and my utter loss, O woe is me.

While she thus lamented, the parson fell down in a swoon; while Reynard lay fleering at a distance, saying, Dame Jollock, be not so grieved, there is many a chapel that has but one bell in it, and that is sufficient to call the good wives together, there is something yet left, therefore be not discontented.[65]

And the moral of the story is 'by the cat's going unwillingly, signifies prudence not to venture upon an undertaking against cunning crafty men, lest we be unadvisedly ensnared, as the cat was in hopes of mice.'[66]

One rather rare romance made a brief appearance, price 3*d.*, in the 1740s. This was *The history of Sir Eger, Sir Grahame, and Sir Gray Steel.*[67] This was long popular in Scotland,[68] though the earliest extant text only dates from the middle years of the seventeenth century.[69] The story is a chivalric one of two sworn brothers, Sir Grahame and Sir Eger. Sir Eger is beaten by Sir Graysteel, and Grahame pretends to be Eger and defeats Graysteel. However, it does not appear to have had a lasting appeal in eighteenth-century Ulster. Another tale that makes a brief appearance is the *History of Fortunatus.*[70] This was apparently first put in print in 1509, on the continent, and was popular ever since.[71] Fortunatus, the son of a sadly reduced Cypriot citizen, goes abroad to try his fortune. After numerous adventures of the usual sort, he awakes from a sleep to find standing in front of him a fair lady with her eyes muffled. She turns out to be the goddess of Fortune, who has power to bestow one of six gifts: wisdom, strength, riches, health, beauty, and long life. Fortunatus chooses riches, and the goddess gives him a purse, which will always produce ten pounds in the coin of the country where he should happen to be, whenever he put his hand into it.

[65] Ibid., pp 30–31.
[66] Ibid., p. 31.
[67] See appendix I, nos 23, 29, 34.
[68] T. F. Henderson, *Scottish vernacular literature* (3rd. ed., Edinburgh, 1910), pp 38–9.
[69] Mabel Van Duzee, *A medieval romance of friendship: Eger and Grime* (New York, 1963), p. 5.
[70] See appendix I, no. 86.
[71] John Ashton, *Chapbooks of the eighteenth century* (London, 1862), p. 124.

After further adventures, which make him wish that he had chosen wisdom, he arrives home to find his parents dead. He builds a palace and three tombs, one for his parents, one for the wife he intended to marry, and one for himself and his heirs. After the birth of two sons, he recommences his travels, during the course of which he steals from the soldan of Egypt a magic hat, which enables a man to be wherever he wishes himself to be. The story continues in this vein.

The last of the medieval tales current in eighteenth-century Ulster was *Valentine and Orson*.[72] This was also one of the most popular, and remained so until well into the next century. It was first printed at Lyons in 1489, and there were numerous English editions from the sixteenth century on.[73] The basic plot concerns the two sons of the emperor of Greece, who are born in a forest. Orson is brought up by a bear to become a wild man, and Valentine is brought up by King Pepin, father of Charlemagne. Various adventures follow, including a fight with the Green Knight, another with the giant Ferragus, and an encounter with the dwarf enchanter Pacolet who possesses a magic flying wooden horse, together with other combats with various ogres. The preface is worth quoting, in order to give the flavour:

Among many histories, as well antient as modern, which have in former times borrowed our English phrase to speak withal, this (gentle reader) here of Valentine and Orson, sons to the emperor of Greece, now once again reprinted, craves free passage of thy acceptance, and puts itself to the censure of those historiographers, who make invention the eldest daughter of the seven sciences. . . . It is furnished with much state of matter, elegancy, and invention, and deck'd forth with many fair models and lively pictures, all pertinent and agreeable to the subject of the history, which I have caused to be newly cut, not only to make it carry the more grace in reading, but more lustre in heroic atchievements [*sic*] of knightly adventure. For here may the princely mind see his own model; the knightly tilter his martial atchievements; and the amorous lady her dulcit [*sic*] passages of love. . . . The history, for the strangeness, may well bear the title of courtly contents, for indeed it is a garden of courtly delights, wherein grow flowers of an extraordinary savour, that give scent in the bosom of nobles, ladies, knights, and gentlewomen: it gives also a working to the minds of dull country swains, and, as it were, leads them to search for martial atchievements, befitting many pastimes. Herein is also contained the true difference betwixt art and nature; for in Valentine is comprehended the education of art; and in Orson the true working of nature; for being both one emperor's sons, the one brought up in a prince's palace, the

[72] See appendix I, nos 34, 74, 76, 98, 105, 107, 111, 112, 132.
[73] Ernest A. Baker, *The history of the English novel: the age of romance* (London, 1924), p. 246.

other among savage beasts. . . . If you desire to see the care and trouble of
kings, here they are; if for courtly tournaments and combats of princes, here
they are; if you desire to know the battles of martial champions, here they are;
if of travels of knightly adventures, here they are; if of the sorrows of distress'd
ladies, here they are; if of strange birds and savage education, here they are; if
of friends long lost, and their joyful meeting again, here they are; if of charms
and enchantments, here they are; if of long captivities and imprisonments,
here they are. . . .[74]

It is amusing to note the reference to the illustrations being 'newly
cut' – in the edition from which this quotation has been taken they
look as if they had been cut by an apprentice with a blunt hatchet.
    From the late sixteenth century until the late seventeenth
century, a number of writers added to the chivalric canon. Two of
the earliest of the neo-chivalric writers, making the same assessment of the market simultaneously, were Emmanuel Forde and
Richard Johnson. Forde was the author of *The history of Parismus*,[75]
first published in 1598,[76] a euphuistic chivalric romance which
imitated the sort of Spanish work that had turned the head of Don
Quixote. Richard Johnson produced a work that rivalled the
History of Valentine and Orson in local popularity – the *Seven champions
of Christendom*.[77] First published in 1596/7,[78] it is an amazing
production which, like *Valentine and Orson*, lasted locally until well
into the nineteenth century. The heroes were seven saints, and the
story starts with a paragraph that catapults the reader straight
into a non-historical past: 'Not long after the destruction of Troy,
sprung up the seven wonders of the world, the seven champions of
Christendom; St George for England; St Denis for France; St
James for Spain; St Anthony for Italy; St Andrew for Scotland; St
Patrick for Ireland; and St David for Wales.'[79]
    This beginning is probably specifically designed to prepare the
reader mentally for a strictly fantastic story, peopled by heroes
who bear hardly any relationship to the saints whose names they
bear. It is instructive to examine the career of St Patrick, as the
champion most likely to appeal to an Irish audience, though this is
only one thread in the story; all the saints have their own adventures. The champions first meet when St George releases the other

[74] *The history of Valentine and Orson* (Belfast, 1782), p. ii.
[75] See appendix I nos 15, 17, 86, 98.
[76] Spufford, op. cit., p. 233.
[77] See appendix I, nos 15, 17, 76, 86, 98, 105, 111.
[78] Spufford, op. cit., p. 233.
[79] Richard Johnson, *The illustrious and renowned history of the seven champions of Christendom* (Dublin, c. 1840), p. 3.

six, including St Patrick, from captivity in the enchanted cave of the witch Calyb. They then visit Coventry, where they erect a monument and split up. St Patrick comes to Ireland, where he hears one day fearful cries, and drawing his sword he runs to the top of a high hill, where he sees the lamentable spectacle of thirty terrible satyrs, with clubs on their shoulders, dragging six fair maidens along by the hair. They were the daughters of the king of Thrace, and had been turned into swans by an evil giant, who had been killed by St Anthony, who then stole away their sister. They had been restored to human shape by St Andrew. St Patrick attacks the satyrs, killing the chief and forcing the others to flee. He then goes off with the maidens to seek St Andrew. The champions meet again at the court of the emperor of Grecia at Constantinople, many of them with their ladies. They occupy their time in combat with the strongest knights of Greece, Hungary, and Bohemia. On the last night of the journeys, the saints rest their weary limbs 'on their ladies' soft bosoms, solacing in such rapture of pleasure that no pen can express'.[80]

The pagan princes make war on Christendom, and the champions proceed to the Bay of Portugal, with an army of a million men under the generalship of St George. They march to Egypt, where after some adventures St George becomes king. The army defeats the Persian forces, and the champions return to England, then go on a voyage to Jerusalem. In Provence they come on

a beauteous virgin lying on her back in an indecent posture, and coming near they perceived her staked to the ground by the hair of her head, her arms and hands stretched out and tied to two hollow shrubs, and her legs fastened very wide asunder, in a manner as if she had been stretched on a rack. The bashful young knights, at this unusual sight began to retire and cover their faces that were covered with blushes.[81]

They release her. As she explained, she was on the point of being ravished by no less than three deformed Moors. This little piece of frankly pornographic writing can be clearly distinguished from the coarse vulgarity of the jestbooks and the broad humour of *Reynard*.

The champions carry on to Damascus, where St George frees the others from captivity by a giant. They arrive at Jerusalem and then wander off and are captured by a magician during an attempt to avenge a murdered girl who had been raped after being tied to a

[80] Ibid., p. 31.
[81] Ibid., p. 61.

tree (Johnson seems to have been fond of the theme of tying girls to the nearest shrubbery and ravishing them). They are released by St George's sons, and return to their native countries. St Patrick builds his own stone tomb, and lives in it for seven years, with his food passed in through a small hole. He digs his own grave with his nails and shortly afterwards dies. Johnson compiled his work from fragments of old English romances, eked out with his own fantasies. Despite, or perhaps because of, the totally unreal nature of the narrative, it remained perennially popular, at least until past the middle of the nineteenth century.

Cooke[82] and Carleton[83] both mention *Don Belianis of Greece*, first published in 1598.[84] This work has a typical neo-chivalric subtitle:

> . . . containing his many strange and wonderful adventures, viz. his battles with monsters and giants, dissolving inchantments, rescuing distressed ladies, overthrowing tyrants, and obtaining the fair Princess Florisbella in marriage. Together with the heroic deeds of many emperors, kings, princes and knights, with their amorous intrigues, and success in their undertakings.[85]

The plot is also pure neo-chivalry. The emperor of Greece has three sons: Don Belianis of Greece, Don Clarineo of Spain, and Don Lutidamore of Thessaly. Like the *Seven champions of Christendom*, the story has some Irish interest of a purely fantastic kind. Don Belianis, the son who is the hero of the story, travels to Ireland in one of his many adventures. The chief king turns out to be Owen Roe O'Neill. Don Belianis defeats many knights outside Dublin, but is finally forced to take service under O'Neill, who tells him that war has broken out between Connacht and Ulster, over the prince of Connacht wooing the daughter of the prince of Ulster, whom her father intended to marry, against her will, to Fluerston, a giant from the mountains of Carlingford. By killing Fluerston Belianis would save the country from war, and the Princess Honora from dishonour. Belianis sets out for 'Drumore', where the prince of Ulster has his army, accompanied by M'Guire, prince of Munster, father to the valiant Peter, knight of the Keys. They take the city of Drumore, but the prince of Ulster and Fluerston flee to Dundalk. While the prince stays there,

---

[82] *First report of the Commissioners*, appendix, p. 820.
[83] Carleton, op. cit., ii, 235.
[84] Spufford, op. cit., p. 233.
[85] *The honour of chivalry: or, the famous history of Don Belianis of Greece* (Belfast, 1831), back cover.

Fluerston goes to the Carlingford mountains and returns with ten thousand knights, several of them giants. The upshot is that Don Belianis defeats Fluerston and all the good people live happily ever after.

The seventeenth century also produced its crop of chivalry, still popular in the eighteenth. Francis Quarles' *Argalus and Parthenia*,[86] first published in London in 1629, while Quarles was resident in Dublin as secretary to James Ussher, was based on Sydney's *Arcadia*.[87] It is a rather idyllic, pastoral sort of production. The productive Nathaniel Crouch turned out *The history of the nine worthies*.[88] The nine worthies in question were three pagans, Hector, Alexander, and Julius Caesar; three Jews, Joshua, David and Judas Maccabaeus; and three Christians, Arthur, Charlemagne, and Godfrey of 'Bulloigne'. Crouch produced book after book in the late seventeenth century, and his name will occur often in these pages. Dr Johnson gave his works a rather backhanded compliment when he asked a Mr Dilly to procure some of them 'as they seen very proper to allure backward readers'.[89] John Reynolds' *Garden of love and royal flower of fidelity*[90] was a work detailing, in sub-Arcadian prose, the adventures of three foreign princes. Hugh Stanhope's *The fortunate and unfortunate lovers: or the history of Dorastus and Fawnia, and of Hero and Leander*[91] was especially popular in Ulster in the later part of the century, for some reason. The story of Dorastus and Fawnia was first published by Robert Greene in the late sixteenth century, and Stanhope added on the story of Hero and Leander. The chief moral of the tales is that obedience will be rewarded and disobedience punished.

Stories of royal concubines were always popular, and none more so than the *Unfortunate concubines: or, the history of Fair Rosamond, mistress to Henry II, and Jane Shore, concubine to Edward IV*.[92] This sort of material was generally an excuse for a good story about high living and adultery, with a suitably repentant end. Certainly the *Unfortunate concubines* had its moments:

... May it please your majesty, said Alethea, the way that I would have you to take is thus: that you should come into my chamber tomorrow night, a little before bed time, and I will leave you there alone awhile, till I have got my lady

---

[86] See appendix I, no. 34.
[87] *Dictionary of national biography*, xlvii, 92–6.
[88] See appendix I, nos 34, 86.
[89] *Dictionary of national biography*, viii, 14–16.
[90] See appendix I, nos 98, 107, 111, 117.
[91] Ibid., nos 37, 43, 67, 69, 74, 76, 79, 107, 111, 117, 132.
[92] Ibid., nos 34, 37, 43, 49, 67, 69, 76, 79, 86, 107, 111, 117, 132.

Rosamond to bed, whereas I lie with her every night, I will delay the time of my going to bed as I sometimes do, till she is asleep; and I will bring your majesty into the chamber, and you shall go to bed with her in my stead. . . . The king needed no persuasion to follow her but went with her immediately to her chamber and there soon disrobed himself. . . . The king having shut the door, and locked it after Alethea, went into bed with Rosamond, who was fast asleep, not dreaming of the treacherous part Alethea played. The king not willing presently to wake his charming mistress, lay still, but laying closer to her than Alethea used to do, she waked of herself, and not knowing but that it was Alethea that was in her bed. I prithee, governess, said she, for she thought she was, lie further off a little, you crowd so close, as if you would thrust me out of bed.

And now the king thought it a proper time to speak to her thus. My dearest Rosamond, it is not your governess, it is your king that lies so close to you, and thereupon embraced her in his arms, and sure you need not fear that I would thrust you out of bed. . . . Rosamond now found that resistance would be in vain, and since things were gone so far, she had better oblige the King, than to deny him that which he would take whether she would or no – and thereupon, without resisting any further, suffered the king to do what he pleased, which pleased the king so well, that before morning light appeared, he pleased fair Rosamond also.[93]

This story appears to be of mid-seventeenth century origin.[94]

One other late chivalric title to appear was based on the story of Troy, and was usually called the *New history of the Trojan wars and Troy's destruction*.[95] The first book printed in English on this subject was the *Recuyell of the historyes of Troye*, printed in the fifteenth century by Caxton, and the story was perennially fascinating. The *New history* treats

of the lives and mighty actions of Hercules of Greece, and Hector, prince of Troy; of the rape of fair Helen of Greece, and the famous ten years war between the Greeks and the Trojans, at the end of which, that renowned city, which commanded the Asian provinces, was by a stratagem taken and levelled with the ground, with the death of King Priamus, and almost all his numerous issue. As also how Brute, king of the Trojans, arrived in the island of Britain, and conquered Albion and his giants, building a new Troy where London now stands. . . .[96]

---

[93] *The unfortunate concubines: or, the history of fair Rosamond . . . and Jane Shore* (Belfast, 1832), pp 26–31.
[94] Ashton, op. cit., p. 387.
[95] See appendix I, nos 15, 17, 86.
[96] *New history of the Trojan wars and Troy's destruction* (Dublin, *c.* 1840), p. 5.

The wise little Man.

I will sing unto the Lord a new song, and praise him for all his mercies.

He hath taught me to walk in his ways with a benevolent heart and contented mind, and therefore am I happy.

The benevolent man is a partner with all the world: he rejoiceth at the prosperity of all men, and hath therefore a share of all the satisfaction which fortune, wealth, and power can produce.

THE
Whitsuntide-Gift:
OR
The way to be very HAPPY.

A Book necessary for all Families, and intended to be read by *Parents*, as well as *Children* of all Denominations.

Let those who cannot read, learn, that they may be WISE *and* HAPPY.
PLATO.

Adorned with 17 CUTS.

NEWRY:
Printed for the People of all Nations, by D. CARPENTER, and sold by R. KINNIER, No. 33, Fishamble-street and GEO. POWELL, No. 23, Green-street, DUBLIN. [Price only Two-Pence.]

The Whitsuntide-Gift, &c.

it carried into execution the next day, if his Grace would permit them to go to the fair. The Duke consented with a smile, and the next morning they set out for *Tramptington* fair; whither, if you please, Mr. Reader, we will follow them: And for a companion on our journey, pray, send to *Dan. Carpenter's* for the FAIRING.
THE END

CHILDREN BOOKS are Printed and sold by DANIEL CARPENTER, in NEWRY, and by R. KINNIER, No. 33, Fishamble ft. and G. POWELL, Green-ft. DUBLIN.

1. THE Christmas Box, price 1d.
2. The New year's Gift, 1,
3. The Easter-Gift, 2d.
4. The Whitsuntide-Gift, 2d.
5. Goody Two-Shoes, 2d.
6. Giles Gingerbread, 1d.
7. The London Cries, 1d.
8. Tom Thumb's new Play Thing, $\frac{1}{2}$d.
9. The House that Jack built, one $\frac{1}{2}$d.
10. Tom Thumb's Folio, 1d.
11. Entertaining Fables for the Instruction of Children, 1d.
12. A New Riddle Book, price only 2d.

The wise little Woman.

Every woman is always as happy, or as miserable, as she thinks herself. While content dwells in the mind, sorrow can never touch the heart.

Oh let me be cloathed with righteousness, and bear with me the seeds of satisfaction; let me sow them plentifully in every neighbourhood, that the children may rise up and bless me, and the poor pray for my prosperity,

PLATE IV
Newry-printed book for children, c. 1785

CHAPTER 4

Children's Literature, Novels, Plays, Poetry and Songs in the Eighteenth Century

The imaginative world open to the eighteenth-century common reader, as carried round the countryside in the chapman's pack, was not merely confined to religion and chivalric literature. Older genres such as poetry and song were evolving, and new ones were emerging, such as novels proper and books written specially for children – though the traditional works that have just been described were of course not the exclusive preserve of adults. As we have seen, in the case of the hedge schools they formed a major part of the reading material that was available, and indeed it is inconceivable that, as they were scattered round the countryside in such quantities, children would not devour them. Those who could read would naturally seize on any literature of an imaginative or adventurous nature, such as these stories and the chapmen's books containing tales of highwaymen and pirates. After all, this was an age where the literature for children was by and large not of the most entertaining nature.

This was especially true of the first half of the century, where the literature provided was heavily biased in favour of religious material. Some of the religious works mentioned in the previous chapter were intended partly or chiefly to be read by youth, such as Keach's *War with the devil*, and Bunyan's *Pilgrim's progress* could be read as an adventure story. But one little volume stands preeminent, being not only heavily advertised at this time but also the only book to appear on Magee's 1750 chapman's catalogue that was specifically aimed at young children. This was the awful James Janeway's *A token for children,* or in its full title *A token for children: being an exact account of the conversion, holy and exemplary lives, and joyful deaths of several young children.*[1] Janeway's work, first published in 1671, was a product worthy of the man. Janeway believed that children were brands of hell, that nobody was 'too

---

[1] See appendix I, nos 11, 15, 17, 20, 34, 61, 127.

young to go to hell'. [2] The text consists of several stories of the unflinching rectitude of children who die young. They rebuke their contemporaries for frivolity and go to any lengths to bring people to the knowledge of Christ. One even tries to convert a Turk to Christianity by going to fetch his beer for him and so winning his stubborn heart. The book advocates a stern regime – toys are forbidden, especially for some reason whipping-tops – and children are asked to rejoice soberly at the funerals of the blessed. Janeway intended the book to give pleasure; in his seventeenth-century puritan way he could conceive of no pleasure higher than the knowledge of one's own rectitude and ultimate salvation. However, given the fact that the fate of the good child was firstly to be an infernal nuisance, and secondly to have an early death, the book probably had an effect contrary to that intended.

By way of contrast, from the 1740s on we find advertised Isaac Watts' *Divine songs attempted in easy language for the use of children*,[3] first published in 1715. Here at last is children's literature that children could read and enjoy, though Watts was no less concerned than Janeway with the morals of the child. Watts was the originator of 'For Satan finds some mischief still for idle hands to do', and some of his verse is delightful. Consider the cradle song:

> Hush! my dear, lie still and slumber;
> Holy angels guard thy bed!
> Heav'nly blessings without number
> Gently falling on thy head.[4]

Janeway, looking at a sleeping child, would never have had thoughts like that. But Watts was still a man of his time, as shown in such passages as:

> 'Tis dangerous to provoke a God;
> His power and vengeance none can tell;
> One stroke of his almighty rod
> Shall send young sinners quick to hell.[5]

or even:

> Lord, I ascribe it to thy grace,
> And not to chance, as others do,
> That I was born of Christian race,
> And not a heathen, or a Jew.[6]

[2] F. J. H. Darton, *Children's books in England* (Cambridge, 1982), pp 52–6.
[3] See appendix I, nos 29, 53, 61, 68, 69, 74, 100, 107, 109, 114, 117, 124, 127, 132.
[4] Robert Anderson (ed.), *The works of the British poets* (13 vols, London, 1795), ix, 375.
[5] Ibid., p. 369.
[6] Ibid., p. 367.

One other item to appear on the Magee 1750 catalogue of chapmen's books was Nathaniel Crouch's *Winter evening entertainments.*[7] This contained stories and riddles, and was proclaimed by the author to be

> Milk for children, wisdom for young men,
> To teach them that they turn not babes again.[8]

Turning to the later part of the century, we find the field broadening out. One of the features of this period is the number of small, miscellaneous improving volumes produced for the use of youth. Cooke, in his evidence to the Education Commissioners, mentions two that he specifically remembered: the *Lilliputian magazine* and *Youth's instructor,* which have already been dealt with in connection with the hedge schools.[9] But there were others. There was the *Preceptor*[10] by Robert Dodsley, intended for the improvement of young lives; *Forty-two stories, fables and allegories, such as were thought most proper to please, and form the minds of youth;*[11] and, coming right at the end of the period, Hamilton Moore's *Young gentleman and lady's monitor, being a collection of select pieces . . . particularly calculated to form the mind and manners of the youth of both sexes..*[12] This is divided into sections, such as 'Immortality', 'Dress' and 'Mimicking'. Each section in turn is divided into numbered paragraphs. Some of these display interesting sidelights into contemporary manners:

Women are frightened at the name of argument, and are sooner convinced by a happy turn of witty expression, than by demonstration.[13]
 There is nothing so unpardonably rude, as a seeming inattention to the person who is speaking to you. . . . Some ill-bred people, while others are speaking to them, will, instead of looking at or attending to them . . . probably pick their nails or their noses. Nothing betrays a more trifling mind than this.[14]

Proper children's books as distinct from handed down traditional material, pious volumes, instructive works, and miscellanies, began to appear in the later part of the century. One of the first to be marketed in Ulster was Sarah Fielding's *The governess: or, little*

[7] See appendix I, nos 34, 86, 98.
[8] Darton, op. cit., pp 60–61.
[9] *First report of the Commissioners,* appendix, p. 820; above, p. 16.
[10] See appendix I, nos 73, 123, 160; *Belfast News-letter,* 1 Jan. 1760; 3 Jan. 1775.
[11] Ibid., nos 82, 98, 106, 111, 117.
[12] Ibid., nos 156, 160.
[13] Hamilton Moore, *The young gentleman and lady's monitor* (Belfast, 1796), p. 300.
[14] Ibid., p. 307.

female academy. Being the history of Mrs Teachum, and her nine girls.[15]
Sarah was a sister of Henry Fielding, the novelist, and though
there is some attempt at character drawing, the book is really a
collection of stories told by various characters.

The most famous work to make a local appearance was the now
almost unreadable *Sandford and Merton*[16] by Thomas Day, first
published in the 1780s. Day was an extraordinary character, an
admirer of Rousseau and friend of R. L. Edgeworth. He decided
that he needed a wife, went to the orphan asylum at Shrewsbury,
and chose a flaxen-haired beauty of twelve whom he called
Sabrina, and then went to the foundling hospital in London,
where he selected a brunette whom he called Lucretia. He undertook to marry one and maintain the other. He apprenticed the dim
Lucretia to a milliner, and proceeded to try the stoicism of Sabrina
by firing pistols at her petticoats and dropping melted sealing-wax
on her arms. Sabrina eventually married his friend Bicknell, and
two other of his loves became the second and third wives of his
friend Edgeworth. He eventually died riding an unbroken colt
under the delusion that kindness would control any animal.[17]
After all this, the story of *Sandford and Merton* is rather disappoint-
ing. Harry Sandford is a little prig. He prefers dry bread for his
dinner and often goes to his bed supperless that he might feed the
poor starving robins. Tommy Merton is a spoilt little rich boy.
The two are placed under a sententious local clergyman for
education, and there is much moralising along the lines of the
viciousness of the rich and the natural goodness of the poor, with
much 'noble savage' nonsense. Little Tommy is lamentably ignorant, and whenever a camel or a crocodile or the Spartans are
mentioned inevitably asks for information, which is obligingly
given to him with much heavy moralising. The information given
is not always accurate, as when he is informed that the crocodile, if
humanely treated, is quite docile, and will give little children rides
on his back. Luckily the children never meet a crocodile. The story
goes on and on, with Harry becoming even more of a prig, but in
the end he converts Tommy to his ways.

But books somewhat more to the taste of children were
appearing. One was the *New fairie tales*,[18] presumably a selection of
the French stories which became so popular in the eighteenth

[15] See appendix I, nos 103, 111, 117.
[16] Ibid., nos 127, 138, 160.
[17] *Dictionary of national biography*, xiv, 239–41.
[18] See appendix I, nos 68, 86; *Belfast News-letter*, 14 Nov. 1760.

century;[19] another was the *Arabian night's entertainments*,[20] which would have contained a selection of the tales, including such perennial favourites as 'Aladdin' and 'Sinbad'.[21] Local printers also issued little story books, priced at 1*d.* and 2*d.*, often measuring only a few inches in height, and covered in decorated paper wrappers. The vast majority have vanished, but luckily two survive in the archives of the Ulster Folk and Transport Museum. They were printed in Newry in the 1780s by Daniel Carpenter, and both turn out to be piracies of works issued two decades earlier by the famous English printer of children's books, John Newbery. The first is called *The Whitsuntide-gift: or, the way to be very happy. A book necessary for all families, and intended to be read by parents, as well as children.* The imprint grandiloquently reads 'Newry: printed for the people of all nations, by D. Carpenter'. This sounds heavy stuff, and it sounds even heavier when it is discovered that the book consists of short stories illustrative of the ten commandments. But the book is utterly charming, and the stories told to Master Billy and Miss Kitty Smith are told very well and adorned with little woodcuts. The substance of the stories, first published by Newbery in England about 1764,[22] is unremarkable, but the following shows what was considered fit for little children in the late eighteenth century. It illustrates 'Thou shalt not commit adultery.'

In the reign of King James the first, one Ann Waters, having an unlawful and wanton intercourse with a young man in the neighbourhood, and finding her husband some embarrassment to their wicked designs, determined to put him out of the way, and accordingly one night, assisted by her paramour, she strangled her husband, and they buried his body under a dung hill in the cow house. The man was missing, and his wife made such lamentation about him that the people greatly pitied her, and gave all the assistance in their power in searching for her husband. After the search was at an end, and it was imagined that the man might be gone away for debt without acquainting his wife of his intentions, a woman in the neighbourhood dreamed that a stranger told her that Ann Waters had strangled her husband, and hid him under a dung hill. She at first disregarded the dream, but it being repeated several nights, it began publickly to be talked of, and at length they got authority to search the dung hill, where the dead body was found and other concurrent circumstances appearing, the wife was aprehended and convicted of the

[19] Darton, op. cit., pp 85–91.
[20] See appendix I, nos 86, 98, 127.
[21] Darton, op. cit., p. 91; Percy Muir, *English children's books, 1600–1900* (London, 1954), p. 40.
[22] Sydney Roscoe, *John Newbery and his successors, 1740–1814* (Wormley, 1973), p. 271.

murder, which before her execution she confessed, and impeached the young fellow her accomplice, who was also executed.[23]

The book contains advertising for a number of little works, such as *Goody Two-shoes, The house that Jack built,* and *Tom Thumb's folio,* at prices ranging from ½*d.* to 2*d.* Most are printed from the original editions of Newbery, and indeed most of the eighteenth-century books printed in Ireland belonged to this category, at least in the field of imaginative literature. The second of the surviving Carpenter books is *The Easter-gift,* which bears on the title page two lines of verse attributed to Woglog, one of John Newbury's favourite mock authors.[24]

In addition to all the categories mentioned above – the traditional chivalric tales, the religious works, the miscellanies, the new category of children's book proper, and so forth – there was one other source of reading matter: the novels written primarily for adults but adopted by children. Thus Swift's *Gulliver's travels* was available locally through the chapmen,[25] Defoe's *Robinson Crusoe* was available in both large and small versions,[26] and there was likewise an abridged version of Richardson's *Pamela,* under the title of *Virtue display'd,* price 3*d.*[27] This raises the question of what novels were available to the public in Ulster during this century, or at least which novels attained popularity among unsophisticated readers. For a novel to attain popularity among the masses it must only involve a simple exercise of literacy, and not demand a complicated enlightened response towards structure and style,[28] and this is true of those works that achieved popularity in Ulster. A number of mainstream novels did filter down, either whole or in an abridged form, to unsophisticated readers and children – *Gulliver's travels, Robinson Crusoe,* and *Pamela,* as seen above, and also *Moll Flanders,*[29] but the popular novels were anything but sophisticated in form or plot.

The most popular of all is a case in point. This was *The reform'd coquet; or, memoirs of Amoranda. A surprizing novel,*[30] by Mrs Mary Davys. Mrs Davys was born in Dublin in 1674, marrying Rev.

[23] *The Whitsuntide-gift* (Newry, *c.*1785), p. 32.
[24] Darton, op. cit., pp 20–21.
[25] See appendix I nos 65, 68, 98.
[26] Ibid., no. 86.
[27] Ibid., nos 82, 117.
[28] John J. Richetti, *Popular fiction before Richardson* (Oxford, 1969), p. 9.
[29] See appendix I, nos 86, 98.
[30] Ibid., nos 67, 69, 74, 76, 97, 98, 100, 106, 107, 109, 111, 114, 117, 124, 132; *Belfast News-letter,* 13 June 1760.

Peter Davys, headmaster of the school attached to St Patrick's cathedral. After her husband died in 1698, she eventually opened a coffee-house in Cambridge. A lady of a 'hearty and somewhat masculine temperament',[31] who was referred to by Swift as 'a rambling woman with very little taste in wit or humour',[32] she produced the *Reform'd coquet* in 1724. It was first locally advertised in 1760[33] at the usual chapman's book price of 6½d., and rapidly gained in popularity. We are lucky in that we have an account of its reading by an unsophisticated reader, the young William Carleton.

It was a little before this that I met the first thing in the shape of a novel that ever came into my hands. It was published as a pamphlet, but how I came by it I don't recollect. The name was *Amoranda, or the reformed coquette*. She, Amoranda, was a young lady of great fortune and surpassing beauty, and better still for herself, she was the sole mistress of that fortune, responsible to none. Of course, she was surrounded by hundreds of admirers, all suitors for the hand of a lady at once so beautiful and so wealthy. She acted the thorough coquette – encouraged them all, but accepted none. At length one lover made his appearance, a gentleman very superior to her other worshippers, and to him she seemed to give something like a preference; but when he made his proposals she told him that if she were capable of deciding for herself it would be in his favour. In the meantime she preferred her present life; it was better, she thought, to have many worshippers than one. Life with a husband must be an insipid thing, and besides, she preferred being admired to being loved. The disappointed gallant took his farewell, and left her to enjoy the admiration which was so grateful to her vanity. Still she could not banish the image of the last visitor from her memory, and she began to feel something like regret that she did not give him at least a longer trial; however, it was now too late. It seemed that he was so deeply affected by her rejection of his suit, that he went to the continent with the intention of spending the remainder of his life there. This information she had in a letter from himself, and she was deeply affected by it. In the course of a few months afterwards, during the season of autumn, a carriage was passing the public road, which was quite convenient to her magnificent residence; the horses, it seems, took fright at something, the carriage was overturned and an old gentleman of a very dignified and venerable appearance was so severely injured, that it was found necessary to ask Amoranda if she could give him shelter during the illness which was occasioned by the injuries he had received. Amoranda, coquette as she was, possessed a generous and humane heart. She sent her own carriage for him, and he was received by her with a most hospitable welcome. The story then goes on to their conversation during her guest's recovery, and after he became able to walk with her through the beautiful grounds attached to the castle the

---

[31] William H. McBurney, *Four before Richardson* (Lincoln, Neb., 1978), pp xxix–xxx.
[32] Ibid., p. xxiv.
[33] *Belfast News-letter*, 13 June 1760.

venerable sage gained her confidence; she was not at heart a coquette, but she despised men, and took delight in encouraging them in order to secure their punishment by afterwards rejecting them. She said it was her great property that brought the majority of them around her – that she never loved but one, who unfortunately had gone to the continent, and she was never likely to see him again. A few days afterwards his wig became disarranged, by some accident, in her presence, and an artificial nose displaced, and there he stood before her – the only man she had ever loved.[34]

Carleton actually shed tears when he had finished it, out of sheer disappointment that there was no more.

Another peculiar, rather unclassifiable, work that was very popular in the latter half of the century was Solomon Gesner's *Death of Abel*.[35] This, also sold at the familiar price of 6½d.,[36] was an English translation from the original German. It was written in a very high-flown kind of prose poetry:

Henceforth repose in silence, thou soft pipe; no more I render thee vocal, no more I chant the simple manners of the rustic swain. Fain would I raise my voice to bolder strains, and in harmonious lays rehearse of our primeval parents after their dreadful fall. Fain would I celebrate him who, sacrificed by a brother's fury, his dust first mingled with the earth. Come thou noble enthusiasm. . . .[37]

And so Gesner warbles on, invoking his muse. It is difficult to account for the popularity of this, yet the chapmen carried it round the country. William Chetwood's *The voyages and adventures of Captain Robert Boyle*[38] is an interesting narrative. The story is about the rise of an orphan to the estate of gentleman. It involves travel, pirates, love in a harem, separation, and final reunion with loved ones. It has been described as being close to Defoe in the observation of character.[39]

Another novel distributed by the chapmen but lost to mainstream literary history is Mrs Penelope Aubin's *The noble slaves*.[40] The story involves a number of improbable characters in a series of exotic adventures around the world, always saved from calamity by the providence of God and their virtue. The geography and ethnography involved is sometimes peculiar:

[34] William Carleton, *The life of William Carleton* (2 vols, London, 1896), i, 74–6.
[35] See appendix I, nos 76, 79, 97, 98, 100, 104, 105, 107, 108, 111, 114, 117.
[36] *Belfast News-letter*, 30 Apr. 1765.
[37] Solomon Gesner, *The death of Abel* (Belfast, 1827), p. xi.
[38] See appendix I, no. 98.
[39] Richetti, op. cit., p. 211.
[40] See appendix I, nos 86, 92, 98.

The Indian, who proved a Japanese cast on the shore there with his wife and three children, in the Chinese language invited them to his home. The Moor understood him . . .[41]

A further example of this confusion comes when one of the characters explains to another his actions on learning that she had been cast adrift from Mexico in a pleasure-boat:

I no sooner heard of your disaster, but I procured a ship, having visited all the coast of Peru and Canada; missing you there, I determined to go to Japan, it being the nearest coast to which you could be drove.[42]

There is even some fearful talk of lustful Turks.

This completes the survey of novels popular in eighteenth-century Ulster, but one rather puzzling fact remains: all the novels mentioned in this section – that is, all the novels that can be proved to have had widespread popularity – were originally published within the span of five years, apart from *The death of Abel*, which was not English, and anyway hardly a novel; *Pamela*, which was only popularly available in an abridged edition; and *Robinson Crusoe*, which, though published in both large and small editions, does not appear on any of the lists of chapmen's books. Of the novels that do, *Moll Flanders* and *The noble slaves* were published in 1722, *The reform'd coquet* in 1724, and *The voyages . . . of Captain Robert Boyle* and *Gulliver's travels* in 1726. Even *Robinson Crusoe* appeared in 1719. This would suggest that, during one of the great periods of novel-writing in the English language, the unsophisticated provincial readers of Ulster, and presumably elsewhere in Britain and Ireland, were avidly consuming material produced before the true birth of the genre in 1740.

Dramatic works were frequently printed and advertised, particularly in the latter half of the century, but the market for most of these was in Belfast and the larger towns which could afford a theatre. However, three plays did achieve mass popularity at the folk level – Allan Ramsay's *Gentle shepherd*, John Michelburne's *Ireland preserv'd*, and Robert Ashton's *Battle of Aughrim*. *The gentle shepherd*,[43] a Scots pastoral comedy first published in 1725, was vastly popular from the date of the first local advertisement (1731), and probably before that. Editions were published in Belfast in 1743, 1748, 1755, 1768, and 1792, in Newry in 1764,

---

[41] Penelope Aubin, *The noble slaves* (Belfast, 1812), p. 9.
[42] Ibid., p. 21.
[43] See appendix I, nos 17, 20, 23, 27, 30, 34, 37, 48, 67, 68, 70, 79, 80, 97, 117, 124, 132, 137, 140, 144.

1776, and 1793, and in Strabane in 1789, making it one of the most locally reproduced texts of the century. It seems to have been read for its literary merit rather than acted, though there was a performance in 1795.[44]

But the other two texts deserve the title of folk play. The earliest in date is John Michelburne's *Ireland preserv'd: or, the siege of Londonderry*,[45] first published in 1705. Editions of this were published in Belfast in 1744, 1750, and 1759, in Newry in 1774, and in Strabane in 1787, and considering the usage the play got there were probably more, now lost. It is a bombastic piece, set, as the title states, in the times of the siege of Londonderry, where the author was military governor during the events he describes. The Jacobite characters are, in the best traditions of this sort of theatre, moustache-twirling villains:

> Ramsey ... Come Sir Neal, (clapping him on the back) your friend the judge will in four or five days take them into execution: an Irish jury and a good strong gallows will quickly despatch them; but will there be ropes enough?
>
> Sir Neal We must hang them after my country fashion, with gads; you call them in your country, withs; 2 pence a rope to each rebel will be too much expense, we can get a hundred gads for a groat.[46]

Foreign characters have suitable foreign accents:

> Marshall Rosin O miserable! Diable de mutiny; de rebels de rebels are marching into de field and take de advantage by dis mutiny.[47]

But the Ulster folk play *par excellence* was Robert Ashton's *The battle of Aughrim*,[48] first published in 1756. There were Belfast editions in 1767 and 1800, a Newry edition in 1781, and a Strabane edition in 1785, but because of the nature of the play and the consequent heavy wear and tear there were almost certainly many local editions. This 'stupid play' as Carleton called it,[49] was written in heroic verse.

> (Sarsfield and St Ruth fall out)
> Yet know, curst mongrel, here I will not stay;
> I'll quit your camp, then you shall surely find,
> There's not an Irish soul will stay behind,

---

[44] *Belfast News-letter*, 16 Feb. 1795.
[45] See appendix I, nos 28, 33, 37, 57, 67, 69, 79, 90, 97, 117, 129, 132.
[46] Robert Ashton and John Michelburne, *Two historical plays* (Belfast, 1826), p. 62.
[47] Ibid., p. 135.
[48] See appendix I, nos 77, 97, 108, 118, 164.,
[49] Carleton, *Life*, i, 28.

Then with a remnant of my chosen band,
I'll drive your frog devourers off the land,
My eyes like basilisks shall dart you through,
Then will I next the British force subdue.[50]

The battle scenes are described in couplets like these:

Death in each quarter does the eye alarm,
Here lies a leg and there a shattered arm,
There heads appear which cloven by mighty bangs,
And severed quite, on either shoulder hangs.[51]

Carleton describes the popularity of the play:

A usual amusement at the time was to reproduce the 'Battle of Aughrim', in some spacious barn, with a winnowing cloth for the curtain. This play, bound up with the 'Siege of Londonderry', was one of the reading-books in the hedge schools of that day, and circulated largely among the people of all religions; it had, indeed, a most extraordinary influence among the lower classes. 'The Battle of Aughrim', however, because it was written in heroic verse, became so popular that it was rehearsed at almost every Irish hearth, both catholic and protestant, in the north. The spirit it evoked was irresistible. The whole country became dramatic. To repeat it at the fireside in winter nights was nothing: the Orangemen should act it, and show to the whole world how the field of Aughrim was so gloriously won. The consequence was that frequent rehearsals took place. The largest and most spacious barns and kilns were fitted up, the night of representation was given out, and crowds, even to suffocation, as they say, assembled to witness the celebrated 'Battle of Aughrim'.

At first, it was true, the Orangemen had it all to themselves. This, however, could not last. The catholics felt that they were as capable of patronising the drama as the victors of Aughrim. A strong historic spirit awoke among them. They requested of the Orangemen to be allowed the favour of representing the catholic warriors of the disastrous field, and, somewhat to their surprise, the request was immediately granted. The Orangemen felt that there was something awkward and not unlike political apostasy in acting the part of catholics in the play, under any circumstances, no matter how dramatic. It was consequently agreed that the Orangemen should represent the officers of the great man on whose name and title their system had been founded, and the catholics should represent their own generals and officers under the name of St Ruth, Sarsfield, and Colonel O'Neill.[52]

Needless to say, the dramatic presentation ended in bloodshed. The popularity of such a play amongst both protestant and

---

[50] Ashton and Michelburne, op. cit., p. 11.
[51] Ibid., p. 44.
[52] C. L. Graves (ed.), *Humours of Irish life* (London, *c.* 1920)), pp. 131–2.

catholics is explained by the fact that the Jacobite characters such as Sarsfield are portrayed as gallant figures.

Turning to works of poetry, we find that those which either appear on a catalogue of chapman's books or are advertised over a long period are exclusively Scottish, and represent a tradition of surprising antiquity. This was true of Scotland itself: there, as in Ulster, the older Scottish literature was kept alive in the form of popular works until the revival of educated interest in it during the eighteenth century, and by the end of the century the Scottish shepherds could repeat much of Barbour's *Bruce*, Blind Harry's *Wallace*, and Lyndsay's poems.[53] The *Bruce*[54] of John Barbour (*c*.1320–1395) appeared on the 1750 chapman's catalogue. It was with this poem that Scottish literature began to take shape as a distinct national product. Its appeal was clear as a commemoration of the heroism of the Scottish nation.

The life and acts of Sir William Wallace[55] was composed by Blind Harry, also known as Henry the Minstrel, towards the end of the fifteenth century. It is locally advertised until the 1760s, with Belfast editions in 1728 and 1758, the latter modernised and abridged. Its appeal would have been somewhat similar to the above. The works[56] of Sir David Lyndsay (1490–1555) were popular in the first third of the eighteenth century, and there was a Belfast edition in 1714. In Scotland Lyndsay was one of the most popular of the poets, and would have been doubly popular with presbyterians because of his anti-clericalism: he satirises the clergy of his time and advocates the translation of the Bible and confession directly to God.[57]

A puzzling work is *The cherrie and the slae*,[58] by Alexander Montgomerie (*c*.1545–*c*.1615), of which there were Belfast editions in 1700 and 1771. An edition was printed as late as 1813 by J. Buchanan in Londonderry. The interpretation of Montgomerie's poetry is still a matter for debate – the 'cherrie' can be taken to represent good and the 'slae' (sloe) evil, or the 'cherrie' can represent the Roman Catholic eucharist and the 'slae' protestantism. As the work was so popular with Scottish and Ulster

---

[53] David Craig, *Scottish literature and the Scottish people* (London, 1961), pp 112–13, 118–19.
[54] See appendix I, no. 34.
[55] Ibid., nos 14, 15, 17, 20, 54, 68.
[56] Ibid., nos 14, 15, 17, 20.
[57] T. F. Henderson, *Scottish vernacular literature* (3rd. ed., Edinburgh, 1910), pp 201–31; Kurt Wittig, *The Scottish tradition in literature* (Westport, Conn., 1972), p. 97.
[58] See appendix I, nos 7, 17, 68, 84, 97.

presbyterians they obviously put an opposite interpretation on it.
Certainly it has many charming passages of pure poetry:

> About a bank of balmy bews,
> Where nightingales their notes renews,
>   With gallant goldspinks gay;
> The mavise, merl and progne proud,
> The lintwhite, lark, and laverock loud,
>   Saluted mirthful May, . . .
>
> The cushat crouds, the corbie cries,
> The cuckow couks, the prattling pyes,
>   To geek her they begin;
> The jargous of the janglin jays
> The craiking craws, the keckling kays,
>   They deav'd me with their din;
> The painted pown with argus eyes,
>   Can on his maycock call,
> The turtle wails on wither'd trees,
>   And Echo answer'd all . . .[59]

Allan Ramsay has already been dealt with but must be
mentioned here, as the *Gentle shepherd*, though a play, is in many
ways better adapted for reading as poetry than producing on the
stage. Though this tale of rustic courtship, first published in 1725,
is in excellent verse, the action is rather slow and languid.[60]
However, it took Ulster by storm, and was the first new poetic
influence to do so. It held a preeminent place during most of the
century, until in the 1780s a new poet was to change things utterly
and sweep most of the older material away – Robert Burns.
  Editions of Burns' *Poems, chiefly in the Scottish dialect* were
published in Belfast in 1787 (the year of the first Edinburgh
edition), 1789, 1792, and 1800, showing their immense and
immediate popularity. Burns became the idol of every local poet,
though it would be a mistake to assume that because a poet wrote
in a Scottish idiom he was a slavish follower of Burns – as we have
seen, the local poetic tradition was firmly Scottish in tone right
from the beginning to the end of the century, and a recent
examination of the texts of the local 'rhyming weavers' shows that
the influence of Burns on their poetry has perhaps been overva-
lued.[61] Nevertheless, the early and frequent local editions and the

[59] Alexander Montgomerie, *The cherrie and the slae* (Londonderry, 1812), pp 3–4.
[60] *Dictionary of national biography*, xlvii, 230–33.
[61] John Hewitt, *Rhyming weavers* (Belfast, 1974), pp 5–6.

frequent mention of Burns in the works of the Ulster bards show
that even if he was not the first Scottish poet to be popular locally,
and not necessarily a direct literary model, he was immensely
popular and seen as *primus inter pares* by his contemporaries and
immediate successors. For instance, Samuel Thomson visited
Burns in 1794.[62] Thomson, a schoolmaster of Carngranny, County
Antrim, had published his *Poems on different subjects, partly in the
Scottish dialect* in Belfast the previous year. This was dedicated 'to
Mr Robert Burns, the celebrated Ayrshire poet', and contains a
long poem, 'Epistle to Mr R***** B***S', including the following
lines, which perfectly put the influence first of Allan Ramsay and
then of Burns.

> Tho' Allan Ramsay blythly ranted,
> An' tun'd his reed wi' merry glee;
> Yet faith that *something* ay he wanted,
> That makes my Burns sae dear to me.[63]

Turning from poetry to song, we find, not unnaturally, that the
attention of the godly was early drawn to this ephemeral and
potentially disruptive form of entertainment. At a general synod
held in Belfast in 1718, the following resolution was passed.

Complaint being made that there are several obscene ballads printed in
Belfast and dispers'd through the country, the moderator desir'd Mr Kirkpatrick to represent to the printers, that the minister and several other godly
persons take just offense at these ballads, and therefore to advise them not to
print such papers in the future.[64]

None of these ballads has survived, so no contemporary judgment
can be made as to the actual nature of the obscenity. However,
there can be no doubt that thousands of ballad sheets were printed
throughout the century. The selling methods of the ballad singers
have been described in chapter 2. As the century wore on, more
and more 'garlands' were published, in such towns as Belfast (by
James Magee, of course), Newry, and Monaghan. They usually
contained about eight pages, with two, three, or four songs, and
the title pages are usually decorated with small, crude woodcuts,
which sometimes did and sometimes did not bear a relationship to
the texts that followed. They were usually not topical in content,
leaving that field to the broadside ballad. The ones printed in

---

[62] Ibid., p. 5.
[63] Samuel Thomson, *Poems on different subjects* (Belfast, 1793), p. 85.
[64] *Records of the General Synod of Ulster* (3 vols, Belfast, 1890–98), i, 479.

Belfast seem, to judge from the few surviving examples, not to have been particularly Irish in tone, a typical one being *The king and the tinker's garland. In four parts . . . To which are added: 1. The lass of the mill. 2. The miller's wedding*, printed in 1767 by James Magee. Daniel Carpenter in Newry was not averse to printing a mixture of patriotic and general songs, as in the following garland: *Ireland's glory: or, a comparative view of Ireland, in . . . 1776 and 1783. To which are added, 2. Bennet's bottled ale. 3. Admiral Russel's victory. 4. Year fifty-nine.* In Monaghan John Brown was printing a number of garlands containing songs of Irish interest in the 1790s, such as *An answer to Stauka an Vouraga. To which are added II. John and Nelly. III. The phoenix of Ulster. IV. The banks of the Dee.* A huge number of these little garlands must have been carried round the countryside, sold from shops, from market stalls and from door to door. A number of larger songbooks were also published and advertised during the century, but the most popular over a long period was the charming production called *The English archer: or, Robert earl of Huntington, vulgarly called Robin Hood*,[65] sometimes advertised as *Robin Hood's songs.* The story of Robin Hood had been perennially popular, as were stories of the pre-industrial social bandits such as the Irishman Captain Freney, who will be looked at in the next chapter. By the eighteenth century the diffusion of the Robin Hood legend rested almost entirely on the ballads. The number of songs in the collection rose slightly as the century progressed, the advertisements dating from before the 1780s referring to twenty-four songs, those thereafter to twenty-eight. The preface to the Newry 1784 edition reads in part:

> To all gentlemen archers
> This garland has long been out of repair,
> Some songs being wanting, of which we give account;
> For now at last, by true industrious care,
> The twenty-four songs to twenty-eight we mount.[66]

As it was larger, the price was higher (6*d.*); it had been sold for 4*d.* in 1750.[67] The songs are very evocative of a merrie past:

> Robin Hood was a tall young man,
> Derry, derry down,
> And Robin Hood was a proper young man,
> Of courage stout and bold
> Hey down, derry, derry down.

---

[65] See appendix I, nos 23, 29, 34, 68, 97, 115, 124, 159.
[66] *The English archer: or, Robert, earl of Huntington* (Newry, 1784), p. 2.
[67] See appendix I, no. 34.

> Robin Hood went into fair Nottingham,
> With the general for to dine;
> There he was aware of fifteen foresters,
> Drinking beer, ale and wine.[68]

The appeal of these verses is not hard to see, but rather harder to see is the reason why such essentially English songs were popular in Ulster. The answer might simply be the nature of the ballads – the exploits of an outlaw, an always popular theme – or it might be that song, unlike other forms of literature at the popular level, was dominated by the English output. So little survives, but an examination of the handful of garlands that do survive shows indeed that in these the prevailing atmosphere is English, with a scattering of Scottish and Irish songs.

Other larger song books were published, and retained popularity for a time, such as *The goldfinch: a collection of celebrated new songs. . . . To which is added, a select collection of above 100 English and Scots songs*,[69] which was advertised between 1752 and 1767 at the price of 6½d. Some were brought into being by political events, such as the popular *Paddy's resource* by Rev. James Porter, a collection of songs in the United Irishman interest published in Belfast in 1796; others by social movements, such as the popular *Collection of songs to be sung by Free Masons*,[70] whose popularity in the second half of the century was due to the swift growth of freemasonry.

The late eighteenth century was also the era of antiquarianism, and the field of balladry did not escape. So *Popular ballads written in the middle of the last, and the commencement of the present century . . . as examples of the fugitive songs of those times* was printed at Belfast in 1795. Some of the songs would have been better forgotten:

> But at the door keep Babel's whore,
> That she may ne'er beguile again,
> Lest that our nation she once more
> Wi' whoredom may defile and stain.[71]

A far cry indeed from *The English archer*; and luckily most of the songs current during the century, when not being political, were of the healthy 'Black-eyed Susan' sort.

[68] *The English archer*, p. 11.
[69] See appendix I, nos 37, 43, 49, 69, 74, 76, 79.
[70] Ibid., nos 74, 76, 97, 98, 106, 107, 111, 117, 132.
[71] *Popular ballads written in the middle of the last, and the commencement of the present century* (Belfast, 1795), p. 5.

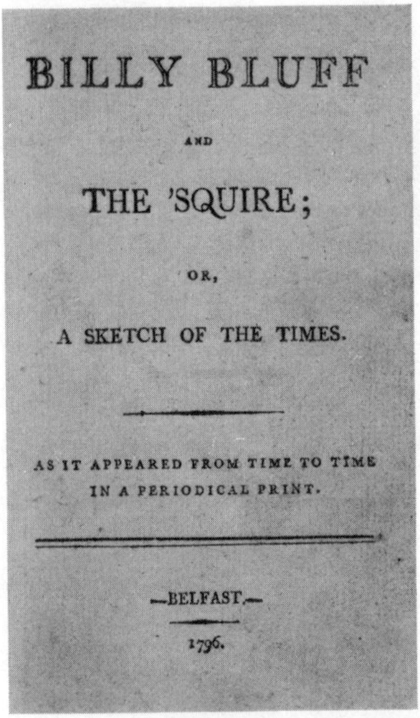

BILLY BLUFF

AND

THE 'SQUIRE;

OR,

A SKETCH OF THE TIMES.

AS IT APPEARED FROM TIME TO TIME
IN A PERIODICAL PRINT.

—BELFAST.—

1796.

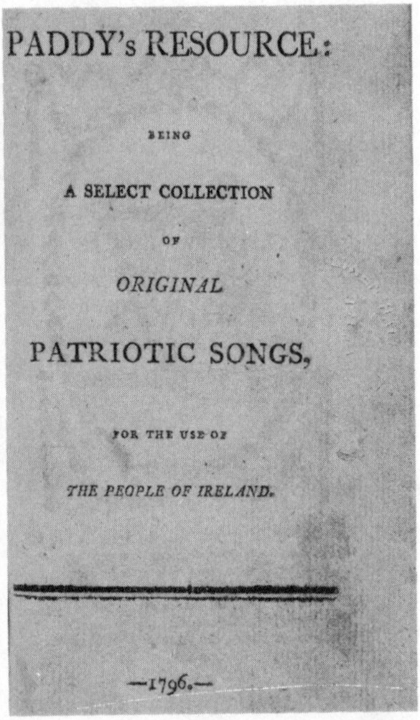

PADDY's RESOURCE:

BEING

A SELECT COLLECTION

OF

ORIGINAL

PATRIOTIC SONGS,

FOR THE USE OF

THE PEOPLE OF IRELAND.

—1796.—

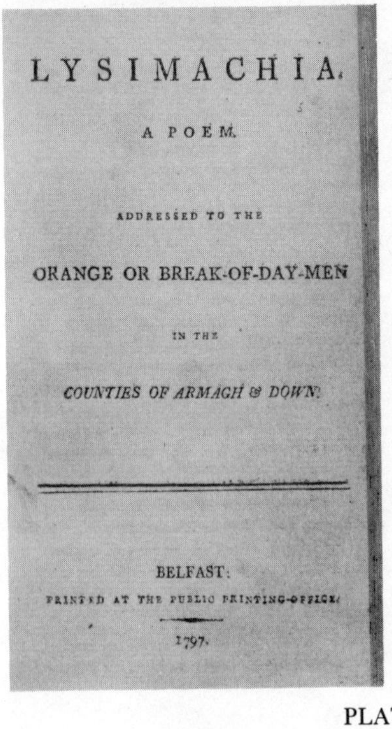

LYSIMACHIA.

A POEM.

ADDRESSED TO THE

ORANGE OR BREAK-OF-DAY-MEN

IN THE

COUNTIES OF ARMAGH & DOWN.

BELFAST:
PRINTED AT THE PUBLIC PRINTING-OFFICE.

1797.

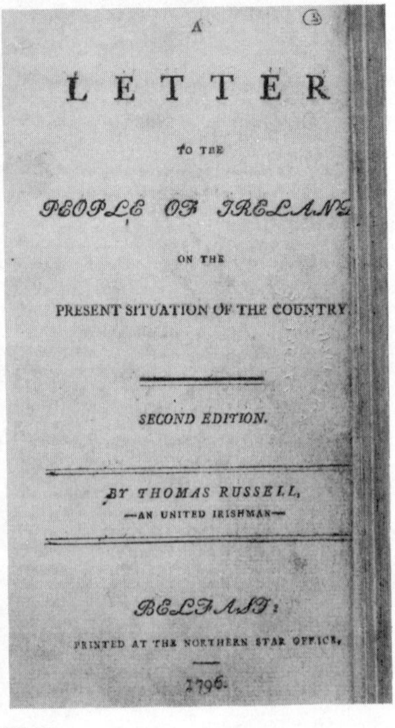

A

LETTER

TO THE

PEOPLE OF IRELAND

ON THE

PRESENT SITUATION OF THE COUNTRY.

SECOND EDITION.

BY THOMAS RUSSELL,
—AN UNITED IRISHMAN—

BELFAST:
PRINTED AT THE NORTHERN STAR OFFICE.

1796.

PLATE V
Radical political productions of the 1790s

CHAPTER 5

Popular Non-Fiction, Politics,
Criminal Biography, and Freemasonry
in the Eighteenth Century

Not all popular literature appealed purely to the religious mind or
the imagination. The same readers who communed internally
with God or travelled to faery lands on magic steeds also lived in a
real world, where they had to eat, live in a community with family,
friends and enemies, and be governed by their pastors and
masters. The literature produced, distributed round the countryside to homes and markets by the travelling chapmen, and bought
reflected this. Some mirrored social aspirations, others dealt with
amusements such as conjuring and jest-telling. But the most
interesting reflected attitudes to authority. As might be expected
from the social class of the readers, these attitudes were unfavou-
rable. The heroes were a mixed bunch, by and large: the covenanter Alexander Peden, Bonnie Prince Charlie, Freney the
highwayman, Billy Bluff. For the masses, one of the main attractions of such figures was the extent to which they stood outside the
established order and threatened it, whether they forecast fire and
brimstone, attempted to change the political order, or merely
removed sums of money from the well-to-do.

Gaining strength as the century progressed was the tendency
towards socialisation. This has already been seen in the growth of
reading societies, but another manifestation was the freemason's
lodge, which between the middle and end of the century became
more and more important in the countryside, and generated its
own literature. But we will begin with a genre less sublime in its
subject matter.

From the early seventeenth century onwards, books of 'compliments' were common. These were little treatises intended to
teach those with no social graces how to write letters, make pretty
compliments to pretty ladies, and even interpret dreams.[1] Ulster

---

[1] Louis B. Wright, *Middle-class culture in Elizabethan England* (Chapel Hill, N.C.,
1935), pp 136–7.

had its share of them. The earliest to be advertised was *The amorous gallant's tongue tipt with golden expressions, being a new academy,*[2] advertised in 1714. This was closely followed by what was possibly a development of it, *The new academy of compliments: or, the lover's secretary,*[3] advertised from the 1730s onward, and, as we shall see, appearing unaltered as late as 1850. The volume commences with various expressions for use on different occasions, and some of the most amusing are contained in the section headed 'To accost a lady, and enter into discourse with her'. A good opening gambit was 'Pardon my rashness, if I presume so far as to proffer my service unto you; your beauty hath so far prevailed over me, that I have long desired to attain to the honour of speaking to you.'[4] Next comes a number of 'witty and ingenious sentences' to help with further conversation. They range from 'You walk in artificial clouds, and heave your wanton lips in sweet dalliances' to 'Your language is more dubious than an oracle.'[5] Further on we come to an amazing section headed 'Witty questions and answers for the improvement of conversation'. They range from the slightly inane ('*Q.* Why is marriage compared to a sea-voyage? *A.* Because if men have not good fortune in it, they are likely to be cast away or ruined') to the slightly funny ('*Q.* What said the tyler [*sic*] to his man, when he fell through the rafters of the house to the bottom? *A.* Well done, i'faith, I like such a servant as thou art, who can get through his work so nimbly') to the risqué ('*Q.* Why is a whore's trade opposite to all others? *A.* Because she sets up without credit, and too much custom breaks her').[6] One wonders what conversation was like before it was improved.

Next follows one of the main sections, 'Instructions for the writing of letters'. This contains sample letters of all sorts, from letters of compliments, couched in high-flown language, to plain country love-letters. After various forms of receipts and so forth, comes 'The silent language'. This enabled people to say things like 'Madam, I am your humble servant' across a crowded room without anyone else being the wiser. In the unlikely event of there being anyone in the room who could understand the man who was gesticulating and snapping his fingers (apart from his lady) he could even change to code, 'I am your humble servant' becoming 'N ym afru hrmblt oturyie', at which point the whole thing

---

[2] See appendix I, no. 11.
[3] Ibid., nos 15, 17, 20, 37, 43, 49, 65, 67, 68, 69, 74, 76, 79, 98, 107, 111, 117, 132.
[4] *New academy of compliments* (Belfast, 1767), p. 8.
[5] Ibid., p. 10.
[6] Ibid., pp 15, 16, 18.

becomes reminiscent of the Black Hand Gang in an old-fashioned children's comic.

There are methods of getting good husbands, the significance of moles, songs, and instructions for dances such as 'Bung your eye'. The whole thing is a vivid picture of what country people thought life in high society would be like, and books like this, distributed by the thousand, encouraged the illusion. There were others, though not so popular. One was John Shirley's *Triumph of wit: or, ingenuity displayed*,[7] which contained poems, the art and mystery of love, canting (slang), and dancing instructions, and *Wit's cabinet*,[8] which contained songs, compliments, instructions for writing letters, dream interpretation, palmistry, and canting.

Another curious volume giving a mixture of useful, or supposedly useful, information and old wives' tales was the *Book of knowledge, treating of the wisdom of the ages*,[9] by 'Erra Pater'. This contained information on astrology, medicine, physiognomy and palmistry, mole interpretation, weather prognostication, husbandry, farriery, and simple accountancy. It was obviously aimed at a rural audience and contained what was apparently the only popularly available agricultural information in print in this era, long before the advent of farming societies on the Ulster scene.

The *Book of knowledge* did contain some medicine, but two medical specialist books were carried by the chapmen, one straightforward, the other frankly falling into the category of folk medicine; indeed, into the category of dirty book. The first was Nicholas Culpeper's *A directory for midwives*,[10] a fairly large book, of which an edition was published in Belfast in 1766. The second was the *Works of Aristotle, the famous philosopher*.[11] 'Aristotle', however, is not by any means 'the famous philosopher' of that name. The *Works* likely owed its origin to one or more hack writers of the seventeenth century,[12] and owed its popularity to a number of causes. Firstly, perhaps in no field of medicine has the occult lingered longer in the popular mind than in the mysterious processes of sex and generation.[13] Secondly, the emphasis on female sexuality seems to show that the book was designed

[7] See appendix I, nos 29, 37, 43, 49, 67, 69, 74, 76, 79, 107, 111, 132.

[8] Ibid., nos 98, 111, 117.

[9] Ibid., nos 15, 17, 20, 34, 68, 98.

[10] Ibid., nos 75, 97, 105.

[11] Ibid., no. 98; *Belfast News-letter*, 3 Jan. 1775.

[12] Otho T. Beall, 'Aristotle's Master Piece in America: a landmark in the folklore of medicine' in *William and Mary Quarterly*, 3rd ser., xx (1963), p. 208.

[13] Ibid., p. 213.

primarily for male readers,[14] and thus the appeal was both to the
curious and to the prurient.

The *Works* consisted of various parts. The main one was the
'Masterpiece'. This consisted of a mass of jumbled 'facts', relating
to generation and pregnancy, such as descriptions of monsters,
descriptions of private parts, ways to beget male or female children (to beget a female, the woman lay on her left side, strongly
imagined a female, drank the decoction of female mercury, and
preferably did all this in Libra or Aries), and ways of foretelling
the sex of the child. The least reliable method of determining the
latter was to see which breast was plumper; the most reliable was
to let a drop of mother's milk fall into a bowl of water: if it floated
the child would be a boy.

The 'Midwife' was usually included with the *Works*. This was a
fairly straightforward piece of obstetrics, varied with a bewilder-
ing array of weird recipes. One for cold distemper of the womb
called for Galengal, cinnamon, nutmeg, mace, cloves, ginger,
cubebs, nedory, cardamum, grains of paradise, long pepper, wine,
sage, mint, balm, and motherwort.[15]

The third piece of hack writing to be usually included was
'Aristotle's last legacy'. This wanders between moral stories and
cures for the gleets, chancres, and buboes. Often included in the
Works are two pieces much older than the seventeenth century, the
'Problems' and 'Physiognony'. The 'Problems', which tradition
says was compiled by the students of the genuine Aristotle, poses,
among more straightforward questions, some which read rather
oddly:

Q. Why has not a man a tail like a beast? *A.* Because man is a noble creature,
whose property is to sit; which a beast, having a tail, cannot.[16]

'Aristotle' foresaw two problems about birds:

Q. Why have birds their stones inward? *A.* Because if outward, they would
hinder their flying and lightness.
Q. How comes it that birds do not piss? *A.* Because that superfluity which
would be converted into urine, is turned into feathers.[17]

The *Works* were not regarded with much favour by the upright and
educated classes. Henry Cooke, when questioned by the Irish

[14] Ibid., p. 217.
[15] Aristotle (pseud.), *Works* (London, *c*.1860), p. 355.
[16] Ibid., p. 437.
[17] Ibid., p. 438.

Education Commissioners, denied that it had appeared in the hedge schools.[18] It was, astonishingly, to remain an under-the-counter book until the early years of the twentieth century.

A more useful book was Hannah Glasse's *Servant's directory*.[19] Priced at the usual 6½d., it contained all that was necessary to qualify a person to act as a servant, with handy recipes. Another workaday book was John Hill's *Young secretary's guide*,[20] already mentioned in chapter 1, and the *Dealer's companion and trader's assistant* improved,[21] of which editions were published in Belfast in 1773 and 1800.

Turning again to less useful arts, we come to Henry Dean's *Hocus pocus: or, the whole art of legerdemain*,[22] which contains some tricks that would nowadays never be allowed into print.

Anoint your tongue with liquid storox, and you may put a pair of tongs into your mouth, without hurting yourself, and lick them till they are cold, by the help of this ointment, and by preparing your mouth thus you may take wood-coal out of the fire, and eat them as you would eat bread . . . take half an ounce of camphor, dissolve it in two ounces of aquavita, add to it an ounce of quicksilver, which is the droppings of myrrh, and hinders the camphor from firing, take also two ounces of hamitatis, a red stone to be had at the druggists . . . and when you intend to walk on the red-hot bar, you must anoint your feet well therewith, and you may walk over without danger, by this you may wash your hands in boiling lead.[23]

'To thrust a piece of lead into your eye, and to drive it about with a stick between the skin and flesh and forehead, until it be brought to the other eye, and there thrust out'[24] was a piece of trickery, as was 'To thrust a dagger into your guts, very strangely, and to recover immediately'. This involved a false belly made of pasteboard and coloured by a painter, and behind this a bladder filled with blood (calf or sheep), behind this again being a metal plate to protect the real belly. There was a cautionary note, one of the few in the book, about a juggler who had forgotten the plate and killed himself.[25]

Witty questions and answers have been mentioned above, but

[18] *First report of the Commissioners*, appendix, p. 820.
[19] See appendix I, nos 67, 69, 74, 76, 82, 107, 111, 117, 132.
[20] Ibid., nos 11, 15, 17, 20, 34, 65, 68, 86, 98; above, p. 19.
[21] Ibid., nos 88, 97, 105, 111, 132, 166.
[22] Ibid., no. 98.
[23] Henry Dean, *The whole art of legerdemain: or, hocus pocus in perfection* (Belfast, 1844), pp 47–9.
[24] Ibid., p. 65.
[25] Ibid., pp 70–71.

there were several popular books devoted purely to jests. Of these, the most popular was a volume entitled *Laugh and be fat*.[26] The frequently scatological Jemmy Carson reveals the coarseness of eighteenth-century life as well as the popularity of the book in Ireland:

'Tis also a great promoter of mirth, for I have known one single fart, that made an escape, raise a laugh of half an hour, and the celebrated author of a book called Laugh and be Fat, proves laughing a very wholesome exercise.[27]

The book was also popular in the hedge schools: it was described as 'a collection of the most indecent stories, told in the coarsest language. . . . the moral sense of the children of both sexes was corrupted, by teaching them to indulge in what was gross and indelicate'.[28] Other jest books were *London jests*,[29] W. Hick's *Coffee-house jests*[30] and George Buchanan's *Jests*,[31] though none of these were as popular as *Laugh and be fat*. The *Belfast almanacs*, published in the latter part of the century, often included, as well as useful information about fairs and markets, numbers of coarse jokes.

Works of travel were becoming more and more popular. The travel book opened up the world, a world that had few boundaries, where there was free and profitable movement, adventure, danger, and great rewards. This was brought out in the fiction of the period: both Mrs Aubin's *Noble slaves* and Chetwood's *Voyages and adventures of Captain Robert Boyle*, dealt with above, had as a theme travel into barely explored parts of the world. In the earlier part of the century Nathaniel Crouch's *Surprizing miracles of nature and art*[32] was a popular little hodge-podge, containing descriptions of birds, beasts, fishes, and flora of foreign countries, with notices of other interesting things. There were two books of voyages proper carried by the chapmen. The earliest in date was Nathaniel Crouch's *Sir Francis Drake revived*,[33] recalling the glories of the Elizabethan age of discovery. The other volume was more topical, being Richard Walter's *Voyage round the world . . . by George Anson*,[34] representing the eighteenth-century leap in exploration.

[26] See appendix I, nos 34, 98, 86.
[27] Jemmy Carson, *Jemmy Carson's collections* (Dublin, 1787), p. 89.
[28] John Edward Walsh, *Sketches of Ireland sixty years ago* (Dublin, 1847), pp 102–3.
[29] See appendix I, nos 34, 65, 68.
[30] Ibid., no. 86.
[31] Ibid., nos 65, 68.
[32] Ibid., no. 34.
[33] Ibid., nos 86, 98.
[34] Ibid., nos 68, 86, 98.

In the field of history, the only work on Ireland carried by the chapmen was the *History of Ireland*,[35] that is, *The history of the kingdom of Ireland* by the indefatigable and almost omnipresent Nathaniel Crouch. This basically dealt with the seventeenth-century wars. The history of England is represented by the *Compendious history of all the monarchs of England*,[36] an adaptation of a work by Crouch – the edition published in Belfast about 1763 brought the story forward to the 1740s – and by W. H. Dilworth's *The protestant hero: or, the life of William III*,[37] which was of both English and Irish interest. The history of Scotland is dealt with in Ralph Griffith's *Ascanius: or, the young adventurer*,[38] a history of the '45 and Bonny Prince Charlie, who is portrayed as more sinned against than sinning.

Ancient history is covered by the laconic entry 'Jews wars' on the 1750 catalogue of chapmen's books, and this must have been an edition of Josephus' *History of the Jewish war*. The 1777 catalogue of chapmen's books carries another brief entry, 'Charles the 12th', and this is certainly Defoe's *Wars of Charles the Twelfth*; Charles, as king of Sweden, was one of the great popular military heroes. The history of America is solely covered by Nathaniel Crouch's *The English empire in America*,[39] which is surprising, as Ulster emigration to America was immense and one would have expected more popular works relating to it.

Turning to politics, we find that every crisis brought forth a host of political pamphlets, which were distributed around the country for a while until they were superseded by the coming of the next crisis. For instance, a long list of pamphlets was advertised in the local press in 1754 'relative to the present political contests in Ireland',[40] and these ranged in price from 2*d.* to 1*s*.1*d.*, the majority being either 3*d.* or 6½*d.* They could be even cheaper: in 1782 a pamphlet called *A letter to a friend, on these caballistic words Repeal and Renounce* sold for a penny.[41] The crises of the later eighteenth century ensured the reprinting of at least one classic Irish political work, William Molyneux's *The case of Ireland . . . stated.* In order to get it read by all classes of people, 'a few gentlemen' got it reprinted at the price of a British sixpence, and,

[35] Ibid., nos 86, 98, 107, 111.
[36] Ibid., nos 34, 64, 65, 68, 86.
[37] See appendix I, nos 58, 68, 86; *Belfast News-letter*, 14 Nov. 1760.
[38] Ibid., no. 86; William Carleton, *Traits and stories of the Irish peasantry* (4th ed., 5 vols, Dublin 1836), ii, 235.
[39] See appendix I, nos 34, 65, 68, 86.
[40] *Belfast News-letter*, 17 Sept. 1754.
[41] Ibid., 2 Aug. 1782.

obviously in order to encourage booksellers and chapmen, noted 'a very large profit from sixteen copies upwards'.[42]

The crisis also resulted in the production of two local classics by Rev. James Porter: *Billy Bluff and Squire Firebrand*, a satirical work, of which two editions were published in Belfast in the eighteenth century (1796 and 1797); and *Paddy's resource*, a collection of songs, again published in Belfast in 1795 and 1796. *Billy Bluff* was being reprinted as late as 1879, and was an extremely effective attack on conservative elements in Ulster, under transparent pseudonyms such as 'Lord Mountmumble' (Robert Stewart, Baron Stewart of Mountstewart). It was responsible for the popular name applied to *Paddy's resource*:

Why, your honour, they [seditious ballads] are galloping over all the country faster than a bird can fly, or a hare can run, and that's the very downright reason they have given them the name they have. – Why, what name have they? – They are all put into one book, your honour, and they are called *Paddy's race-horse*.[43]

But the one author who aroused the ire of the establishment more than any other was Thomas Paine, perhaps because his works savoured not only of revolution but of religious infidelity. His works were disseminated throughout Ulster by the radicals. Henry Cooke testified:

I know perfectly well that the works of Tom Paine and such writers were extensively put into the hands of the people: Paine's *Rights of man*, a political work, and *Age of reason*, a deistical one, were industriously circulated: I know it was very common to drop them on the road, and leave them at the door of the poor man, or push them under the door.[44]

However, not all the activities of the various patriot organisations were of so serious a nature. In 1782, a number of Volunteers from the town of Newtownards put on a performance of the play *The battle of Aughrim*, which hardly needed the advertised singing and dancing between the acts to make it an evening to remember. For good measure, they added the farce *Miss in her teens*.[45]

One rather strange field of literature, which towards the end of the century became entangled with radical politics, was prophecy. The situation in the first three-quarters or so of the century was

---

[42] Ibid., 2 July 1782.
[43] James Porter, *Billy Bluff and Squire Firebrand* (Belfast, 1812), p. 21.
[44] *First report of the Commissioners*, appendix, p. 820.
[45] *Belfast News-letter*, 7 Apr. 1782.

fairly straightforward. There were two prophets whose works appear fairly steadily, and one that makes a brief appearance. At this time there does not seem to be any political significance attached to prophecies. They were part of the Scottish presbyterian tradition before 'modernisation', which has been termed 'prophetic' rather than 'conversionist'; each major religion in the province – presbyterian, anglican and Roman Catholic – tacitly confined its attentions to its own flock, and in the case of the presbyterians there was a fascination with purity of doctrine and polity coupled with a belief in divine intervention.[46]

Of these prophets the oldest was Thomas the Rhymer, or Thomas of Ercildoune, a thirteenth-century inhabitant of Fife who gave his prophecies in rhyme.[47] These prophecies were revered by the ordinary Scots at least until the time of Sir Walter Scott. They were distorted and mutilated at several periods to fit particular events and are suitably vague and apocalyptic:

> At three-burn Grange in after day
> There shall be a lang and bloody fray;
> When a three-thumbed wight by the reins shall hald
> Three kings' horses baith stout and bauld;
> And the three burns three days will rin
> Wi' the blude o' the slain that fa' therein.[48]

But the most popular was Alexander Peden's *Life and prophecies*.[49] Peden was a Scottish covenanter of the seventeenth century, a revered and contumaceous preacher. Part of his local popularity might be explained by the fact that he spent some time in Ulster. He was uncompromising: once, when he was staying at a house in County Antrim,

there was a servant-lass in the house that he could not look upon but with frowns; and sometimes, when at family worship, he said, pointing to her with a frowning countenance, You come from the barn and from the byre reeking in your lusts, and sits down among us, we do not want you or none such. At last he said to William Steel and his wife, Put away that unhappy lass from your house, for she will be a stain to your family, for she is with child and will murder it and will be punished for the same; which accordingly came to pass, and she was burnt at Craig-Fergus.[50]

[46] David W. Miller, 'Presbyterianism and "modernization" in Ulster' in *Past & Present*, lxx (1978), pp 72–3.
[47] See appendix I, nos 15, 17, 29, 124.
[48] T. F. Henderson, *Scottish vernacular literature* (3rd ed., Edinburgh, 1910), pp 19–24.
[49] See appendix I, nos 15, 17, 29, 34, 68, 74, 97, 100, 107, 109, 132.
[50] Alexander Peden, *Life and prophecies* (Cork, 1791), p. 16.

Peden saw God as directly intervening in the most trivial and mundane aspects of life, as did his hearers and readers:

He was preaching one Sabbath night in the said John Slowan's house, a great number both within and without hearing him; where he insisted, shewing the great need and usefulness of seeking and getting spiritual riches brought in an example, if any man of you were going to Belfast or Bellimony, they would be looking their pockets for what they had to bear their charge: One man standing without said quietly, Lord help me, for I have nothing to bear mine; Mr Peden said immediately, pointing to the door, poor man, do not fear; for I have it out of Heaven, as with an audible voice, thy charge shall be borne, and that in a remarkable manner; which rejoiced him to think his case was made known to him, however that man has been mercifully and remarkably supported since, and that in the way of his duty.[51]

Also, in view of later developments, he foresaw more political matters.

The Lord has letten me see the French marching with their armies through the breadth and length of the land, marching to their bridle-reins in the blood of all ranks, and that for a broken, burnt, and buried covenant.[52]

Another prophet to make a brief appearance was James Ussher (Archbishop of Armagh 1625–56), whose *Remarkable prophecies*[53] foretold confusions in church and state, and a great persecution of protestants.

But in the last quarter of the century overt political use began to be made of prophecy. It was a prophetic time, and old favourites such as Peden and Thomas the Rhymer were pressed into service. At a meeting of the United Irishmen at Rasharkin, County Antrim, the following resolutions were passed:

Resolved: That we behold plainly the case of not everyone knowing the prophecies of Thomas the Rhymer, and the propecies of Alexander Peden, all useful to the people in the making our laws, and as many of our brethren cannot read them, and explain them, and tell about them;

Resolved: That Donald O'Kennedy will read to the county of Derry, and that Archy Woods will read to the county of Antrim, and that they tell the French news to everybody, and dispute with all who dare to contradict them.[54]

At the same time strange, Peden-like figures appeared in the countryside, such as the covenanter Gibson:

[51] Ibid., p. 53.
[52] Ibid., p. 38.
[53] See appendix I, no. 86.
[54] Samuel M'Skimin, *Annals of Ulster* (Belfast, 1849), pp 49–50.

The religious services of the day, if such they may be called, seldom concluded in less than six hours, and his texts of scripture were always taken from the book of the Revelations, the eighteenth chapter of which seemed to be his favourite. These harangues were always of a political nature, and the texts applied in such a manner as to impress his bearers that it was the word of God which inculcated upon them certain duties, while, in reality, they were inflamed to deeds of rebellion, tyranny and murder. On entering upon his mission, he, at times, so far forgot himself as to relapse for a moment into his holy hatred of popery, by introducing the antiquated dogmas of his sect, in allusion to the man of sin, and an old jade dressed in scarlet, dyed with the blood of the saints, said to reside near Babylon. These untimely slips of his reverence were overlooked by the hearers with a truly Christian forbearance, for which kindness he was afterwards sure to make amends by pointing out the immediate destruction of the British monarchy.[55]

One prophecy, *The vision of St Malachias*, which stated on the title-page that it was printed in 1776, but sounds suspiciously later, made similar claims about the British monarchy.

When eighteen centuries from Christ
Are near compleat and full,
And Britain's crown shall imitate
That of the Great Mogul,
Imposing slavery on all
Who its dominion own
Then shall it stand a hazard great
On ground to tumble down.[56]

In the 1790s the prophecies flooded off the presses, and millenarianism, combined with a real feeling that God was working to change the social order (especially when events in France were considered), spread over the country. In the single year of 1795, for instance, the following works were published: *An examination of the scripture prophecies respecting the downfall of Antichrist . . . and the late revolution in France shewn to be plainly foretold* (Belfast); *Extracts from the prophecies of Richard Brothers* (Belfast); *Prophetical extracts particularly such as relate to the revolution in France* (Strabane); Robert Fleming's *Rise and fall of Antichrist* (Belfast); and *The shaking and translation of heaven and earth*, by John Owen (Belfast and Monaghan editions), recalling the popularity of prophecy in England during the troubled 1640s.[57] With the coming of the new century, the

[55] Ibid., pp 53–4.
[56] *The vision of St Malachias, one of the most famous successors of St Patrick* (Belfast, 1776), p. 29.
[57] Christopher Hill, *The world turned upside down* (Harmondsworth, 1975), pp 87–106.

prophetic urge seems to have left the presbyterians and been replaced by 'conversionist evangelicalism'.[58] It was revived, mainly by catholics in the more southerly parts of Ireland, in the 1820s in a rather different form.

If characters such as the covenanter Gibson with his apocalyptic sermons were outside the bounds of the establishment's way of life, so too were the highwaymen and raparees, whose doings were celebrated in a number of small books. One of the best-known was John Cosgrave's *Genuine history of the lives and actions of the most notorious highwaymen*, of which an edition was published in Belfast in 1776. This was better known as *Irish rogues and raparees*,[59] and indeed in the Belfast edition this wording was used as the running title along the tops of the pages. It was one of the books, along with the life of Redmond O'Hanlon and the life of Captain Freney, that were recollected by Henry Cooke;[60] and Carleton also remembered the life of Freney and *Irish rogues and raparees* as being available in the hedge schools.[61]

The life and adventures of James Freney is the best known of the individual biographies. Freney was born in County Kilkenny,[62] and was accepted into a 'big house' as a pantry boy. He advanced himself somewhat, and then in 1724 his mistress died, and he married and set up in business in Waterford. He fell foul of the other traders because he was not free of the city, and moved to Thomastown, County Kilkenny, where he got into debt. He fell in with a former member of the 'Kellymount gang' who had been pardoned as an informer, and got into bad ways. There is some attempt on his part to give himself a sort of picaresque, Robin Hood, Dick Turpin image – once when he robbed a man of fifty pounds he returned a part of the money for expenses towards the rest of the journey. He took part in a number of rather squalid burglaries; a large part of a highwayman's life seems not so much to have consisted of romantic 'your money or your life' exploits as of breaking and entering with a liberal amount of grevious bodily harm. His Turpin self-image extended to the name of his horse, which was called Beef-stakes, though the animal died rather unromantically of the staggers. After his capture, he asked for pardon and in return offered to inform on a number of his associates and keep the country clear in future. Rumours followed

[58] Miller, op. cit., p. 85.
[59] See appendix I nos 86, 98.
[60] *First report of the Commissioners*, appendix, p. 820.
[61] Carleton, op. cit., p. 234.
[62] James Freney, *Life and adventures* (Belfast, 1835).

about mass informations, but eventually the gang was taken and executed and Freney pardoned because of his valuable information. Lord Carrick tried to raise a subscription to help Freney and his family to leave the kingdom, but as the local gentry refused to assist him he was forced to raise money by writing his life story. Posterity saw two different Freneys. Mid-twentieth-century nationalism saw him as a chivalrous knight, with his betrayals excised from the record, who took part in adventures and thrilling escapes, his only victims the establishment, that is the representatives of British rule;[63] while John Edward Walsh, who was certainly chronologically nearer to him, described him as 'a mean-looking fellow, pitted with the smallpox, and blind of an eye . . . he was a coarse, vulgar, treacherous villain, much of the highwayman, and nothing of the hero'.[64] Despite this, the influence of Freney is seen in the following, dating from 1790.

Whereas on Thursday night last, between the hours of nine and ten o'clock, after all the servant-men, who slept in an outhouse, had retired to the beds, except the butler, a desperate set of fellows entered Doctor Lill's house of Barn-hill, in the county of Tyrone, and in a most outrageous manner, abused and desperately cut his butler, who had given them opposition; and had it not been for the cries and shouts of the family, which were heard by the neighbours of Stewarts-Town, who humanely ran to their assistance, they would have gained their ends, and perhaps would have committed murder, as they fired a shot at Mrs Lill, who was calling out of the window for help; but fortunately the shot missed her, and broke the pane of glass next to where she was standing. Two of the fellows who entered the house had black faces, one of which had a shirt on, hanging from the top of his head, leaving his face open to the mouth. The third was a well-looking fellow, about 5 feet 9 inches high, seemed to be between thirty and forty years of age; he had on a brown jacket and striped waistcoat – *Sailor-like;* was not disguised; said he was called the 'bold Capt. Freney'.[65]

This vividly shows the influence of Freney's story long after his death and, as we shall see, well into the next century. Not all the rogues were Irish: *The English rogue . . . To which is added, the life . . . of Jonathan Wild,* by the seventeenth-century hack writer Richard Head, occurs,[66] as does W. H. Dilworth's *History of the bucaniers of America.*[67] In addition, of course, there were innumerable last dying speeches, sold by such as Tantra Barbus.

One influence that made itself felt in the latter part of the

---

[63] Terence O'Hanlon, *The highwayman in Irish History* (Dublin, 1932), pp 97–105.
[64] John Edward Walsh, *Sketches of Ireland sixty years ago* (Dublin, 1847), pp 106–7.
[65] *Belfast News-letter,* 28 Dec. 1790.
[66] See appendix I, no. 86.
[67] Ibid., no. 68; *Belfast News-letter,* 14 Nov. 1760.

century was freemasonry. Though there may have been a lodge at Omagh in 1724, the first warranted lodge in Ulster was established in 1737.[68] The movement rapidly spread throughout the countryside, and by the end of the century its influence was everywhere felt, expressing itself, for instance, in the works of the weaver poets.[69] The local lodge in a rural area was a place for the males to meet and discuss matters; without entering into a discussion about the sociological significance of a secret society (or a society with secrets), it can be said that the facility to meet and socialise in this way was of great importance.

The rise of freemasonry is dramatically charted by the fate of John Bunyan's *Solomon's temple spiritualised.*[70] This does not make an appearance at all in the first half of the century, at a time when other works of Bunyan were at the height of their popularity. Suddenly in the 1750s it does appear and remains steadily popular thereafter. Three other masonic works to appear on the same 1777 catalogue of chapman's books were the *Pocket companion for freemasons;*[71] *Solomon in all his glory: or the master-mason. Being a true guide to the minutest recesses of masonry, both ancient and modern*[72] and *A collection of songs to be sung by freemasons . . . To which is added, Solomon's Temple, an oratorio.*[73] One work to be printed locally, in 1782, was Laurence Dermott's *Ahiman Rezon: or, a help to a brother,* first published in England in 1764. Few books on freemasonry have had such an influence.[74] It also contained, like the *Collection of songs,* the oratorio *Solomon's temple.*

The freemasons went in for lighter entertainment, as well. In the same year that the Volunteers of Newtownards put on a performance of the folk play *The battle of Aughrim,* accompanied by songs and dances, the freemasons of Moira, County Down, did exactly the same for the benefit of the poor,[75] thus linking the bourgeoisie of County Down with the peasantry of Carleton's Clogher Valley. The eighteenth century was a century that saw wide differences in class, in wealth, and in education, but also saw traces of the disappearing common culture of an earlier epoch.

---

[68] J. H.. Lepper, P. Crossle and R. E. Parkinson, *History of the Grand Lodge of Free and Accepted Masons of Ireland* (2 vols, Dublin, 1925–57), i, 117–19.

[69] Donald Akenson and W. H. Crawford, *James Orr, bard of Ballycarry* (Belfast, 1977), p. 26.

[70] See appendix I, nos 43, 49, 67, 69, 74, 86, 98, 105, 106, 107, 117, 132, 155.

[71] Ibid., nos 37, 67, 69, 74, 76, 97, 98, 107, 111, 117, 132.

[72] Ibid., nos 98, 106, 107, 111.

[73] Ibid., nos 74, 76, 97, 98, 106, 107, 111, 117, 132.

[74] Lepper, Crossle, and Parkinson, op. cit., p. 236.

[75] *Belfast News-letter,* 8 Jan. 1782.

PLATE VI
Interior of a national school
From *Sequel No. 1 to the second book of lessons* (Dublin, 1866), p. 5

CHAPTER 6

Education and Literacy, 1800–1850

Although changes in popular reading habits in Ulster are discernible in the eighteenth century, particularly towards its end, in the nineteenth century the pace of change increased enormously. Though the older literature such as *Valentine and Orson* and like tales proved surprisingly resilient, with the coming of the mass production of cheap reading matter in a very few centres, chiefly London and Edinburgh, and with relatively cheap and speedy transport, local identities tended to be ironed out; and this tendency was immeasurably accelerated by the fact that during the first half of the century a very large number of individuals and groups were actively attempting to change ordinary reading habits, with varying success, and at the same time mass education accompanied by increasing literacy was spreading across the land.

Of the societies that were engaged in elementary education the oldest was the Incorporated Society for Promoting English Protestant Schools in Ireland, founded in 1733 with an avowedly proselytising aim. Though a large amount of space is usually devoted to it in educational histories, it was never of any great importance in educational terms, having only a few thousand children under its care,[1] if care is the right word to describe the often horrifying conditions under which the children were kept. Though each child was supposed to be taught reading, writing, arithmetic, and the principles of the established church, in practice these charter schools were a mass of abuses and sometimes run for the exclusive financial gain of the master, as (more recently) were old-fashioned jails in the southern states of America. At one time or another there had been ten such schools in Ulster,[2] but by 1825 there were only two – one for girls at Ballycastle, County Antrim, and one for boys at Strangford, County Down, as well as a day school at Ray, County Donegal. The two boarding schools between them only catered for 157 children. Rev. Elias Thackeray, who visited the Strangford school in 1818, thought the

---

[1] *First report of the Commissioners*, p. 14.
[2] Ibid., appendix, p. 25.

master 'a giddy man, and not fit for such responsibility'.[3] In the same year he reported of the Ballycastle school: 'In reading, spelling, writing and arithmetic, evident pains have been taken',[4] but a different picture was painted at the examination by the Commissioners of one Catherine Carthy, aged about nineteen:

. . . I recollect then that I went into Ballycastle.
How long did you stay there? – Five or six years.
. . . Had you been taught to read and write before you left Ballycastle? – Not very well.
Can you write now? – Very indifferently; not more than my name.
Can you read? – I am a very middling reader.[5]

Somewhat more important, but again of little mass appeal, were the schools attached to the Association Incorporated for Discountenancing Vice, and Promoting the Knowledge and Practice of the Christian Religion, founded in 1792. In its infancy, this strongly established church body distributed Bibles, prayer-books, and religious and moral tracts at reduced prices, originally on a very small scale. By 1825 they were running about 250 schools throughout the whole country, which taught English reading (chiefly through the medium of the scriptures), writing, arithmetic, and general instruction. The schools were open to all persuasions, and though the established church catechism was used, only members of that church were obliged to use it.[6] Of the schools sixty were in Ulster: fifteen in Cavan and ten in Down, with the other counties having between seven and two.[7]

Another group was the London Hibernian Society for Establishing Schools and Circulating the Holy Scriptures in Ireland. This was the most aggressive of the proselytising societies,[8] originating in 1806. Although the society ostensibly did not proselytise – 'The London Hibernian Society positively disavows that their object is to make proselytes from the Roman Catholic to the protestant communion'[9] – this does not sit comfortably with another of its statements:

The great body of the Irish wander like sheep, that have no faithful shepherd to lead them. Legendary tales, pilgrimages, penances, superstitions,

[3] Ibid., appendix, p. 99.
[4] Ibid., appendix, p. 69.
[5] Ibid., appendix, pp 257–8.
[6] Ibid., pp 31–3; appendix, p. 340.
[7] Ibid., appendix, pp 406–15.
[8] D. H. Akenson, *The Irish education experiment* (London, 1970), p. 82.
[9] *First report of the Commissioners*, p. 69.

offerings, priestly domination, the notorious habit of reconciling sanctimonious accents and attitudes with abandoned practices, and all that shocks and disgusts in the mummery of the mass house, cannot fail to fix a mournful sentiment in the heart of every enlightened and pious observer.... The manoeuvres of its priests are so various, so subtle, and alas! so efficient. ... The hope, therefore, that the Irish will ever be a tranquil and loyal people, and still more than piety and virtue will flourish among them, must be built on the anticipated reduction of popery.[10]

By 1823 there were 653 day schools in connection with the society in Ireland, of which 326, with 31,702 scholars, were in Ulster.[11] This again does not go with the statement of the society some years earlier that the main thrust of its efforts should be in those regions where Roman Catholics were in the majority (the 'confessed region of popery').[12]

The regulations of the society show how the average pupil was expected to progress, and are interesting from this point of view:

Pupils entered in the following classes must be qualified to pass into the next class in succession, within the following periods:

Alphabet class, in two months.
Junior spelling class, in four months.
Senior spelling class, in three months.
Spelling-book readers, in three months.

Allowing six months from the alphabet to entrance into the senior spelling class, and six months from commencing in that class for qualifying to enter the testament class.

Writing

Each pupil is to commence writing on entering into the spelling-book reading class.

Cyphering

Each pupil on entering the testament class is to commence the study of figures.[13]

However, the schools themselves seem to have been of widely differing standards. The 1825 education enquiry summed them up thus:

The funds of the society are not of such amount as to enable them to erect and furnish suitable school houses, or to allow adequate salaries to the teachers;

[10] Ibid., p. 66.
[11] Ibid., p. 67.
[12] Ibid., p. 66.
[13] Ibid., p. 68.

and the schools are frequently opened in remote and obscure districts, where little assistance can be obtained from local patronage or superintendence. Accordingly, of those schools of the society which we personally visited, we found, that with the exception of such as were in connection with the Society for the Education of the Poor of Ireland, or the Association for Discountenancing Vice, or under the superintendence of powerful local patrons, the buildings in general were common cabins, and sometimes mere hovels. The masters are usually from the lowest ranks of the peasantry, and have themselves frequently received but very little education . . . The great object of the schools . . . is the reading of the scriptures.[14]

Indeed the New Testament was the main class book in the London Hibernian Society's schools, and Captain George Pringle stated to the Commission that though the society did not object to the Kildare Place Society's books, it would prefer that they were not in its schools.[15] The children in fact appear to have had to commit so much scripture to memory in the evenings that they had no time to read anything else.[16] Especial scorn was reserved for those books commonly found in the hedge schools: 'nonsensical . . . containing fairy tales, the history of St Patrick, the seven champions of Christendom, the Scapular, &c., or at the very best Aesop's fables.'[17]

About 1820 an auxiliary branch of the society was established in Belfast with the Marquis of Donegall as president.[18]

However, one society stands head and shoulders over the rest for its educational methods, and, more importantly in the present context, for its vast influence on the course of popular reading habits in Ireland. This was the Society for the Education of the Poor of Ireland, more commonly known as the Kildare Place Society, from its abode. The society was formed in Dublin in 1811, and was managed by a committee consisting of people from different religious persuasions. Its principles were to establish schools which both in their government and admission policies should be uninfluenced by religious considerations, and in which the Bible, without note or comment, should be read by all pupils who had attained sufficient proficiency in reading, excluding as well all catechisms and books of religious controversy. It was to be understood that the Bible was not to be used as a school book from which children should be taught to spell or read. The society

14 Ibid., p. 81.
15 Ibid., appendix, p. 691.
16 Ibid., p. 490.
17 P. J. Dowling, *The hedge schools of Ireland* (Dublin, 1935), p. 82.
18 *Belfast News-letter*, 9 June 1820; *Belfast almanac, 1821*, p. 35.

received its first parliamentary grant, of £6,980, in the session of 1814–15.[19]

As far as the schools went, the society went on from strength to strength, starting with eight schools in connection by 1816, and rising to 1,634 by 1830.[20] There was always a greater proportion of applications to establish schools from Ulster than from any other province – J. D. Jackson gave the following reasons to the Education Commission in 1824:

> In the first place, in a great many counties in the north, there is a thicker population of resident noblemen and gentlemen who would be interested in the establishment of schools than is to be found in the extensive counties which constitute the province of Munster, and amongst the middling and lower orders themselves, there is a great desire in the north to have an improved description of schools established; there are a great many descendants of Scotch ancestors, and a great many manufactories established in the north, where a description of persons different from the common peasantry in Munster may be found.[21]

On the 5 January 1827, out of 1,477 schools connected with the society, no less than 803 were in Ulster. Down and Antrim lead, with 155 and 151 schools respectively, and at the bottom of the list come Cavan and Monaghan, with 45 and 35 schools respectively.[22]

One of the first things that the society did was to cast about for suitable school books. Like all the other societies, the Kildare Place Society was horrified by the material in use in the common pay or hedge schools, which not only consisted of such old fashioned works as the *Arabian nights* and the *Seven champions*, but of more objectionable fare such as *The feast of love, The effects of love, The school of delights* and *The history of Philander Flashaway*.[23] Indeed it is interesting to note that contemporary critics of popular reading material almost totally ignored any distinction between different types of such material: either it was officially approved and written by the commonality's betters with some sort of moral uplift as the ultimate aim, or it was to be utterly and uncritically condemned, whether it was a medieval romance or *Nocturnal revels*. The society's aims deprived it of the Bible as a basis for the curriculum, and

[19] *First report of the Commissioners*, p. 39.

[20] R. M. Martin, *Ireland before and after the union with Great Britain* (2nd ed., London, 1848), p. 210.

[21] *First report of the Commissioners*, appendix, p. 431.

[22] *Fifteenth report of the Society for Promoting the Education of the Poor of Ireland* (Dublin, 1827), pp 78–113.

[23] *First report of the Commissioners*, p. 43.

the only other textbooks suitable for the education of the lower orders were the publications of the National Society for Promoting the Education of the Poor in the Principles of the Established Church. But books written for English anglican children would never do for a non-sectarian Irish school system.[24] Lindley Murray's *English reader* was non-sectarian, but it had not been written for poor children and was priced at between three and five shillings.[25] There was no alternative for the society to the creation of its own books.

By the end of 1813 two volumes had appeared: the *Dublin spelling book* and the *Dublin reading book*. In their first form, indeed, they were not books proper, but a series of tablets, each mounted on a card, and of sufficient size to be suitable for class purposes. This was certainly an economic method of supplying textbooks to a school, whatever its other merits or demerits; the spelling book cost 5*s*. and the reading book 8*s.d.*, and the committee of the society reckoned that one of each should do a school of several hundred children for some years 'if reasonable care be taken by the teachers'.[26] Other textbooks followed.

However, the society was also engaged in an undertaking that was to have a more profound effect on Irish reading habits. In 1814 a Cheap Book Society had been established in Dublin, with the purpose of providing literature of a healthy kind, cheaply. However it appeared that its resources were not equal to the task.[27] In 1816 the Cheap Book Society handed over its effects to the Kildare Place Society, with one book ready and others in preparation. The Kildare Place Society had felt that it was little use teaching the Irish to read if they then rushed to their local chapman and bought copies of undesirable writings, and the only alternative was to write, print, bind, and distribute material in direct competition with the pernicious literature, alongside it, through the same outlets. The format was to be similar to the objectionable material – small in size, with woodcuts, though well produced. It does not seem to have been stated policy, but in fact none of the Kildare Place publications bear the name of the society on the title page or elsewhere, presumably so as not to frighten prospective purchasers wary of being got at. One result of this 'protective mimicry' is that the volumes are seldom recognised as

[24] J. M. Goldstrom, *The social content of education, 1808–1870* (Shannon, 1972), p. 55.
[25] Ibid., p. 56.
[26] H. K. Moore, *An unwritten chapter in the history of education* (London, 1904), pp 218–19.
[27] Ibid., p. 215.

Kildare Place Society publications today, and when they appear in the catalogues of antiquarian book dealers (as they frequently do, having been produced in such quantities) they are almost invariably catalogued under the heading 'chapbooks', for which a higher price can be asked.

A special book committee was appointed, whose members at first tried to write the books themselves, with results lost to posterity. They had the sense to employ a very competent literary assistant, Rev. Charles Bardin.[28] This man, nowadays unknown, probably had a greater effect on Irish reading habits, and was more widely read, than many a famous mainstream literary author. The strictest care was taken in the composition of the little books, so that there should not be the slightest suspicion of proselytising intent – one whiff of this and the whole structure on which the society was built would come tumbling down. By early 1817 seven books had been printed, four were in the press, one was awaiting final approval, and several others were in progress.[29] The works had astonishing success. Moore states, quoting a letter of January 1818, that the works were not 'advertised in the newspapers or in any of the usual modes',[30] but this policy must have been either short-lived or not firm policy at all, for the society took an advertisement in the *Belfast News-letter* in November of the same year, advertising sixteen volumes at prices ranging from £2.2s. a hundred for copies bound in sheep, and £1.10s. a hundred for copies bound in grain (sheepskin with the hair side outside) to single copies at 8d. each bound in sheep, 6d. bound in grain.[31]

At the beginning of 1819 there were twenty-seven volumes on sale, and by 1831 there were seventy-nine titles, by which time a grand total of 1,464,817 volumes had been issued.[32] But the grant was discontinued by parliament with the setting up of the national system of education in 1831, and the output of the society naturally slowed; but by 1842 a grand total of 1,698,062 volumes had been issued.[33]

In view of the importance of works produced by the society and their effect upon reading habits, it would be as well to look at their compositon. Charles Bardin was literary assistant from 1818 until 1827, during the main thrust of book production. He wrote,

[28] Ibid., p. 244.
[29] Ibid., p. 245.
[30] Ibid., p. 247.
[31] *Belfast News-letter*, 17 Nov. 1818.
[32] Moore, op. cit., pp 247–8.
[33] Martin, op. cit., p. 210.

rewrote and edited the books, under very strict superintendence
by the committee:

> Sometimes the kind of book wished for is suggested by the committee, and I
> am directed to prepare it; when I suggest the book myself, if the plan is
> approved of, I compile or compose it according, as the case may be;
> sometimes abridge it from another work, and submit it to the book sub-
> committee; when thus prepared, it is referred to one of the members of the
> committee, who gives it an attentive reading, and returns it with his
> observations; if I agree with him in the corrections suggested by him, I make
> them accordingly, and if not, I state the reasons of my dissent, and the
> committee decide upon them. When thus corrected, the book is referred to
> another member of the committee, who sees the corrections suggested, and
> the manner in which they have been attended to; indeed, it often comes back
> to me three or four times, circulating through the members till it meets their
> approbation; two of them at least must sign the recommendation to the
> general committee.[34]

Even after Bardin's departure to become curate of Dundalk, he
undertook to supply copy for some books each year, and indeed
was in connection with this part of the society's work for nearly
fifteen years more.[35]

The reasons for all this care in the production of the books were
of course not only to ensure that the books were well written,
informative, accurate, and entertaining, but perhaps above all to
ensure that they did not in the slightest offend Roman Catholic
opinion. In this way they were largely successful, though of course
it was extremely difficult to offend such opinion in, for instance, a
work of voyages to the Arctic regions. The society, however,
occasionally did run foul of adverse criticism, despite its care. On
one occasion, in Westport, a catholic clergyman objected to the
possible use of the Kildare Place volumes in his school. It turned
out, upon examination, that the books were already in the school,
and used with his approbation, but that he did not realise that they
were the books in question.[36] As has already been pointed out, the
books nowhere bear the name of the society.

Another objection was made, by a priest in Waterford, to the
volume *Travels of Mungo*. Mungo was a sagacious dog who travelled around on a sort of grand tour, and obviously had a very
impressionable mind. In 1820, the society received a complaint

[34] *First report of the Commissioners*, appendix, p. 463.
[35] Moore, op. cit., p. 257.
[36] *First report of the Commissioners*, appendix, p. 433.

that one of the volumes, entitled *Travels through Italy*, contained a passage 'injurious to the religion of which these poor children are members'. The society was able to point out loftily that it had never published a work entitled *Travels through Italy*, but upon enquiring they discovered that the passage referred to was the following, from *Mungo*.

It seemed there existed a weak and wicked law that every murderer who could take refuge in a church was safe from his pursuers, no one daring to seize him in so sacred an asylum. They had always friends to supply them with food, and in time to provide their escape. My master was one evening intently surveying some painting in an obscure part of the church, when one of these wretches, wrapped in a long cloak, with murder and revenge scowling on his dark countenance, glided by us. Even I shook with fear at the assassin's sight; and my master, casting toward him a look of horror, left the place. I pretend not to say that this disgusting circumstance hastened him away, but on the following day we took our leave of Rome.

This does indeed give a rather gothic-horror air to the churches in Rome, but the committee 'certainly did not concur in opinion with the reverend gentleman'; nevertheless they graciously expunged the passage from the next edition.[37] One other objection was made to a passage in the *History of the widow Reilly*. The passage referred to the custom of waking the dead, and stated that the deceased person was beyond the reach of the living, and no longer in want of their help. It was objected that this was contrary to the doctrines of the catholic church, in that the dead were not beyond the reach of the living, inasmuch as the prayers of the living might benefit them. The committee thought this was a groundless objection, but nevertheless printed no new edition.[38]

Moving from the objections to popularity, we find that Bardin in his evidence before the education inquiry in 1824 gives some figures.[39] The usual edition was 10,000 copies, though 15,000 had been printed of Aesop's *Fables*, 60,000 copies of this having been sold since April 1817. Of *Elizabeth: or, the exiles of Siberia* 65,000 copies had been printed since 1817, of *History of Joseph* 35,000 since November 1816, of *Robinson Crusoe* 35,000 since 1817. Voyages and shipwrecks were popular: for instance, 30,000 copies of Cook's *Voyages* had been printed since April 1820. What was not popular is very telling. Bardin stated that the *History of Isaac Jenkins* and the

---

[37] Ibid., appendix, pp 464, 623.
[38] Ibid., appendix, p. 464.
[39] Ibid., appendix, pp 464–5.

History of the brothers were the least popular, and shrewdly stated the reason:

> ... the stories are good, and I think deserve to be popular; but there are some didactic essays at the end of the books which make them unpopular; one is advice to servants; another, an essay on savings banks.[40]

In other words, people did not like being got at, and could see a moral sermon a mile off. But nevertheless 20,000 of each of these 'least popular' books had been sold since the end of 1816 or the beginning of 1817. 20,000 copies of the *Cottage fireside* had been printed and 15,000 sold since the middle of 1821; and this was a didactic volume, consisting of a series of conversations between a grandmother and her grand-daughter during which much advice is given respecting potatoes, pigs, spinning, gardening, nursing, and the advantages to be gained from a frugal and moral life.

The society took a loss upon the sale of the Cheap Books. According to Samuel Bewley school requisites were not sold at a loss: Cheap Books sold at wholesale prices made a loss of about 50 per cent, and those sold retail, bound, made a small loss. The reason was simple: the whole object of issuing the library was to supplant what was regarded as pernicious literature, and the mode arrived at was to induce the wholesale buyers 'who were the fountain that supplied the bad books' to buy the society's publications, allowing them adequate profit if they sold at the same retail price as the society itself, which was the same price as the pernicious literature. The books were sold in quires to the dealers, who retailed them bound. The books bound by the society mainly went to the society's schools as grants. Those bought in quires by wholesalers were distributed round the country by hawkers and booksellers in the country towns.[41]

The books were not only sold on the market but, as stated above, grants of complete sets were made to all the schools in connection with the society. Either one or two sets were normally sent to a school, and if the number of pupils exceeded one hundred the number of sets was frequently increased to four. The society pointed out that 'it is not intended that they should be *given* to the children, but that they should become the foundation of a library, attached to the school, and be *lent* to the most deserving pupils. A cheap mode of rewarding the meritorious is thus provided, and moral and instructive works are more likely to be thus read, when

[40] Ibid., appendix, p. 465.
[41] Ibid., appendix, p. 446.

lent, than if they were actually the property of those who borrow them' – an argument hard to follow.[42]

But the society went further – it made a grant of complete sets to any school, organisation, or even individual who would 'provide for the preservation of the books, and the permanent application of them to the purposes intended'.[43] In 1823, in Ulster, apart from schools in connection with the society, the following bodies received grants of complete libraries: thirty-three schools, Sunday schools, and lending libraries in Carrickfergus, Drumbeg, Tildarg, Markethill, Templecarn, Dunkineely, Killybegs, Magherafelt, Stewartstown, and Arboe.[44] In 1826 thirty-one schools and Sunday schools received grants, as well as lending libraries in Ballymena, Ballycastle, Ballyconnell, Moyallen (this was a tract lending library), Dungiven (the 'Dungiven Association'), Maghera, Coleraine, Glasslough, Caledon, and Castlewellan.[45] In 1827 there were forty-nine schools and Sunday schools, but fewer lending libraries – these were at Tartaraghan and Rathfriland.[46] Thus when one considers that every school in connection with the society in Ulster (more than eight hundred in 1827) had a complete set, or several sets, together with the sets held in other institutions, added to the numbers simply sold by the hawkers and booksellers, it is not surprising that these publications had a very strong effect on reading habits; and when one comes to examine the popular lists of Belfast booksellers, especially Joseph Smyth, the air of Kildare Place is all-pervasive.

The war was not all victories, though. Malachy Daly, an inspector of the Kildare Place Society, was questioned by the Education Commissioners in 1824. Daly had been on a tour of inspection of the north-west, and was not impressed by the usage that the libraries got. 'In general they did not make much use of them; and in many of the schools, I have generally found fault with them for not using them. . . . Sometimes I found them altogether, and sometimes tossed about the room; but I have examined the scholars in the histories, and found them deficient in their knowledge of them.'[47] In the bookshops and pedlars' packs Ulster was still putting up a fight for the old order. Samuel Bewley was forced to admit, again in 1824, in reply to the question 'Have the society

---

[42] *Sixteenth report of the Society for Promoting the Education of the Poor of Ireland* (Dublin, 1828), p. 117.

[43] Ibid., p. 122.

[44] *Twelfth report of the Society* (1824), pp 80–81.

[45] *Fifteenth report of the Society* (1827), pp 114–15.

[46] *Sixteenth report of the Society* (1828), pp 110–11.

[47] *First report of the Commissioners*, appendix, p. 532.

succeeded in putting that class of books out of the market?' that 'to the southward we found no instance of those pernicious books being reprinted; that those on sale were remains of old editions that were printed, probably, before we began; at Belfast they have continued to print some of them of a very bad kind.'[48]

A complete list of the cheap publications of the Kildare Place Society is given in appendix V. There were twelve of a religious nature, all totally non-controversial (except for a few doubtful points, mentioned above). They consisted of such works as *Scripture zoology, Manners and customs of the Israelites,* Sturm's *Reflections* and so forth. There were ten 'instructive in arts or economy'. These consisted of such titles as the *Cottage fireside,* already mentioned, *Hints to farmers,* the *Cabinet of arts* and *Richard MacReady, the farmer lad. Richard MacReady* tells the story of a poor farmer lad whose father is a bit of a layabout who chooses to live in a hovel rather than work hard to better himself. Richard, however, succeeds in doing well, and becomes a prosperous farmer. There is much good advice to the peasantry *en route.* Next came ten works on natural history, including one on an early nineteenth-century preoccupation – *Animal sagacity, exemplified by facts.* It was books of this nature that were satirised by Dickens's *Pickwick papers* in the story of the sagacious dog that would not pass the gamekeeper's notice. A more typical volume is *Natural history of remarkable trees, shrubs and plants.* This ranges from such mundane local items as flax to the anchar or poison tree of Java (including a long account of the mythical upas tree). In true *Coral island* style it includes the wax tree, the butter tree, the coffee tree, the cotton tree, and the tallow tree.

The largest section is that which includes voyages and travels, one of the most popular sections, after *Elizabeth* and Aesop. This contained thirty-two volumes. It had a long section of travel books organised geographically. This was amazingly detailed – three of the volumes, for instance, are *Travels in south-eastern Asia, Travels in south-western Asia* and *Travels in northern Asia.* There were shipwreck stories, such as *Shipwreck of the Alceste and Medusa,* adventures like *Dangerous voyage of Captain Bligh,* curiosities such as *History of Prince Lee Boo* (a native of the Pelew Islands who was brought to Britain), and accounts of famous voyages such as those of Anson and Columbus.

Finally there was a miscellaneous section of fifteen titles. This contained fiction like the popular *Elizabeth, or the exiles of Siberia* and *Robinson Crusoe,* the *New Robinson Crusoe* and *History of the Robins*

[48] Ibid., p. 445.

– a popular eighteenth-century children's book. There were *Amusing stories* and *Mungo the traveller*, whose remarks on Rome caused such grave offence. There was *Isaac Jenkins*, whose heavy moralising put people off. And there was a rather charming little compendium, entitled *Selection of poems*. This contains a number of poems which would one day be parodied, such as 'My mother', by Ann and Jane Taylor:

> Who fed me from her gentle breast,
> And hush'd me in her arms to rest,
> And on my cheek sweet kisses prest?
> > My mother.[49]

There is the original of the 'Sluggard', by Isaac Watts:

> Tis the voice of the sluggard, I heard him complain
> You have wak'd me too soon, I must slumber again;
> As the door on its hinges, so he on his bed,
> Turns his sides, and his shoulders, and his heavy head.[50]

There is even the following, by Robert Southey:

> You are old, Father William, the young man he said;
> The few locks that are left you are gray;
> You are hale, Father William, a hearty old man,
> Now tell me the reason, I pray.[51]

The original Father William, rather boringly, remembered his God and did not abuse his health.

With the cessation of the parliamentary grant in 1831 the influence of the Kildare Place Society, outside the field of teacher training, began to fade, but the library of cheap books had an enormously strong effect on the contents of the popular reading lists of the two main Belfast distributors of such literature, Simms & M'Intyre (in an earlier venture into popular publishing than the one they are generally credited with) and Joseph Smyth. These will be dealt with in Chapter 8.

Sunday schools have been mentioned several times in the course of this chapter; they were an important part of the early nineteenth-century educational system, often underrated today, partly because the name nowadays smacks of purely religious

---

[49] *Poems selected from the works of approved authors* (Dublin, 1825), pp 16–18.
[50] Ibid., p. 44.
[51] Ibid., p. 150.

education. But in the early nineteenth century they were more than that. The origin of the Sunday school movement lies in the late eighteenth century, as we have seen. The early nineteenth-century schools had more to do with education proper than with religious education. For instance, the first major Sunday school in Belfast (there had been earlier ones) opened in January 1802 'for the reception of children whose circumstances would not admit their attending any daily school. . . . The committee and teachers agreed to give a preference to applicants who were in the station of servants and apprentices, as it appeared to be their last opportunity of school improvement.' By 1804 there were 120 pupils on the books, 'instructed in spelling, reading, writing, and arithmetic'.[52] A building was erected in Frederick Street in 1810–11, and by 1812 nearly 500 boys were taught during the week and the same numbers with about 250 girls on Sundays,[53] its title now being the Sunday and Lancasterian Schools. By 1833 it had become the Frederick Street National School,[54] and its career can be seen to have little in common with today's Sunday schools. The secular bias in this particular example is explained by the fact that the schools promoters were well known local liberals.[55] The conservatives were alarmed at this, and formed their own school, which eventually developed into the Brown Street Primary School. This is not the place for a detailed history of individual educational institutions, so the tortuous evolution of this school can thankfully be left aside. However an account of the school in 1825[56] gives a good picture of the curriculum: there were 156 boys reading the Bible and Testament, 28 were at the second spelling book, 36 were at the first spelling book, and 58 were learning letters and monosyllables. The figures for girls were 156, 58, 39, and 64 respectively, and a clear understanding seems to have existed that the purpose of learning to read was to read the Bible. This was due to the influence of the Sunday School Society for Ireland. Founded in 1809, its object was 'to promote the general establishment of Sunday schools for the religious instruction of the people, and the principle by which its proceedings are governed is thus explained . . . it shall promote the establishment and facilitate the conducting of Sunday schools in Ireland, by disseminating the

[52] *Belfast Almanac, 1804*, p. 47.
[53] *Belfast Almanac, 1812*, pp 42–3.
[54] *Belfast Almanac, 1833*, p. 53.
[55] Aiken McClelland, 'The early history of Brown Street Primary School' in *Ulster Folklife*, xvii (1971), p. 53.
[56] *Belfast News-letter*, 15 Apr. 1825.

most approved plans for the management of such schools, by supplying them with spelling books, and copies of the sacred scriptures, or extracts therefrom, without note or comment. . . .'[57] The Society had two schools and 87 scholars in connection in 1810, and by 1825 claimed 1,702 schools and 150,831 scholars.[58] The Sunday schools were strongest in Ulster, and it was claimed that the proportion of scholars here was one in sixteen of the population (compared to one in 354 in Munster). Indeed in 1825 there were nearly four times as many scholars in Ulster as in the other three provinces combined.[59] These figures alone make the Sunday schools one of the more important factors in the introduction of literacy in the earlier part of the century, and as will be seen, in the introduction of books as well, through their libraries.

The works distributed by the society itself were fairly limited in scope: Bibles, Testaments, spelling books one and two, alphabets, and the oddly named 'Freeman's card'. These materials were used as the school books, and in themselves seem to have provided a satisfactory method of attaining literacy. But a great number of Sunday schools had libraries as well. Some of these libraries would have consisted simply of the publications of the Kildare Place Society – as we have seen, that society made many grants of complete sets of its cheap books to Sunday schools. But others were somewhat larger, and it is instructive to examine those in one Ulster county – Down.

The Sunday School Society itself, as the parent body, was interested in the subject of libraries. In 1822 they were advising that 'a library may be commenced at a moderate expense at the present day', quoting the publications of the Kildare Place Society and those of the Religious Tract and Book Society.[60] One of the earliest and strongest Sunday-school libraries in the county was in Rathfriland. There was a Sunday school there by 1819,[61] and by December 1821 the Rathfriland Sunday School Union had established a library of religious books 'for the use and benefit of the different schools in connection with the union, both for teachers and scholars; and the books are received and read with great avidity by them, and are calculated to do great good'.[62] Less than a year later the library had evolved yet further:

[57] *First report of the Commissioners*, p. 61.
[58] Ibid., p. 63.
[59] Ibid., pp 62–3.
[60] *Sunday School Society for Ireland: monthly extracts*, xxi (1822), p. 183.
[61] T. Bradshaw, *General directory of Newry, Armagh* . . . (Newry, 1819), p. 53.
[62] *Sunday School Society for Ireland: monthly extracts*, xxviii (1822), p. 136.

... and in this part there seems to be a desire implanted in the breasts of the rising generation for scriptural and historical information; and in order to stir up, and keep alive this thirst for knowledge, we have established a tract library (the tracts were purchased at the Tract Society, Dublin). These we lend weekly to the children, many of whom read them with alacrity and delight; and many of their parents are so delighted with them, that they are desirous to pay for them, so that they may become their own property. Another library is established here, entitled the Rathfriland Sunday School Union Circulating Library. To this the teachers of Sunday schools in connection with the union have access; those that teach in our school receive these books weekly as the children receive the tracts. These two institutions have been set on foot through the instrumentality of Sunday School exertion; and we may now say, without deviating from truth, that Rathfriland abounds with light, information, and improvement.[63]

The Rathfriland correspondent of the Sunday School Society possessed both rosy-tinted spectacles and a knack for composing purple prose – his (or possibly her) comments on the envisaged home life of the deserving poor in Rathfriland area are worth quoting.

It is pleasant to relate how patiently the parent sits (after returning from his days labour, clearing up the coals, or turning the faggot, whilst the child reads over a number of pages of moral or divine truths, put into his hand through the circulating library, and on the Lord's day, when more of his children may be gathered round the kind parent's hearth, they will sit and read a few chapters, verse about, in their Testament, and point out some portions of scripture which they must have committed for next Sabbath morning.[64]

This is a view from the top end of the social ladder; and the actual parent, in a rural region near Rathfriland, possibly brought up on a diet of the *Seven champions* and the ideals of the United Irishmen, with the values of Regency Britain brought to his table via the press and such echoes of the press as percolated to him through the medium of reading circles and common gossip, may have viewed his tract-quoting offspring with less ardour than the writer imagined. But the fact still remains that literacy was gained. By 1835, there were 30 schools in connection with the Rathfriland union, and the circulating library contained 888 volumes.[65] The movement was expanding rapidly, but even so not all Sunday schools could hope to attain these dizzy heights: Backnamullagh, County Down, for instance, with an attendance of 300, had by

[63] Ibid., xli (1823), pp 338–9.
[64] Ibid., xxviii (1822), p. 132.
[65] *Newry Commercial Telegraph*, 16 June 1835.

1821 formed a library of about 140 volumes.[66] But Rathfriland was not unique – in 1837 the Kilmore Sabbath School Union had a library of about 700 books, and five schools in connection.[67] All in all these little libraries were a powerful stimulus to reading – the schools taught the art, and while most of the contents of the libraries consisted of religious works and tracts, there would have been more miscellaneous matter and, above all, numerous sets of the Kildare Place libraries.[68]

Of the other schools, perhaps the least distinct entity was the network of schools established under acts of Henry VIII and William III, commonly called parochial schools. Several of these schools were maintained by the clergymen, but the 1825 Commission found that a practice noted in 1810 still generally prevailed 'for the incumbents of parishes in which schools are kept to allow the schoolmaster forty shillings per annum as his salary; and whenever this small stipend (utterly inadequate at present) is paid by the clergyman to a schoolmaster, the school is called a parish school'.[69] About a third of the parochial schools in Ireland were in connection with the Association for Discountenancing Vice, and others derived aid from such bodies as the Kildare Place Society.[70] In the ecclesiastical province of Armagh (roughly corresponding to Ulster) there were in 1825 436 benefices and 337 parochial schools, educating a total of 16,498 scholars, of which two-thirds were protestant.[71]

Even more assorted than the parochial schools were the pay schools, usually called hedge schools. A rosy glow often surrounds these schools in the present-day imagination, and the impression is often given that Ireland abounded with people lacking a seat to their trousers but quoting Virgil and Homer. The reality was different, as has been shown in Chapter I, and as can be imagined when it is considered that there was nothing at all to stop anyone setting up a school anywhere and teaching the most arrant nonsense – unless the parents were able to spot this and not send their children. This type of school was decribed in 1812.

That instruction, except in a very few instances, extends no farther than reading, writing, and the common rules of arithmetic, and the prices paid are

[66] *Sunday School Society for Ireland: monthly extracts,* xxx (1822), p. 163.
[67] *Downpatrick Recorder,* 16 Dec. 1837.
[68] Sunday School Society for Ireland, *Hints for conducting Sunday schools* (9th ed., Dublin, 1844), p. 127.
[69] *First report of the Commissioners,* p. 37.
[70] Ibid., p. 37.
[71] Ibid., appendix, pp 14–15.

on an average ten shillings per annum for reading, seventeen shillings and
fourpence where writing, and one pound six shillings where arithmetic is
added: but even this limited instruction the masters are very ill qualified to
give, having been themselves taught in schools of a similar description, and
consequently deficient in information, unacquainted with regular plans of
education, and unaccustomed to that discipline, from the steady and tem-
perate enforcement of which some of the best advantages of education are
derived. The poverty of the lower classes of the people, which limits the
recompense of the masters to the low rates above-mentioned, and thus holds
out no temptation to a better class to undertake the office of instructors,
produces effects, if possible, still worse, by incapacitating them from purchasing such books as are fit for children to read: whence it frequently happens,
that instead of being improved by religious or moral instruction, their minds
are corrupted by books calculated to incite to lawless and profligate adventure, to cherish superstition, or to lead to dissension or disloyalty.[72]

One good aspect of the pay schools that struck the 1825
Commission was the pragmatic manner in which the schoolmaster dealt with a religiously divided attendance. Each child was
taught the catechism of its own church by the master, and
religious animosity was at a minimum. The Commission were
evidently rather uneasy at the spectacle of a protestant schoolmaster quite happily teaching catholic children out of a catholic
catechism – it rather smacked of a complete lack of any belief
whatsoever, or an abandonment of principle in order to bring in
more pupils. They were nevertheless much taken with the religious harmony that prevailed in many schools.[73]

With a few honourable exceptions, the reading material supplied was the usual reading material of the countryside, undiluted
for younger readers. The 1825 Commission gives a list of books
found in the various schools in Donegal, Kildare, Galway, and
Kerry, but unfortunately does not say which work was found in
which county.[74] The list is very long, and contains a goodly
proportion of the material that has been mentioned above in
dealing with the eighteenth century, and a miscellaneous collection of novels. There are also a number of howlers: the presbyterian catechism found is described as 'Shorter's' – poor Larger
does not seem to have been patronised.

Despite all this, or perhaps because of it, a very great number of
Ulster children learnt at least the rudiments of reading at these
schools, and if some schools were very bad (and descriptions of

[72] Ibid., appendix, p. 416.
[73] Ibid., p. 92.
[74] Ibid., appendix, pp 553–9.

bad schools and worse schoolmasters are not wanting) some were
better and some must have been very good indeed.

A beautiful example of the work and character of some of the
best of these hedge schoolmasters, without concealing their faults,
is provided by a little book of a hundred pages printed at Omagh
in 1822: *A logical essay, on the syntax of the English language*, by Samuel
Alexander. It contains a two-page list of subscribers, one of which
must have been very annoyed to find himself described as 'phila-
moth'. The work, and especially the preface, is written in a rotund
style favouring many long words, but the letters of commendation
written by his schoolmaster friends, and printed in the work, show
to good advantage the style favoured by these hedge scholars, but
ridiculous to a modern reader. Bernard Maginnis, teacher of
mathematics in Clones, writes:

Who, possessing candour or discernment, that will not instantly confess, that
the mutual dependence you take notice of between the subject and the
attribute, bids defiance to any refutation? . . . Is it to be supposed that the
shadow of a doubt could overspread the mind of any thinking being that your
unacquaintance of the learned languages would disqualify you for the task?
No, . . . what greater difficulty can be presented to your mind in forming a
syllogism on grammar, than a prosyllogism on mathematics; I am persuaded
a person conversant with both will pronounce the latter the more difficult.
Proceed my friend, the illiterate attacks of pedantry are no more capable of
retarding the progress of true genius than the exhalations of a marshy ground
can stop the bounds of a courser; both proceed from soft foundations
producing a weak and insignificant progeny.[75]

Francis M'Kinzie, philomath, from Dungannon, writes more
succinctly:

I have perused your manuscript on the elucidation of English syntax. I think
from the symmetry of its sublime and scientifical arguments, it ingeniously
merits the favour and esteem of the most eminent professors of academical
institutions.[76]

It is to be feared, however, that the work launched by Mr
Alexander so hopefully did not attain a wide circulation.

In 1831 an event occurred that was to change the face of
education in Ireland: the creation of the 'national' system of
education. This is not the place to go into the administrative

[75] Samuel Alexander, *Logical essay, on the syntax of the English language* (Omagh, 1822),
pp xxvii–xxviii.
[76] Ibid., p. xxviii.

history of the creation and development of the system. The
number of national schools increased rapidly: 789 in 1833; 1,978 in
1840; 4,321, with 480,623 pupils, in 1849.[77] Some were new
schools, others were pay schools and schools connected with the
societies, others were schools run partly or wholly by charity. For
instance, of the large Belfast schools, the Weekly or Sunday
School, set up in 1802, had, via various changes in name and
method, become the Frederick Street Lancasterian National
School by 1833;[78] and the Donegall Street School, commenced in
1829 under the patronage of William Crolly, catholic bishop of
Down and Connor, had joined the national system in 1832.[79]

One of the first problems facing the national board was that of
providing the schools with a properly graded series of textbooks,
and Rev. James Carlile was entrusted with the task of producing
these. In order to gain a little breathing space, Carlile sanctioned
for temporary use the books of the Kildare Place Society and a
slightly edited set of those produced by the Catholic Truth
Society.[80] In 1834 four lesson books were available, and by 1850
there were forty-one titles on the list: ten readers, four anthologies
of secular and religious verse, the *Agricultural class book*, *Lessons on
the truth of Christianity*, and manuals on needlework and accountancy. All the schools needed was here except a work of Irish
history, and this was too controversial for the Commissioners to
publish the agreed text. These publications, and especially the five
books of lessons, were the prescribed literary diet of generations of
Irish children. The image of the world projected by these readers
was a Christian, if non-sectarian one; and though religion was not
a strident, dominant theme, the class structure was shown as
God-ordained. But it was possible for a sober, industrious man to
pull himself up the ladder, at least for a rung or two.

The net result of all this effort, by so many societies and
individuals, over the years, was to produce a more literate society.
The reasons were different: to make a living; to enable people to
read the Bible; to convert catholics into protestants; to improve
social conditions – one clergyman even noted 'the influence of a
paper currency in promoting education among the lower classes'
in the parish of Dungiven.[81] But the means used was to teach

---

[77] D. H. Akenson, *The Irish education experiment* (London, 1970), p. 140.
[78] *Belfast Almanac, 1833*, p. 53.
[79] Ibid., p. 53.
[80] Goldstrom, op. cit., pp 63–4.
[81] William Shaw Mason (ed.), *A statistical account: or, parochial survey of Ireland* (3 vols,
Dublin, 1814–19), i, 330.

people, first of all and most importantly for our purpose, to read. By the middle of the century how much had been achieved? At least one writer, commenting on education in the parish of Carnmoney, County Antrim, shortly after the middle of the century, had no doubts.

Then there were but three schools within the bounds of the parish, and some of these no better than hedge schools. *Now* there are seven spacious and well-finished buildings set apart for the education of youth, presided over by well-educated and efficient teachers, and supplied with excellent books and every facility for acquiring information, within the same bounds, and three more immediately in our neighbourhood.[82]

Good education was, however, by no means spread evenly over the countryside. As table I, derived from 1851 census,[83] shows, there were large differences between urban and rural areas, though the precision of the figures is impossible to ascertain. What is certain, nevertheless, is that there was a great advance on the eighteenth century, however imperfect our understanding of literacy in that century. An almost totally literate society, where the vast majority of the citizens would be able to read and comprehend an extended text, was, however, some way off by the 1850s.

Table I: Literacy, 1851

| | population aged 5 and over | percentage of population aged 5 and over | | |
		who can read/write	who can read only	who can neither read nor write
ANTRIM				
males	109,886	54	27.6	18.4
females	120,909	35.4	43.3	21.3
total	230,795	44.3	35.8	19.9
ARMAGH				
males	85,097	41.9	23.2	34.9
females	90,276	23.6	33.4	43
total	175,373	32.5	28.4	39.1

[82] W. O. McGaw, 'Notes on the parish of Carnmoney, Co. Antrim' in *Ulster Folklife*, i (1955), p. 53.
[83] *The census of Ireland for the year 1851. Part VI. General report*, pp 380–528 [2134], H.C. 1856, xxxi, 524–672.

The printed word and the common man

Table I: (*continued*)

	population aged 5 and over	percentage of population aged 5 and over		
		who can read/write	who can read only	who can neither read nor write
BELFAST				
males	40,935	59.9	22.5	17.6
females	47,602	40.5	36.7	22.8
total	88,537	49.5	30.1	20.4
CAVAN				
males	78,085	41.1	19.9	39
females	78,888	22	27	51
total	156,973	31.5	23.5	45
DONEGAL				
males	106,127	30	19.9	50.1
females	117,079	14.7	23.2	62.1
total	223,206	22	21.6	56.4
DOWN				
males	135,024	53.2	25.1	21.7
females	150,972	34.8	38.6	26.6
total	285,996	43.5	32.2	24.3
FERMANAGH				
males	51,147	45.6	20.6	33.8
females	53,733	24.7	32.2	43.1
total	104,880	34.9	26.6	38.5
LONDONDERRY				
males	83,234	44.8	28.5	26.7
females	89,259	26.7	41.3	32
total	172,493	35.4	35.1	29.5
MONAGHAN				
males	62,246	41.1	23.1	35.8
females	66,597	20.1	32.1	47.8
total	128,843	30.2	27.8	42
TYRONE				
males	113,495	41.8	24.2	34
females	117,165	22.8	35	42.2
total	230,660	32.1	29.7	38.2

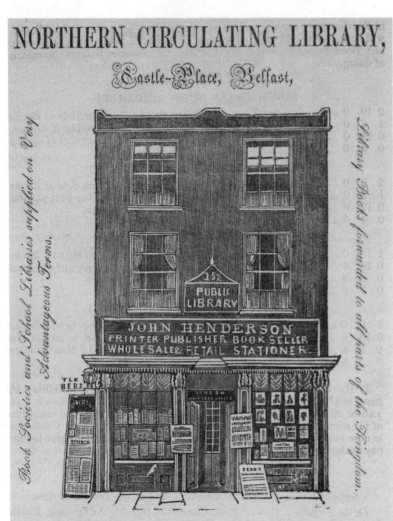

PLATE VII
Henderson's bookshop and circulating library, Belfast
From *Henderson's new Belfast directory* (Belfast, 1843), p. 16

CHAPTER 7

The Distribution of Printed Material, 1800–50

As we have seen, the rapid development of educational systems in Ireland during the first half of the nineteenth century led to a situation where more and more people were in a position to read printed material. A matter of some importance, especially in a time of improved communications, is the manner in which this printed matter actually reached the reading public. A number of elements, such as libraries and newspapers, were involved, but the most obvious source was the local bookseller in all his numerous manifestations. First, there were the larger bookshops proper, in Belfast and the larger towns. Then there were the shops which sold books but mainly concentrated on other merchandise, such as groceries. Thirdly, there were the travelling chapmen; and finally, at the very bottom of the heap, there were the ballad singers and petty purveyors of chapbooks and speeches, lower than the chapman proper – boys, petty thieves, and people little better than beggars.

To take the bookshops proper first, an idea of the network towards the middle years of the century can be gleaned from the entries in Slater's *Directory* for 1846.[1] This lists 118 towns in Ulster, ranging from the very small to Belfast, which was of course the largest of the towns, and as the capital of Ulster had the largest number of bookselling entries – eighteen. Of the other towns with populations over 7,000, Armagh had four, Londonderry had five, Newry had five, and Newtownards (suffering from proximity to Belfast) had two.

There were eight towns with populations between 4,000 and 7,000 and these all had bookshops. Ballymena had two; Coleraine had four; Enniskillen, Lurgan, Monaghan, and Strabane each had three; Downpatrick and Lisburn each had one.

Of the ten towns with populations ranging from 3,000 to 4,000, only one had no bookshop – Donaghadee. Of the rest, Larne, Dungannon, and Limavady boasted three, Cookstown, Cavan,

---

[1] *Slater's national commercial directory of Ireland* (Manchester, 1846).

and Carrickfergus had two, and Ballyshannon, Bangor, and Banbridge one each.

Significantly, of the twelve towns with populations ranging from 2,000 to 3,000 nine had no bookshops, only Ballymoney with two, and Letterkenny and Omagh with one, keeping the flag flying. Of the eighty-three towns listed with populations under 2,000, only four had bookshops: Garvagh, Donegal, Maghera, and Tandragee. Some of the smaller shops were simply described as stationers.

From these statistics it would seem that virtually every town with a population over 3,000 possessed at least one bookseller, while it was very rare for a town with a smaller population to possess one. This left large tracts of the countryside relatively bookseller-free: for instance in Donegal there was one in Letterkenny, one in Donegal town, and one in Ballyshannon. Antrim (excluding Belfast), with an almost exactly similar population over five years of age, boasted ten. This reflects differences in both literacy and economic standards. Some of these shops, especially those in the smaller towns, were not only booksellers. Robertson of Garvagh (population 851), for instance, was also grocer, ironmonger, and hardware merchant; and to those few booksellers in towns with populations under 3,000 the same would probably apply.

Below this there was an even larger number of shops that sold books of a popular kind, but as too small a part of their trade to mention — how many shops today possess a small paperback display? Henry Cooke was referring to the late eighteenth century when he mentioned the grocers in the villages selling books,[2] but this method of distribution continued. This end of the trade is particularly shadowy, as is that of the travelling chapman during this period. However, the pages of such directories as Bradshaw's *Newry* (1820)[3] are littered with the names of chapmen and hawkers, some of whom carried a selection of popular literature with them on their rounds.

Oddly enough, we are on surer ground when dealing with the most debased form of bookselling of all — ballad-selling and the distribution of printed material by the utterly destitute. The reason is simple: the people who took part in it were recorded because they fell foul of the respectable citizen. They made a particular nuisance of themselves in Belfast in 1815 and 1816. At the Carrickfergus assizes in March 1816 a boy, Robert Bedford,

---

[2] *First report of the Commissioners*, appendix, p. 280.
[3] T. Bradshaw, *General directory of Newry, Armagh* . . . (Newry, 1819).

was indicted for stealing a pocket book containing about £80 in August 1815.[4] The plaintiff, Hugh McCulloch, told the court that he had gone to an office and taken out his pocket book to extract a note when he 'observed the prisoner close to him with a basket in which were some small books he was selling. He was twice desired to go out of the office, but he still refused, and pressed them to buy books. The same boy he had observed dogging him the same morning into two other houses.' Another witness had observed Bedford in the office 'plaguing them to buy books'. The upshot was that Bedford was sentenced to be transported for seven years.

In May of the same year (1816) the *Belfast News-letter* sourly noted that 'the town has been sadly annoyed by itinerant ballad-singers, who collect crowds of people, especially at each end of Bridge Street, so that passengers cannot get forward. The constables should be ordered to prevent them.'[5] But it was not just the trouble of squeezing through a crowd of people that offended some people. A gentleman, signing himself 'Observer' wrote to the paper in August, in reply to one 'X.Y.Z.' who had complained about the nuisance caused by ringing of bells and calling of auctions. 'Observer' noted that there were far worse annoyances. He mentioned heaps of mud (presumably a euphemism) and the offal cast out of butchers' shops. He goes on:

Again, I suppose this gentleman strung the lyre of Apollo, or courted the happy retreat of the muses, for he never thinks the least harm arises from the delightful harmony, and exquisite composition, that day and night resounds about our corners, emanating from the musical and poetical talents of our regular ballad-singers. This gentleman is not at all afraid of his pockets being picked by the hoard of thieves that are dispersed through such crowds – crowds, that in the noon-day stop up the passage of men of business, and make the communication between shop and shop difficult and perilous. He is not afraid of the morals of his servants being corrupted by the purchase of ballads containing the most obscene language. Surely these annoyances of public comfort ought to be put down – they and the suppliers of such abominable, immoral, and licentious publications.[6]

The trade that distributed printed matter had indeed a very wide base.

As has been shown above in considering education, there was a wide variety of libraries attached to local schools, some small, others – especially those connected to the Kildare Place Society – not so small, and containing useful works of entertaining instruc-

[4] *Belfast News-letter*, 22 Mar. 1816.
[5] Ibid., 31 May 1816.
[6] Ibid., 5 Aug. 1816.

tion. But there were other libraries where those below the middle classes might obtain reading material during this half century. From the point of view of the student of Ulster vernacular poetry, the most important were the reading societies. These, as seen above, were becoming frequent in Ulster in the late eighteenth century, and became even more frequent in the early years of the nineteenth. There were various types, depending on the organisation of the society, but for the purposes of the present study they may be divided into two types: those composed of people from the middle classes or upwards, and those whose membership consisted of the literate lower orders. The first type can by no means be ignored, as they frequently acted as patrons to the local vernacular poets by allowing them access to their shelves. Most towns in east Ulster, especially County Down, possessed a society of this type, as indeed did Belfast in the shape of what was to become the Linen Hall Library. One was the Banbridge Reading Society, founded in 1795,[7] and described by John Gamble in 1812 as 'a neat little public library, where I found a respectable collection of books'.[8] The local weaver poet Joseph Carson was made a member in 1827, and celebrated the occasion by writing a brace of poems.[9] They are rather high-flown in tone:

> Ye chosen members of this fane of knowledge,
> Enlighten'd guardians of the classic train, . . .

Another of these societies (and there were many in County Down at this time) to attract the attention of a vernacular poet was the Rathfriland Book Society. The poet was Hugh Porter, and in 1811 he wrote a poem addressed to the president and other members of the Rathfriland Book Society, the gist of which was a plea to be allowed to read the *Lady of the lake*. The poem does not bear quotation in whole, but one stanza illustrates the main difficulty of these town-based societies for the literate of more humble means:

> O, if I some great something were,
> An' had as muckle cash to spare,
>   As might mak' me a member,
> And ye wad sic a wretch admit,
> Ye'd see how saucily I'd sit
>   Amang ye ere December.[10]

---

[7] Richard Linn, *History of Banbridge* (Banbridge, 1935), pp 6–7.

[8] John Gamble, *A view of society and manners in the north of Ireland, in the summer and autumn of 1812* (London, 1813), p. 41.

[9] J. Carson, *Poems, odes, songs and satires* (Newry, 1831), pp 42–5.

[10] Hugh Porter, *Poetical attempts* (Belfast, 1813), pp 154–7.

Apart from the question of what Burns would have thought of this, this raises one query. To what extent did the subscriptions of the town reading societies (leaving out any class difficulties) put an obstacle in the way of the literate common person? Luckily we know some of the subscription rates charged. The Downpatrick Literary Society (founded 1793) published its rules in 1801.[11] They show that a considerable outlay was required of its members. Each member had to pay one guinea as admission fee, and a monthly subscription of one shilling British. In addition there was a system of heavy fines. A folio or quarto could be kept out twenty-eight days, an octavo eighteen, a duodecimo or pamphlet seven. After this there was a fine of 2*d*. a day (apart from country members, who were allowed a further seven days). There were fines for losing or abusing a book. Every member who failed to attend the monthly meetings paid a fine of one British sixpence, and if a committee member, two British shillings. This, perhaps deliberately, put the society beyond the reach of the ordinary person.

At a meeting of the Ballynahinch Reading Society held in 1834 the opinion was expressed that with a moderate entry fee of about 10*s*. and a subscription of 6*d*. a month many had it in their power to have a fairly extensive reading.[12] This was less than the previous rate but still an amount to think carefully about on the part of the less well-off. In 1837 the monthly subscription of the Banbridge Reading Society was 2*s*.,[13] while about the same time the subscription to the Newtownards Book Society was 12*s*. for the first year and 10*s*. thereafter, with a life subscription of six guineas.[14] The Portaferry Literary Society (established 1786) had an entrance fee of £2, and this was in fact reduced before 1834 from £5.[15]

The Comber Society for Acquiring Knowledge had an admission fee of £3 in 1828,[16] and every member had to pay 8*d*. at each meeting, 5*d*. to be spent on 'contingencies' and 3*d*. on books. Every member leaving the meeting without the permission of the president had to pay a fine of 5*d*., and any member absent for three months had to pay 6*d*. a quarter. Any person wishing to use the

---

[11] *Catalogue of the books in the library of the Down Literary Society* (Downpatrick, 1801).

[12] *Belfast Commercial Chronicle*, 29 Nov. 1834.

[13] Ordnance survey memoir for the parish of Seapatrick (Royal Irish Academy, Dublin, Box 25, Down III, vii).

[14] Ordnance survey memoir for the parish of Newtownards (R.I.A., Box 24, Down III, ii).

[15] Ordnance survey memoir for the parish of Ballyphilip (R.I.A., Box 23, Down I, xiii).

[16] *Rules of the Comber Society for Acquiring Knowledge* (Belfast, 1828).

society without joining in the property had to pay a deposit of 15*s*.
and 1*s*.3*d*. a month.

In County Antrim the Kilroot and Dobbs Land Library[17] had a
small entrance fee of 2*s*.6*d*., but a savage system of fines: for
declining an office in the society, 6*d*.; for missing a meeting, 1*d*.; for
failing to return books by the appointed hour, 6*d*.; for not addressing the chair when addressing the meetings, 1*d*.; for entering the
club room in a state of intoxication, 1*s*.; for swearing, or blas-
phemy, or speaking obscene language, 1*s*.; for proposing a deistical, obscene, or blasphemous work, 1*s*.; and for proposing a book
on party politics, or religious controversy, or introducing these
subjects into conversation, 1*s*. All this shows that these societies
were for the middle classes, though they occasionally let a local
poet have the run of their shelves.

Of more importance to the ordinary literate person were the
many small artisan-based, and especially weaver-based, reading
societies that covered the face of Down and Antrim especially.
When William Anderson published his *Collection of moral, instructive, and descriptive poems* in 1830[18] an extensive list of local reading
societies subscribed to the volume. These were the Ballycroon
Reading Society, followed by the Boardmills Reading Society, the
Ker Reading Society, the Crossgar Reading Society, the Lessons
Reading Society, the Laverick Reading Society, the Moneyrea
Reading Society, and the Donaghmore Reading Society. These
formed a close network of reading societies some four or five miles
distant from one another. There is no reason to suppose that these,
and even smaller societies, did not cover at least the eastern part of
Ulster. While the works which they contained were not part of
popular culture, as the societies were an attempt at self-
improvement, they would have contained that reading material
which the common man wished to read and could not individually
afford, unlike the chapbooks and chapmens' books which he or she
could readily buy.

James Orr, the Bard of Ballycarry, was no gentleman – he was a
weaver, a small farmer, a one-time rebel and a drunk. Yet he was a
pillar of his local reading society:

> The sun has set in smiles, and pensive eve
> Sheds soft'ning dew-drops on the thirsty soil;
> The slow-pac'd swains the cultur'd landscape leave,
> And from their work-shop stalk the sons of toil.

---

[17] Bookplate, dated 1837, in possession of Dr H. G. Calwell, Belfast.
[18] W. Anderson, *Collection of moral, instructive and religious poems* (Belfast, 1830).

My sweet associates, kind in thought and looks,
Who all my toils, and all my pastimes share;
Attend the reading circle with your books,
And sensibly converse away your care.[19]

In the eighteenth century, or at least in the first three-quarters of it, if a person below the middle class wished to read a book that was rather expensive by his standards, he had two choices: he could buy the work by hook or crook (a fact occasionally recorded for posterity by the inclusion of his name in a subscribers' list) or if he was very lucky a member of the local gentry could patronise him (in the strict, rather than the pejorative, sense) by allowing him to use his library. The little social difficulties occasionally caused by the latter practice are nicely summed up in the following anecdote, told by the eccentric John Moore Johnston, Lord Moira's rent-collector at Ballynahinch.

One day I had taken a book out of the library to read at my own house, but instead of bringing the same book back, I happened to put one of my own of the same size in my pocket (White's beauties), which I put on the shelf in the library; when I went home, I found that I had committed a mistake, and returned immediately with the right book, but in the mean time a certain clergyman (I can assure my readers, not the Rev. Mr James Forde, who is *an honest man*) found my book as my name was in it, and I imagine supposed I had intended to substitute the one for the other.

When I came into the library his lordship asked me if I had taken a book out of the library; I told him I had, but had replaced it with one of my own in mistake; he said he believed I spoke the truth, and spoke against the clergyman in rather harsh terms. However this anecdote shews the malignancy of some of the clergy, of bad principles, such as Voltaire's, Hume's, Pain's [*sic*], principles, etc. or perhaps of no principles at all.[20]

Despite Johnston's ascription of revolutionary principles to the clergyman concerned, it seems clear that what was running through the clergyman's mind was the thought that he had at last got something on the little upstart. This was a constant risk during the period of patronage. With the arrival of the reading society, the common man could have access to the literature he wanted, on his own terms.

What sort of material was in the reading society libraries? Unfortunately the surviving catalogues are from the middle-class town societies. These show very clear preferences. Travel, geography, history and biography took up 50 per cent of the stock in

---

[19] James Orr, *Poems on various subjects* (Belfast, 1935), p. 274.
[20] J. M. Johnston, *Heterogenea, or medley* (Downpatrick, 1803), pp 70–71.

Downpatrick,[21] 46 per cent in Belfast,[22] 50 per cent in Limavady,[23] and 39 per cent in Comber.[24] All these remarkably consistent figures belong to the period 1801–*c.* 1828. In contrast, imaginative literature in the same towns took up the following respective percentages: 21, 5, 32, and 22.

By way of contrast, the smaller, artisan-based reading societies seem to have concentrated on imaginative literature. One writer stated in 1814:

> In any library of this kind that I have seen, or in any catalogue of such that I have examined, I have observed that they were generally composed of works in the belles-lettres, to the exclusion of every book treating even remotely of the sciences. In a few, indeed, encyclopaedias were to be found, but the exception in their favour arose not so much from the scientific as the miscellaneous matter they contained.[25]

The small rural societies can thus be sharply distinguished from the larger town-based ones. They show an overwhelming interest in imaginative literature of one sort or another, as one would expect both from an examination of their reading habits at an earlier period and from the published work produced by this class in the shape of vernacular poetry.

Though in the eighteenth century reading societies were regarded with suspicion as being hotbeds of radicalism, it would appear that by the early nineteenth century they were seen in some quarters at least as a positive force. A person using the pen name 'Censor' wrote in the *Belfast Monthly Magazine* in 1812:

> Perhaps few things, in our day, have contributed so much to this very desirable object [the progress of civilisation] as the establishing of reading societies, commonly called book clubs. So conspicuous is this, that the people of those districts where they have been held for a length of time are *far* superior in general information to those in which none have ever been established. . . . A few persons, who I think may be properly called bedar-keners, have stated several objections against such societies, the chief of which is, that, according to them, some books of an immoral tendency have been at times introduced. This, perhaps may be true in a few instances, yet it would certainly be both illiberal and impolitic to deprive mankind of the means of obtaining information, for the errors of a few. . . . We should

---

[21] *Catalogue of the books in the library of the Down Literary Society* (Downpatrick, 1801).
[22] *Rules of the Belfast Society for Promoting Knowledge, with a catalogue* (Belfast, 1808).
[23] *Catalogue of the Newtownlimavady Library* (Belfast, 1815).
[24] *Catalogue of books belonging to the Comber Society for Acquiring Knowledge* (Belfast, *c.* 1828).
[25] *Belfast Monthly Magazine*, xii (1814), p. 376.

therefore give no ear to such weak objections, which are really unworthy of the present age, savouring rather of the reveries of fanatical monks, than the language of this age, already not a little conspicuous for laying the hoe of reason to the roots of superstition.[26]

It was also remarked of the reading society in Saintfield in 1815: 'In the town there is a book club of later institution, the publications in which are of respectable character, and their effect on the morals of its members seems favourable.'[27] By the middle of the century, however, the reading societies were in decline.

During the first half of the nineteenth century there were other library influences on popular reading habits, apart from the reading societies and the educational libraries, such as those supplied by the Kildare Place Society and the Sunday schools. There were the mechanics' institutes, such as those founded in Belfast in 1825,[28] Portaferry in 1828,[29] and Downpatrick in 1841.[30] The idea of the mechanics' institutes was admirable, in that useful instruction and rational reading material would be provided for the artisan class; but unfortunately they never really got off the ground, and since they never affected more than a tiny proportion of the working classes they are included in this survey more for the sake of completeness than for any importance they had. Their decline was noted by T. E. C. Leslie in 1852,[31] and the reason was not far to seek: they had ceased to be organisations of the working classes, and instead had become middle-class institutions.

Similarly a number of factories and mills provided some sort of library provision for the workers. One of the earliest, at John Martin's mill in Killyleagh, was in existence by 1840, in which year its praises were sung: it was stated that 'the workers at Mr. Martin's mill enjoyed many important advantages, which ought to contribute to the advancement of the [Total Abstinence] Society. They had an excellent library, and a most commodious news-room, well supplied with newspapers and magazines of the day, accessible to all of them. The men who enjoyed such benefits

[26] Ibid., ix (1812), p. 98.

[27] H. H. Wolsely, 'Statistical account of the parish of Saintfield, 1815' (MS, Linen Hall Library, Belfast).

[28] R. G. Morton, 'Mechanic's institutes and the attempted diffusion of useful knowledge in Ireland' in *Irish Booklore*, ii (1972), pp 59–74.

[29] Ordnance survey memoir for the parish of Ballyphilip (R.I.A., Box 23, Down I, xiii).

[30] *Downpatrick Recorder*, 13 Feb. 1841.

[31] T. E. C. Leslie, *An inquiry into the progress and condition of mechanics' and literary institutions*, part 2 (Dublin, 1852).

128   *The printed word and the common man*

had no excuse to resort to the public house, in order to spend their evenings comfortably.'[32] A similar library, at the Gilford works of Dunbar, M'Master & Co., was in existence by 1840. Of this it was remarked:

It is with more than ordinary pleasure we refer to the well selected library and reading-room that has been established at Gilford, through the exertions of Hugh Dunbar, Esq., and others. The objects of the institution are, to give the labouring and mechanical classes an opportunity of improving themselves, during their leisure hours. The library already contains many popular and useful works, and a few newspapers, of a literary character, are also received. Two copies of the *Whig* also are taken for the use of the reading-room. As a useful adjunct to this institution, a temperance society has been established in the neigbourhood, . . . we are certain that, under such direction, and with the valuable cooperation of the people of Gilford, the institution to which we refer will, ere long, elevate the moral tone of the working classes to exert a considerable influence on society generally, in that district.[33]

Allied to these types of libraries were those provided by landlords for their tenantry. As early as 1836, for instance, Lord Roden had a loan library for his tenants, contained in a picturesque cottage in the village of Bryansford.[34] The nature of the library is not stated, but as the notice of it immediately follows the statement that the noble lord was solicitous for his tenants' spiritual welfare it can be safely assumed that it contained thoroughly uplifting literature.

A rather different library seems to have been organised by the Johnston family of Ballykilbeg. The Johnstons were progressive enough to procure a set of the Kildare Place Society's publications for their tenantry, if one can judge from the fact that the two known survivors of the library[35] are both Kildare Place Society library books: *The history of little Jack, a foundling; together with the history of William, an orphan,* and *Natural history of remarkable trees, shrubs and plants.* These both bear the manuscript annotation 'Ballykilbeg Lending Library'. The books were given out gratis, according to a note in the Johnston family's own family newspaper, printed on their private press.[36]

Another source of printed material for the ordinary person was

[32] *Northern Whig,* 30 Apr. 1840.
[33] Ibid., 26 Dec. 1840.
[34] B. W. Noel, *Notes of a short tour through the midland counties of Ireland, in the summer of 1836* (London, 1837), pp 58–9.
[35] In my possession.
[36] *Ballykilbeg Newspaper,* 1 Dec. 1846.

the congregational library. These tended to be very small, and such works as they held tended to be of a rather earnest character, as indeed one might expect. The catalogues of a few survive. The library belonging to the Seceding Congregation of Ballynahinch in the 1830s contained about 180 volumes of Christian literature.[37] The library of Clough First Presbyterian Church contained 274 volumes in 1842, of which the vast majority were on religious subjects. However it did include a small number of general books, mainly works of travel. It also possessed the autobiography of Archibald Hamilton Rowan, *The life and death of Lord Edward Fitzgerald*, and J. Wade's *History and political philosophy of the middle and working classes*.[38] The catalogue of the congregational library of the Newry Unitarian Congregation was published in 1856,[39] and was probably rare in that the majority of the 686 works listed were not on religious subjects. Religion accounted for 31 per cent, travel and geography 19 per cent, novels 16 per cent.

Yet another minor source of reading material for the working classes came from religious libraries not specifically attached to any church. Such was the Moyallen Tract Lending Library, which received in 1826 a grant of books from the Kildare Place Society.[40] Another was the Crossgar Religious Reading Society, of which an interesting account is given in 1829.

This society, which embraces the parishes of Kilmore, Killileagh, Killinchy, Saintfield, Ballynahinch, and Inch . . . has for its object the procuring, at the least possible expense to *individuals*, of religious publications (and religious publications only) of every description. The fundamental principle of the Society, which is totally abhorrent from every species or degree of proselytism, is that every member in rotation (*no matter what may be his church*) shall nominate such book or work as he may think proper; whereupon it shall be purchased by the society, if its price be not too great for their funds. By one of the rules, no observations, nor discussions upon either religious or political subjects are allowed at the meetings of the Society. The consequence of these fair and honest principles is that there are on the list of members persons of various creeds, Roman Catholics, protestants, and presbyterians, both Old and New Light.[41]

[37] Catalogue of books belonging to the congregation of Seceders in Ballynahinch (MS, Edengrove Presbyterian Church, Ballynahinch).

[38] *Catalogue of the Sunday School and congregational library belonging to the First Presbyterian Congregation, Clough* (Downpatrick, 1843).

[39] *Catalogue of the library of the Unitarian Presbyterian Congregation Needham Place, Newry* (Newry, 1856).

[40] *Fifteenth report of the Society for Promoting the Education of the Poor of Ireland* (Dublin, 1827), p. 114.

[41] *Northern Whig*, 2 Apr. 1829.

It was also noted that there was a great want of books, but the want could hardly have been greater than that experienced by the Gilnahirk Religious Reading Society, which had the audacity to print its rules and library catalogue about 1833.[42]. This society had only marginally more books than rules.

The temperance movement was also active in promoting small libraries for the working man, and indeed all the types of library undertaken from a religious and social point of view tended to be very like one another. The temperance movement arrived in Ulster in 1829 and rapidly spread, though before the end of the 1830s the teetotal movement (which regarded the temperance people as being even worse than the drunks) was making rapid strides. Small libraries were started in such towns as Newtownards,[43] Bangor,[44] and other towns. However, they never really amounted to very much.

It is difficult to get information on the (commercial) circulating libraries. Those for which records remain were strictly intended for the middle classes, such as Greer's in Newry, where the cheapest annual subscription was £1.10s. in 1826,[45], and of the ninety-eight users whose names can be recovered from his ledger[46] only twenty-six cannot readily be identified from printed sources. Viscount Newry was a member, as was the retired Admiral Wolseley. It is not likely that many artisans used the library, or indeed would be encouraged to do so. However most villages would have had at least one shop that had a shelf or two of books for hire, and this practice is alluded to in an article in the *Ulster Monthly Magazine* in 1830:

We cannot affirm, indeed, that the people were destitute of materials for their study and edification. They had the religious manuals of our tract societies, of which the majority were puerile in thought, scanty in facts, vulgar in composition, and illiberal in tendency. Equally inferior in execution and stimulating in their incentives, were the political pamphlets which were scattered in thousands over the country. . . . To this coarse, ill-assorted, and pernicious banquet was added the sweetened poison of our village-bookstalls and circulating libraries.[47]

The sweetened poison of the bookstalls would have comprised

[42] Gilnahirk Religious Reading Society, *Rules and catalogue* (Belfast, *c.* 1833).
[43] *Northern Whig,* 6 Oct. 1840.
[44] Ibid., 12 Nov. 1840.
[45] *Newry Commercial Telegraph,* 25 July 1826.
[46] Account book of Robert Greer, Newry, 1826–30 (P.R.O.N.I., Mic. 40).
[47] *Ulster Monthly Magazine,* i (1830), p. 86.

chapmen's books, and that of the circulating libraries would have consisted of novels, some of them perhaps a trifle risqué.

During this period, as well, the newspaper press became almost completely democratised. At the beginning of the nineteenth century, papers were luxuries with incredibly small circulations by today's standards. The reason for the high price of newspapers was that they were subject to a very high tax, which at the beginning of the century stood at 2*d*.[48]

The English and Irish stamps were consolidated at 1*d*. in 1836[49] (the English stamp duty having been raised to the dizzy heights of 4*d*. in 1815). Again there was the advertisement duty, which in 1800 was 1*s*., in 1810 was raised to 2*s*., and in 1815–16 to 2*s*6*d*., being reduced to 1*s*. in 1833.[50] A consequence of this high rate of taxation in the early part of the century was a high price per issue – about 5*d*. This of course put it out of the way of the ordinary reader, and even some of the commercial classes had a cause for complaint. In 1831 the *Northern Whig* observed:

In consequence of the infamous taxes on knowledge, with which the press of these countries is burdened (taxes we expect a reformed house of commons will speedily wipe away), the generality of persons are deprived of reading at their own houses the best newspapers and periodicals of the day. A London daily newspaper costs £10; and, in this age of enquiry, very few would be contented with studying the reflections, and perusing the contents of less than, at least, half a dozen London journals. . . . In short, only men of very large fortunes can indulge in these luxuries – luxuries now become necessaries.[51]

If this was the position of the middle classes, the position of the ordinary reader can be imagined.

Another factor affecting the usefulness of the newspaper press at this time was the smallness of the circulation, largely caused by the taxes upon knowledge mentioned above. And the numbers issued were sometimes astonishingly small. Of the stamped provincial papers in 1831 the bulk had circulations under 400.[52] Nevertheless, there was one way by which those less well off had access to newspapers. In Holywood at the time of the peninsular war 'several would join to buy a number of the *Belfast News-letter* or of

[48] C. P. O'Neill, *Newspaper stamps of Ireland* (Enniskillen, 1978), pp 19, 21.
[49] Ibid., p. 29.
[50] W. G. Wheeler, 'The spread of provincial printing in Ireland up to 1850' in *Irish Booklore*, iv (1978), p. 10.
[51] *Northern Whig*, 14 Nov. 1831.
[52] R. L. Munter, *History of the Irish newspaper* (Cambridge, 1967), p. 89.

the *Commercial Chronicle*; or, through the kindness of a richer neighbour, a sight of one of these papers would be obtained, and one would read while many would attentively listen.'[53] At about the same time John Gamble mentioned that country employers would often read newspapers to their labourers after the day's work was finished,[54] and in Belfast in the 1820s newspapers were carried around and left at houses for 1*d*. an hour.[55] By these means, and indeed by word of mouth beyond the immediate circle of readers – for even more than today the printed culture and the oral culture were far from distinct – the newspapers had a profound effect. A circulation of less than four hundred to cover half a county may not seem much, but when one reflects that the original paper might be seen and read by dozens of people, and discussed far beyond that circle, and that it came out week after week (meaning that in a year a single paper with a circulation of 300 would produce 15,600 separate printed items), the provincial press assumes its rightful importance. The importance has perhaps been masked indeed by bibliographical convention, which will accord ten years of a local newspaper, comprehending more than one hundred and fifty thousand printed items, the same space in a bibliography as a sermon printed in an edition of one hundred.

Apart from the commercial suppliers of literature, that is the publishers and the booksellers of all types, the educational suppliers (mainly and most importantly the Kildare Place Society, in the first half of the century), those libraries available to the less well-off, and the newspapers, there was one more large source of printed matter for the common person in Ireland: the tract society. The main national tract-distributing society was the Association for Discountenancing Vice, and Promoting the Knowledge and Practice of the Christian Religion, already mentioned in connection with the schools attached to it. They were massive distributors of tracts, and from 1800 to 1824 979,826 religious books and tracts were sold on account of the association.[56] In August 1815 the association announced that, 'strongly impressed with the great laxity of morals prevalent among the lower classes in the north of Ireland, and the evident advantage that would consequently

[53] C. M'Alester, *A sketch of the life and literary labours of the late Robert Sullivan* (Belfast, 1870), pp 6–7.
[54] Gamble, op. cit., p. 219.
[55] Thomas Gaffikin, *Belfast fifty years ago, now (1894) seventy years ago* (3rd ed., Belfast, 1894), p. 29.
[56] *First report of the Commissioners*, p. 37.

result from the distribution of good moral and religious tracts',[57] they were setting up a branch in the diocese of Down and Connor. The association saw its duties as promoting above all the cause of the established church, as evinced by the report of the Down and Connor branch for 1819.

> In presenting the subjoined report . . . to the subscribers and the public, the committee beg leave to advert to the quarterly increase which is manifest in the numerical sales: a fact which is more deeply interesting in the present times, when daring infidelity has been abroad, as it amounts to a demonstration that the *demand* for the sacred volumes which contain the revealed will of God, for the excellent liturgy of the Church of England, and for the well digested tracts which enforce the moral and benevolent duties of life, as the fruit of a living faith, is *increasing* and *progressive* in the north of Ireland.

Apart from Bibles, prayer books, and so forth, the branch recorded the sale of 1,740 tracts,[58] not really a lot to make such a fuss over. Desmond Bowen notes that though the clergy of the established church in the south had little to do and were therefore led into 'mischief' such as thrusting tracts at people who only wanted food, those in the north of Ireland were busier, and in addition had to watch their flanks for presbyterian incursions into their congregations.[59] This would explain the lack of progress on this front.

The presbyterians, indeed, were not far behind in the field of tracts. The Belfast Religious Tract Society was established in 1815[60] and, commencing in 1816, it published an impressive list of at least sixty-six tracts. The first of these was *The history of little Jane, the young cottager*, a very large tract of sixty pages, which sold at £1 per hundred. The most noticeable thing about the tracts at first sight is that they are not overtly anti-catholic. The impression given by the southern-organised Church of Ireland bodies is that their main object is the conversion of catholics to that church, while the concern of the Belfast Religious Tract Society publications is a simple need for salvation, thrift, honesty, and so forth. One indeed deals with conversion: *The advantage of reading the scriptures, exemplified in the history of James Byrne . . .*, a twelve-page tract published in 1816 (B.R.T.S. 7), has the hero, a catholic weaver from Athy, reading some leaves from a New Testament and being converted, but even this one is not strident.

---

[57] *Belfast News-letter,* 11 Aug. 1815.
[58] Ibid., 22 Feb. 1820.
[59] Desmond Bowen, *The protestant crusade in Ireland, 1800–70* (Dublin, 1978), p. 29.
[60] *Belfast Almanac, 1850,* p. 76.

The tracts convey a picture of the ideal lower orders: moral, Christian, honest, sober, and cleanly. They also convey a picture of the ideal reading habits of these lower orders. B.R.T.S. 2, *The dairyman's daughter*, deals with the reading material owned by the very religious daughter of an aged and poor dairyman. She had read few books apart from the Bible and the Common Prayer Book (the latter, surprising in the publication of a presbyterian body, can be explained by the publishing history of these tracts, to be dealt with shortly.) These were Doddridge's *Rise and progress,* Romaine's *Life, work and triumph of faith,* Bunyan's *Pilgrim's progress,* Alleine's *Alarm,* Baxter's *Saint's everlasting rest,* a hymnbook, and a few tracts.

B.R.T.S. 66, *Parental duties,* an undated twelve-page tract, fulminates against popular reading material:

> The indiscriminate use of circulating libraries, and the company of many young persons who resort to them, should be assiduously guarded against, as frequently leading to the most destructive consequences. The real tendency of the greater part of the reading furnished by novels and romances is to mislead the understanding, corrupt the heart, and prepare the way for a dissolute and vicious course of practice. Indeed not a few of the books alluded to, deserve to be burned by the hands of the public executioner. The writer speaks from his own knowledge, when he says, that some of the worst of this kind, jest-books, &c. are printed upon very coarse paper, and hawked among servants from door to door . . . And yet so deluded are the multitude, that these things pass current *for innnocent amusements.*[61]

The purpose of the tracts is explained by B.R.T.S. 5, *The history of Susan Ward,* a sixteen-page tract.

> Before I finish this little book, let me inquire what impression has been made on your mind while reading it? Are you convinced that, though you are ignorant, your ignorance will be no hindrance to your becoming a true Christian, provided you pray for divine teaching? Do you believe the things that have been told you? . . . But if you lay the book, and all concern about its contents, aside altogether, you have read to no purpose but to increase your future condemnation.[62]

These tracts do not appear to have been composed locally, but had been copied direct from tracts published elsewhere. They would appear, indeed, to have been republished versions of tracts printed by the Liverpool Religious Tract Society. The house style,

---

[61] *Parental duties* (B.R.T.S. 66; Belfast, *c.* 1816), pp 7–8.
[62] *The history of Susan Ward* (B.R.T.S. 6; Belfast, 1816), p. 15.

including the style of numbering, is copied exactly, and there are other close similarities. For instance B.R.T.S. 12, *The African widow*, bears a woodcut on the title-page showing a black woman under a tree. The Liverpool Religious Tract Society 112 has the same illustration, but the Belfast tract has the tree copied almost exactly, the woman reversed, and an almost totally different background. B.R.T.S. 37, *Friendly hints to a servant*, copies the woodcut on L.R.T.S. 12, but exactly reverses it, and B.R.T.S. 25, *The history and adventures of Ben the soldier*, bears a woodcut which is a slightly different reversed version of the woodcut on L.R.T.S. 135. All this explains the non-local tone of the tracts. No figures are readily available for the numbers distributed, but in view of the large numbers of titles published the distribution must have been large. The society sold them at prices varying from 1*s*.4*d*. to £1 per hundred, depending on the size.

Of course the tracts and such material as the Kildare Place Society volumes were produced with the idea not of commercial profit, but rather of self-improvement. The Kildare Place Society books at least were truly popular in that large quantities were actually bought directly by the ultimate readership; but, as in the eighteenth century, the most correct insights into contemporary taste emerge when purely commercial factors come into play. These factors can be seen at work in the productions of two worthy successors of James Magee of Belfast.

ASCANIUS,

OR, THE

YOUNG ADVENTURER

BELFAST:

PRINTED BY JOSEPH SMYTH,

HIGH-STREET.

PLATE VIII
Popular book of Joseph Smyth, 1841

CHAPTER 8

The Popular Lists of
Joseph Smyth and Simms & M'Intyre

In the first half of the nineteenth century the small popular book changed its appearance. For the whole of the eighteenth century the physical form remained fixed: a duodecimo of about 144 pages, bound in some cheap leather such as sheepskin, or in plain blue paper. During the early years of the nineteenth century, though the book still usually contained about 144 pages and the format was still the duodecimo, sheepskin bindings disappeared, to be replaced by printed paper covers, with the title and publication details printed on the front and often, as well, a woodcut illustration. The rear cover often bore a list of other books available from the publisher. These changes came gradually, but by 1830 the transformation was virtually complete locally. The majority of Kildare Place Society publications that survive are in the earlier style of binding, but a few have printed paper covers,[1] and these were almost certainly issued from around 1830 onwards.

It was a time of great technical advances in the production of books. Paper was being produced by a mechanical process instead of the old method of hand manufacture; the metal press and then the power of the steam engine superseded the old cumbersome wooden presses; and the invention of stereotyping meant that new issues of books could be cheaply produced almost indefinitely from moulds without the labour of resetting the type each time. These advances contributed greatly to the success of two Belfast firms of printers and publishers who between them virtually monopolised the production of popular literature in Ulster at this time – Joseph Smyth and Simms & M'Intyre. Both issued large numbers of books with printed paper covers, bearing on the back a list of other publications in the series available from them. These printed lists, which vary from copy to copy, provide a valuable insight into early nineteenth-century local popular reading habits, and show very

---

[1] *Catalogue of the Bradshaw Collection of Irish books in the University Library, Cambridge* (3 vols, Cambridge, 1916), ii, 1292–3.

clearly the rapidly evolving nature of popular taste between the later eighteenth century and the middle years of the nineteenth. Joseph Smyth first appeared at the turn of the century,[2] and from an early stage concentrated on the popular material, printing in 1800 Ashton's *Battle of Aughrim* and the *Cattle keeper's guide*.[3] By 1803 he was in partnership with S. Lyons, a partnership that was to last until 1810. From then on he published and printed an extremely heterogeneous list, which even included, in 1816, an editon of Pastorini's *History of the Christian church*,[4] a book which in the 1820s was to become the *bête noire* of Irish protestants, being accepted by the peasantry as prophesying the end of the protestant churches and, by extension, of British rule in Ireland. By the middle of the 1820s, however, he was already embarked on his series of small paper-covered books, which encompassed both the older literature and the newer input, especially that of the Kildare Place Society.

The Kildare Place Society may have thought that it was displacing popular literature everywhere except in Belfast, but an examination of the books produced by Smyth and by a Dublin printer and publisher called C. M. Warren shows otherwise. There were very close commercial relations between the two printers. The relationship indeed was so close that both appeared indifferent to any credit that accrued from a publication; an indifference that seems to have stemmed from a purely commercial attitude, as one would expect when dealing with the popular end of the market. For instance, an examination of *The life of Captain James Cook* reveals the fact that according to the title-page, the accepted bibliographical criterion, the printer was 'Joseph Smyth, 34 High Street, Belfast'. However, the paper cover, on those few copies that still retain this feature without being rebound by enthusiastic librarians, states 'Dublin: printed by C. M. Warren, 21 Upper Ormond Quay'.[5] Conversely, a copy of Elizabeth Hamilton's *The cottagers of Glenburnie* bears on the title page the legend 'Dublin: printed by C. M. Warren' and on the paper cover 'Belfast: printed by J. Smyth'.[6] There are numerous examples of this sort of thing among those copies of Smyth's publications that are still extant in the original paper covers. There even exist two

[2] John Anderson, *Catalogue of early Belfast printed books, 1694–1830* (Belfast, 1890), p. 45.

[3] Ibid., p. 45.

[4] Ibid., p. 57.

[5] *Life of Captain James Cook* (Belfast, n.d.).

[6] Elizabeth Hamilton, *The cottagers of Glenburnie* (Dublin, n.d.).

issues of Aesop's *Fables* (1840), identical in every respect and clearly made up from the same sheets, with the exception of the title-pages, which respectively claim the volume for Smyth and Warren.[7] This printing of two different title-pages is rather puzzling in view of the carelessness with which they regarded this sort of thing in other volumes. It certainly was not an increasing sensitivity or an early example, since the Belfast title-page bears the date 1840, by which time the partnership was well established, and another volume with a Belfast title-page and a Dublin cover bears the date 1845.[8]

They did not both carry or advertise the whole of the joint series. For instance Warren included the following titles, which Smyth never advertised: *Joe Miller's new Irish jest book, Life of Lord Edward Fitzgerald*, Hamilton's *Catechism of the history of Ireland*, and Hugh O'Reilly's *History of Ireland*.[9] Smyth was probably not willing to have his name associated with anything too overtly nationalistic in tone, though his list did, in fact, include Challoner's *Think well on't*, a catholic classic, and *Life and actions of Robert Emmet, leader of the insurrection of 1803*. Challoner, oddly enough, does not appear to have been carried by Warren.

In all, the total number of books advertised by Smyth, from the earliest dated survivor from the series – Allan Ramsay's *Gentle shepherd* (1826) – until the last, *The history of Sir William Wallace* (1841, but with the paper cover and advertisements dated 1850), is ninety-eight. Of this number, thirty-five have been located bearing Smyth's imprint. This seems at first glance to be an astonishingly low figure. The lowness of the figure for surviving copies is, however, easily explained. In the first place, a number of the books advertised by Smyth as being in his series may in fact bear Warren's imprint and be thus hidden. Even if Warren's name was on the title-page and Smyth's on the paper cover, the paper cover might have been discarded when the book was being rebound by a library. Librarians of the past were not always careful to instruct the binders to retain the printed wrappers. Perhaps more importantly, a large number of the 'missing' works can be explained in a different way. Of the total number of works advertised, thirty-eight of the titles are identical with the titles of Kildare Place Society books, and of these titles only five are represented by titles printed by Smyth. These are Aesop's *Fables*,

---

[7] Aesop, *Fables* (Belfast, 1840; Dublin, n.d.).

[8] Bernardin St Pierre, *The Indian cottage* (Belfast, 1845).

[9] Robert Burns, *Poetical works* (Dublin, n.d.), rear cover.

Byron's *Narrative* (a shipwreck story), Marie Cottin's *Elizabeth or the exiles of Siberia*, the *Shipwreck of the Alceste* and the *Life of Captain James Cook*. Again, only three of the Kildare Place Society's titles, out of the thirty-three that have no known Belfast edition, have not disappeared between the advertisement in the 1835 Smyth edition of Allan Ramsay's *Gentle shepherd* and Ralph Griffith's *Ascanius* (1841). And of these three one at least, Josephus's *History of the siege and destruction of Jerusalem*, was available from Warren. It would therefore seem that Smyth simply bought these Kildare Place Society books and sold them alongside his own, making no distinction in his advertisements. Thus the society's publications, instead of displacing books like the *Seven champions of Christendom*, were, for the period that they were available, simply absorbed into the canon. And when they ceased to become available in sufficient numbers, they disappeared from his shelves and his popular list.

The complete list is detailed in appendix VI, where the books are arranged alphabetically, and added details show the period during which the book was printed and advertised (as far as this can be ascertained) and also whether the book appeared on the Kildare Place Society list, that of Warren (again as far as this can be ascertained), and that of Simms and M'Intyre, whose popular lists will be examined later below. Of the list, twelve are mainly religious in tone. Of these five are Kildare Place Society books, all of which disappear after the middle of the 1830s except Josephus, which as explained above was probably kept alive in the Warren edition. Of the remainder, the most interesting are, firstly, Robert Russell's *Seven sermons*, which was of course the book that gave us the first list of chapmen's books back in 1750; then Edward Ward's *Female policy detected: or, the arts of designing women laid bare*, which needs little explanation, though perhaps some of the advice might be a little out of date, as the author died in 1731. Of interest also are Richard Challoner's *Think well on't*, and *The protestant's trial (in controverted points of faith), by the written word*, a work disproving the protestant point of view. It is perhaps significant that this work, though in the Smyth series and with the standard advertisement list on the rear paper cover, bears, instead of the usual imprint, the legend 'Belfast: printed for the booksellers', and is only advertised in one other advertisement list, that on Allan Ramsay's *Gentle shepherd* (1835). Of the other works, their stay on the list seems to have been of short duration. Indeed, if we pick the steadily advertised ones we are left with a religious list consisting of Challoner's *Think well on't*, Josephus, Robert Russell's *Seven sermons*, and Ward's *Female policy detected*, with the possible surreptitious addition of *The protestant's trial*.

When we come to the traditional fare, it is interesting to see how much of this survives the strongest attempts of the Kildare Place Society and other organisations to sweep it out of existence. Of those having their basis in classical times, Aesop of course holds preeminence, and was not, of course, one of those of which the Kildare Place Society disapproved. Ovid's *Art of love*, which also survived, was. Of the medieval tales the *Seven wise masters and mistresses of Rome* was still listed, as was *Valentine and Orson*, both revealing extraordinary staying power, being sold well into the Victorian era. Of the neo-chivalric romances a goodly number remained available. Richard Johnson's *Seven champions of Christendom, The honour of chivalry: or, the famous history of Don Belianis of Greece*, and John Reynold's *Garden of love and royal flower of fidelity* were still flourishing, as was Hugh Stanhope's *Dorastus and Fawnia and Hero and Leander, The unfortunate concubines: or, the history of Fair Rosamond . . . and Jane Shore*, and the *New history of the Trojan wars and Troy's destruction*. This raises the whole question of why some chivalric and neo-chivalric romances became popular in Ulster and some did not. For instance, some of the most popular of the *genre* in England were *Guy of Warwick, Montelion knight of the oracle, Palmerin of England*, and *Bevis of Southampton*. Yet no trace of them has been discovered in Ulster during the period under review. It would seem that there were strong local prejudices, as indeed one would expect.

Accounts of voyages, travels and shipwrecks take up twenty titles, but when these are examined nineteen are found to be Kildare Place Society volumes, which disappear after the middle of the 1830s. Four travel books were printed by Smyth himself, and it is significant that the three dated ones are all published after 1843, when the supply of Kildare Place Society books would have been drying up. Three of the Smyth books are in fact new editions of Kildare Place Society books: *Life of Captain James Cook*, Byron's *Narrative*, and *Shipwreck of the Alceste . . . also . . . the Medusa*. The latter two were printed in 1844 and 1846 respectively. Published in 1843 was *Voyage and adventures of Sir Francis Drake*. As we have seen, Drake's voyages and adventures were popular from the eighteenth century, but for some reason they were never included in the Kildare Place series.

A number of the volumes dealt with the practical and not so practical aspects of human life. Several volumes on social behaviour appear, such as *The accomplished gentlemen; or, principles of politeness, and of knowing the world, . . . to which is now added, the economy of human life* (the first part apparently adapted from Chesterfield's letters to his son), *The modern polite letter writer*, and, astonishingly,

The new academy of compliments, which, as we have seen, was first advertised back in the 1730s. That this was never intended for any but an unsophisticated audience is shown by the fact that it remained unchanged from the middle years of the previous century: a book published in 1833 and advertised through 1850 advised people to say things like 'as a kind sun to a new-born spring, so are your gracious favours to my new born soul',[10] suitably witty remarks included such as the following: '*Q*. What is the suddenest and most successful way of addressing a widow? *A*. Briskly tell her, you come to plough her up that she may lie fallow no longer,'[11] and people were still advised to gesticulate to one another in sign language and write in code 'God bless King George, and keep us from popish slavery.'[12]

Of more practical use were a few titles, four of them Kildare Place Society publications – three of them useful and moral advice to the peasantry and one, *The cabinet of useful arts and manufactures*, of more use to the urban artisan. Two were published by Smyth: *The cattle keeper's guide: or complete directory for the choice and management of cattle* (cattle being used in the broad sense of farm animals generally), and Mrs Stavely's *Housewives' guide: or, a complete system of modern cookery*, of which editions were published in 1831 and 1839.

Moving back to the less useful of the social graces, we have two jest books, the *Irish humourist*, advertised from 1826 to 1835, and the *Banquet of wit*, advertised from 1835 to 1850, and which therefore probably succeeded one another as his standard jest book.

Natural history does not appear to have been a strong suit, as it is represented by only two titles, *Animal sagacity* and *The picture of the seasons*, both Kildare Place Society publications. History proper is represented by a number of titles, none of them Kildare Place publications. Hangovers from the history of the previous century are Ralph Griffith's *Ascanius: or, the young adventurer* (dealing with the '45) and *The history of Sir William Wallace, the Scottish patriot*. Dealing with events in the very late eighteenth century and the early nineteenth century are, firstly, *A narrative of the Irish rebellion . . . in 1798*, of which Smyth published an edition in 1844, though it had been advertised a few years earlier. This took a fairly even-handed approach. The origins of the United Irishmen are accounted for by an unpopular French war, a rapacious soldiery,

---

[10] *New academy of compliments* (Belfast, 1833), p. 14.
[11] Ibid., p. 18.
[12] Ibid., p. 71.

and the suspension of habeas corpus. The Orangemen are accused of ejecting many of the opposite party from their houses and lands. Though massacres of the protestants took place in the south, 'from the principles of the northern people, better educated, . . . the insurgents of this quarter [were not] deliberately guilty, except in one instance, of the plunder, devastation, and murder of the southern.'[13] The troops were often as great a danger to the loyal protestants as to the rebels. The grand moral at the end of the book is thus stated:

Since, from experience of the event, civil wars in any part of Ireland, except some northern counties, must from whatever cause excited, be justly expected to assume a religious complexion of the most bloody hue, Irish protestants ought to be convinced that the political separation of their country from Britain by a popular insurrection must involve their extinction and that consequently an infrangibly determined adherence to their British connexion is necessary for their safety.[14]

In other words unionism, tempered by a certain pride in the thought that if Ulster protestants did rebel, at least they could do it properly.

Another work dealing with the United Irishmen was *The life and actions of Robert Emmet*, of which Smyth published an edition in 1842. This work is quite sympathetic to Emmet, and regrets that 'Emmet did not live to behold the triumph of the catholic cause, that happy accomplishment of one of the great measures to which he devoted fortune and life.'[15] This was not exactly a sentiment that would appeal to the average representative of Ulster unionism and protestantism, but by and large the publishers of popular material did not seem to worry too much about the complexion of the material they sold as long as the sixpences kept coming in and they did not fall foul of the law. Two foreign biographies were also sold: the *Life of General Jackson* (presumably Andrew Jackson, who nobly defended New Orleans in the war of 1812–14 and later became president of the U.S.A.) and J. G. Scott's *Life of Napoleon Bonaparte*, published by Smyth in 1835, a factual and mainly admiring biography. There is only one item representing politics, and by this time it represented rather history. This was James Porter's *Billy Bluff*, the one United Irish satirical work to enter the field of popular literature and remain there. Pirates were out by this time, but highwaymen were still in, and still represented by

---

[13] *A narrative of the Irish rebellion* (Belfast, 1844), p. 84.
[14] Ibid., p. 144.
[15] *Life and actions of Robert Emmet* (Belfast, 1842), p. 10.

the two titles that Henry Cooke testified to having read in the late eighteenth century:[16] *Irish rogues and rapparees* and the *Life and adventures of James Freney.*
There was a fairly long list of novels in the advertisements. Many of these have long lapsed into relative obscurity. Titles such as Elizabeth Hamilton's *The cottagers of Glenburnie: a tale for the inglenook,* Goethe's *The sorrows of Werter: a German story,* Goldsmith's *The vicar of Wakefield,* and Swift's *Travels of Lemuel Gulliver* (Lilliput and Brobdingnag only) need no comment. But few non-specialist readers today are familiar with two works by Bernardine St Pierre – *Paul and Virginia* and *The Indian cottage.* The first is a sickly, affecting tale of love on a tropical island. The second is a rather odd story about a learned doctor who visits India to acquire knowledge, and seeks it at the home of a simple 'paria'. He learns from nature to want nothing. On his return from Calcutta he sends ninety books of manuscript to the Royal Society, who deposit them in the British Museum, 'where, at this very hour, the literati and journalists are still employed in making from them translations, concordances, eulogies, philipics, criticisms & pamphlets'.[17] But the scholar admits that the most useful facts he learnt were that 'truth is to be sought with a simple heart, it is not to be found out of nature; and is to be communicated to men of worth only.' To which he added: 'there is no real happiness without a good wife.'[18] The last half of the book consists of bits and pieces of classical biography and the like.

Then there is the volume constantly advertised simply as *Lady Lucy.* This must be the work mentioned in the Education Commissioners' list of books found in Irish schools: *Life of Lady Lucy, daughter of an Irish lord, who married a general officer and was by him carried into Flanders, where he became jealous of her and a young nobleman, his kinsman, whom he killed, and afterwards left her wounded and big with child in a forest.*[19] It sounds more exciting than the others on the list. It was by Mrs Aubin, of *Noble slaves* fame.

A genre new to this period was the sea story proper. One of the first was John Davis's *The post-captain: or, the wooden walls of England well manned.* This is a humorous story, with characters such as Captain Brilliant, Lieutenant Hurricane, Purser Nipcheese, Dr Gallipot, Midshipman Echo, and so forth. There is lots of good dialogue, and an extract will show the flavour of the work.

[16] *First report of the Commissioners,* appendix, p. 820.
[17] St Pierre, op. cit., p. 71.
[18] Ibid., p. 71.
[19] *First report of the Commissioners,* appendix, p. 555.

'Come, Hurricane, drink your wine, Here's to the wind that blows, the ship that goes, and the lass that loves a sailor.'
Here the conversation was interrupted by the entrance of Flora, who came down under the pretence of finding her smelling bottle.
The captain and lieutenant rose to receive her.
'Captain', exclaimed Flora, 'do you know I have lost my smelling bottle, and Mr Factor [her husband, a very old man] is angry with me for it.'
'Angry with such loveliness!' exclaimed Captain Brilliant. 'Good Lord.'
Flora had insensibly taken a seat next the captain, who was caressing her fine form. The lieutenant expressed his apprehension that he was wanted upon deck, and withdrew from the cabin. . . .
'You have sweet lips, Flora. Notwithstanding my love of fighting, I would rather engage them than an enemy's frigate.'
'For shame, Captain', said Flora.
'Another pull?' cried the captain.
'My dear Brilliant!' said Flora.
'A long pull, Flora, a strong pull, and a pull both together.'[20]

In other words, the book can be read with enjoyment, at least in chunks, which is more than can be said for most of the ones mentioned here. There is one puzzle. Smyth advertised it from 1841 through 1850, but an edition was printed by Hugh Clark in Belfast in 1830 exactly in the Smyth format. Possibly Smyth took over Clark's stock about 1840. Oddly enough, almost exactly the same can be said of another in this mode, *The patriotic sailor: or, adventures of a naval life.* Advertised by Smyth between 1835 and 1850, the only known Belfast edition was printed by Archer & Sons in 1841. Again, it is a good read, set in the Napoleonic period. *Life on board a man of war* is presumably a naval story as well.

Coming to the novels for children on the lists, we find three Kildare Place Society volumes. Of these, Joachim Henrich Campe's *New Robinson Crusoe* and Marie Cottin's *Elizabeth: or, the exiles of Siberia* both retained popularity through 1850, the latter, at least, being reprinted by Smyth. The *New Robinson Crusoe* is somewhat in the Rousseau manner, but is more honest and realistic,[21] and *Elizabeth* is an affecting story about Polish exiles in Siberia. The third of the three Kildare Place stories is Mrs Sarah Trimmer's *History of the Robins.* First published in 1786 as *Fabulous histories*, it was one of the most popular children's books of the later eighteenth and early nineteenth centuries. Mrs Trimmer is one of the giants of the juvenile literature of her age, solid, stolid, and

---

[20] John David, *The post captain* (Belfast, 1830), p. 29.
[21] F. J. H. Darton, *Children's books in England* (3rd ed., Cambridge, 1982), p. 144.

good.[22] The *History of the Robins* tells the story of a family of robins, and is intended to convey to the readers a moral message about living in general and cruelty in particular. Even more moral than Mrs Trimmer was Mrs Sherwood, represented by two titles, *The history of Lucy Clare* and *The history of Susan Gray*. They are both extremely boring and pious, and the author would certainly *not* be amused by *The post-captain*. Rudolf Erich Raspe's *Baron Munchausen* needs no comment.

In the field of the short story or miscellany we have a number of categories. Firstly there are three Kildare Place Society publications: *Miscellany: or, evening's entertainment; Entertaining medley, with true and curious anecdotes*, and the *Scrapbook: or, a selection of interesting and authentic anecdotes*. These little compilations are worthy miscellaneous compilations. The *Entertaining medley*, for instance, deals with the Eddystone lighthouse, a moving bog in Galway, enormous serpents, the tarantula, sufferings in the Black Hole of Calcutta, carrier pigeons, camels, the Polish dwarf, and the Irish giant, among many other unrelated things, and *en route* attacks fairy tales: 'sometimes amusing, they nevertheless are of little use, and even do mischief, by holding forth what is not true, and thus misleading the reader.'[23] *The scrapbook* is somewhat similar, dealing with Dutch workhouses, the Hindoos, mourning dogs, Granville Sharp, clever animals, snake destroyers, tiger hunters, and so on. Despite the attack on fairy stories mounted by the Kildare Place Society, there is no sign of their disappearing from the popular lists. The *History of the tales of the fairies; being a collection of entertaining stories, translated from the French* showed a steady popularity. These were of course not Irish fairy stories, but such stories as the Blue Bird Prince and Princess Florina, and Prince Avenant and the beauty with locks of gold, and so on. The *Arabian night's entertainment* would be a version of the famous stories.

Irish stories were not missing. There are two volumes of these, and it was these (or rather Warren's edition presumably) that Thackeray purchased, among others of that ilk, at Ennis in 1842. Speaking of them he says

Two of the little yellow volumes purchased at Ennis are entitled 'The Irish and Hibernian Tales'. The former are modern, and the latter of an ancient sort; and so great is the superiority of the old stories over the new, in fancy, dramatic interest, and humour, that one can't help fancying Hibernia must have been a very superior country to Ireland.[24]

[22] Ibid., p. 158.
[23] *Entertaining medley* (Dublin, 1826), p. v.
[24] W. M. Thackeray, *The Irish sketch book* (London, 1903), p. 212.

The 'Irish tales' referred to is probably the volume *Modern Irish tales and stories,* of which Smyth published an edition in 1837. This consists of a number of short stories such as 'The Dublin shoeblack', 'The Hibernian mendicant', and 'Kate Connor', of nineteenth-century literary derivation. For instance, the story 'Shane Fadh's wedding' is a cut-down version of the story by Carleton, about one-seventh the length of the original story. Thackeray might, however, have been alluding to *Irish legendary tales and stories,* which appears on both the Warren and, as will be seen, the Simms & M'Intyre lists. This also consists of 'literary' works. The 'Hibernian' and much superior volume is the *Royal Hibernian tales.* This work is quite important as being 'the earliest known collection of Irish popular tales or *Märchen*',[25] and stories from it were reprinted by W. B. Yeats in *Fairy and folk tales of the Irish peasantry,* by Andrew Lang in *The red fairy book,* and indeed by Thackeray in the *Irish sketch book.*[26] The whole volume, with the omission of one tale 'worthless from a folkloristic standpoint' has been reprinted in *Béaloideas,* the journal of the Folklore of Ireland Society.[27]

Finally, though of course all the above could have been read with enjoyment by children, there is one avowedly juvenile title in the section. This is *The new Lilliputian magazine,* of which an edition was printed by Smyth in 1819. It does not appear to have been reprinted, and it ceased to be advertised after 1833.

There is a small number of titles in the field of poetry. The Kildare Place Society's *Selection of poems* was used until the middle of the 1830s, and then Smyth printed his own *Elegant poems* in 1835, which was the one advertised thereafter. The other poetic miscellany was the Kildare Place Society's *The bee.* Finally we have the rather unclassifiable prose-poem, Salomon Gesner's *The death of Abel,* surviving from the previous century.

In the field of drama two volumes also continue uninterruptedly from the previous century. The first is *Two historical plays. The battle of Aughrim. Ireland preserved,* the former play being by John Ashton, the latter by John Michelburne. Two editions were published in the series, the twenty-third in 1826 and the twenty-fourth in 1830. As well as being read, it was still being acted in the Irish countryside, as a production of the *Battle of Aughrim* was seen by Thackeray in Galway in 1842.[28] Indeed the *Battle of Aughrim* surely

---

[25] Séamus Ó Duilearga, 'The Royal Hibernian Tales' in *Béaloideas,* x (1940), pp 148–9.

[26] Thackeray, op. cit., pp 212–28.

[27] Ó Duilearga, op. cit., pp 148–203.

[28] Thackeray, op. cit., pp 203–12.

achieves the status of being the only genuine Irish folk play, for, through frequently printed and by a known author, it continued to be acted by unsophisticated players or even by the peasantry themselves, as we saw above, for an equally unsophisticated audience. The remaining play is the perennial *Gentle shepherd* of Allan Ramsay.

Two books of songs appear, or rather one appears briefly and the other is never advertised at all. *Robin Hood's garland* is a familiar composition from the previous century, but advertisements have only been traced between 1841 and 1846. Possibly, by this time, the market for songs was changing and people no longer wished to sing the familiar traditional songs – the latest music-hall comic song would have been preferable. The other title is puzzling: *The mariner's compass: a selection of favourite naval songs.* Smyth printed an edition in the usual format in 1828, but not a single advertisement for it could be traced. Like *Robin Hood's garland*, it must have somehow missed the market, and naval songs by Dibdin and others were not appreciated. It would have been a rare mistake by Smyth, who was able for about a quarter of a century to keep a fairly large and constantly changing popular list in being. The idea of a cheap, paper-covered series of popular works, issued in a uniform format, was in existence over a century before Penguin Books were thought of, and Smyth was an adept at the art of keeping such a list in existence. Smyth must have died or retired between December 1850 and December 1851, as the *Belfast almanac* for 1851 was issued by him, and that for 1852 was issued by Alexander Mayne, who described himself as 'successor to Joseph Smyth'. Mayne does not appear to have continued the series, as no volumes have been discovered with a date after 1850. Smyth's last effort seems to have been a reissue of *The history of Sir William Wallace*, as a copy in the Linen Hall Library of the 1841 edition has the date 1850 on the front cover.

The history of the Smyth series may therefore be briefly summarised. It seems to have a reasonably constant size of about fifty titles at any one time. The first traceable book in the format with a definite date on the title-page is Challoner's *Think well on't* (1823), but the earliest book with both a date and a list of other books in the series to be traced is Ashton and Michelburne's *Two historical plays* (1826). As seen above, the last date connected with the series is 1850. In between these dates the series went through a number of changes. The most drastic was the removal of the Kildare Place Society volumes in the middle of the 1830s. As mentioned at the beginning of this chaper, Smyth had close commercial relations with C. M. Warren of Dublin, but he nevertheless printed a good

few of the works himself – in the few cases where the name on the
title-page differs from the name on the printed cover, it is safe to
assume that the printer is the one named on the title-page, and
that the other had the paper covers printed locally for those that he
was distributing. Smyth occasionally produced a number of works
of a particular genre in clumps. For instance, *Don Belianis, Valentine
and Orson, The seven champions,* and the *Unfortunate concubines* were all
printed in 1831–2, and the *Voyages and adventures of Sir Francis Drake,*
Byron's *Narrative,* and the *Shipwreck of the Alceste* were all produced
during 1843–6, probably in response to a demand for voyage
literature stimulated by Kildare Place Society books that were no
longer available. He appears to have been a careful man as well:
the *Unfortunate concubines* is printed in the series, but not advertised;
the *Protestant's trial* appears with the imprint 'Belfast: printed for
the booksellers' (though with his list on the back cover); and Hugh
Porter's *Billy Bluff,* though frequently advertised, appears in at
least one Belfast edition which bears all the marks of a work in the
series but with the coy imprint 'Belfast, printed for the purchasers,
1840'.

Smyth would appear to have been a good businessman, but not
as good as Simms & M'Intyre. This Belfast printing and
publishing firm started in the 1790s with a couple of out-of-work
compositors, and ended in the 1850s having revolutionised the
whole business of publishing cheap fiction, not just in Ireland but
in the English-speaking world. This is what the doyen of
nineteenth-century bibliography, Michael Sadleir, has to say
about the 'Parlour Library' that Simms & M'Intyre commenced
in 1847.

It is, presumably, because the study of nineteenth-century publishing history
is of comparatively recent date, that the sensational importance of the Parlour
Library as an innovation in cheap book-making has not previously been
realised. 'Sensational', nevertheless, the venture was, alike in its courage,
efficiency of handling, and success; and perhaps the most remarkable feature
of the whole affair is that it originated in Ireland, was undertaken by a firm of
printers who had not previously been general publishers at all, and was neither
underwritten in London nor relied – except in the ordinary way of business –
on the support or money of the English trade. Certainly its immediate and
overwhelming popularity transformed it in a few weeks from a local Irish
speculation into an international property of great value. A London office was
acquired, and a London address added to the Irish address which at the
outset stood alone in the imprint of the first volume.[29]

---

[29] Michael Sadleir, *XIX century fiction* (2 vols, Cambridge, 1951), ii, 146.

Simms & McIntyre certainly merit this praise and more, but Sadleir very much underrates or is unaware of the previous publishing history of the firm, treating them as a firm of printers who got a bright idea as a bolt from the blue. Before the Parlour Library was thought of, they were already well established as the publishers of a popular series for the local market, and this was not even the first series on which the firm had embarked.

The history of the firm goes back to the year 1797, when the office of the *Northern Star* was raided and wrecked and two compositors thrown out of work.[30] Their names were D. Simms and J. Doherty, and together they acquired equipment and started to print on their own account. They separated in 1803, and in 1807 Simms entered into partnership with one M'Intyre, and we meet with the joint names in imprints. It was the sons of the founders, John Simms and James M'Intyre, who later conceived the Parlour Library. The firm specialised in such matters as educational works, but very early on showed a willingness to embark on small, paper-covered uniform series. By 1820 they had five titles in print of their first series, priced at betwen 6½d. and 2s.6d. That they regarded themselves primarily as publishers and not as printers, as early as this, is proved by the imprint on these little volumes: 'Belfast: printed by T. Mairs & Co. for Simms & M'Intyre, Donegall Street'.[31] By the following year they had twenty-six works in the series, all paper-covered in a uniform style, and priced at between 6½d. and 4s4d. a volume. The vast majority were priced at under 3s. The contents were 'literary' rather than popular, though the list did include such favourites as *The vicar of Wakefield*, *The death of Abel*, and *Paul and Virginia and Elizabeth* (in one volume.[32] The significance of the series is that it gave the firm valuable experience in producing a cheap series, though not as cheap as the next that they embarked on, which was the direct rival of that issued by Joseph Smyth. It is difficult to date this series accurately, as the firm was very shy about dating title-pages; but the earliest date to be found is 1836 and the latest 1842, so it probably lasted from the early or middle 1830s to the launching of the Parlour Library, which would have left little time for other things.

A fair number of the works on the Simms & M'Intyre list are also represented on that of Joseph Smyth, but there is no evidence

---

[30] 'The Parlour Library' in *Irish Book Lover*, ii (1911), pp 133–5.

[31] Robert Blair, *The grave: a poem* (Belfast, 1820), titlepage.

[32] John Langhorne, *The correspondence of Theodosius and Constantia* (Belfast, 1821), rear cover.

of any economic collusion such as occurred between Smyth and Warren of Dublin. What evidence there is points the other way: for instance, they published editions of Aesop's *Fables* within a year of each other, Smyth in 1840 and Simms & M'Intyre in 1841. The books are physically very like those of Smyth: the same size, with title and so forth printed on the front paper cover and a list of other books in the series on the rear cover. They were sold at 6*d*. each, the standard price for this sort of thing, or could be got half-bound for 8*d*.

All the titles so far discovered are listed in appendix VII, which also indicates whether the title occurs in the lists of the Kildare Place Society, that of Smyth, or that of Warren. It can be seen that, like Smyth, Simms & M'Intyre sold the Kildare Place Society titles alongside its own as long as they were available. Indeed, a number of Kildare Place Society volumes with paper covers name the firm of Simms & M'Intyre as agents.[33] It is also probable that, being good businessmen, the two Belfast firms would sell each other's books, acquiring them wholesale in the normal commercial manner, and then in turn retailing them from their shops or selling them in quantity to the travelling chapmen and people whose business it was to keep country shops supplied. The list is smaller than that of Smyth, but in subject content is roughly comparable; the exceptions are mainly in the field of history and biography, where the Simms & M'Intyre list is very much weaker, and in the field of novels, where their list is somewhat stronger.

Of the religious works, a number are unique to the Simms & M'Intyre list. These are the *Abridgement of the Christian doctrine*, the *Grounds of catholic doctrine*, and Cooke on the *Larger catechism* – a nice mix. Another title unique to the list is *Bible stories, adapted for young persons*. Of the remainder, all are represented on Smyth's list (one is Challoner's *Think well on't*) and of these two are also Kildare Place Society publications, though both of these had been reprinted – the *History of Joseph* by Simms & M'Intyre themselves in 1837, and Josephus was available in a Warren edition. It will be noted that both the Smyth and Simms & M'Intyre lists include catholic works. Years before catholic emancipation the printers of Belfast – protestant printers – were turning out catholic literature. In the eighteenth century, with very minor exceptions, catholic material was supplied from Dublin, but this position changed in the first half of the nineteenth. It should be stressed, however, that the vast majority of books produced for popular consumption were read by the literate of all persuasions.

---

[33] *Catalogue of the Bradshaw Collection*, 1292–3.

In the field of catholic religious publishing we find Joseph Smyth both as a printer and as a printer-publisher. In 1816 appeared Pastorini's *General history of the Christian church, from her birth to her triumphant state in heaven*, with the imprint 'Belfast: printed for M. Dawson, by J. Smyth'. 'Pastorini' (Charles Walmsley, bishop of Rama) wrote this fairly substantial volume in order to prove from the Apocalypse the eventual triumph of the catholic church. The book itself is a rather earnest tome, but its main significance in Irish terms is that a pamphlet purporting to be Pastorini's prophecies achieved mass circulation in the 1820s, foretelling the violent overthrow of the protestant churches in 1825.[34]

In the following year, 1817, Smyth published in an edition of the Douai *New testament*. Smyth had several catholic books on his popular list, but he had also printed *England's conversion and reformation compared* (1817), *Grounds of the Catholic doctrine* (1822) – oddly enough, advertised on the list of Simms & M'Intyre but not on his own –, and John Power's *The New testament by way of question and answer with illustrations taken from the holy fathers* (1827). Simms & M'Intyre published the *Poor man's manual of devotions* in 1818, and in 1832 Rev. P. Baker's *Devout communicant*. By then they were actually advertising 'Catholic books, published and sold by Simms & M'Intyre', the list of which is reproduced in appendix VIII.

But by 1829 the catholics of Ulster were in a position to supply some of their own reading materials. By that year there was a Belfast Catholic Book Society in existence, as this imprint appears on a copy of *An explanation of the prayers and ceremonies of the holy sacrifice of the mass*. In 1831 it printed the *Office for the dead: to which are added the devotions of the sacred rosaries*, and from the same year dates an advertisement of the society, which listed the books that were generally supplied.[35] First came the books of the Dublin Catholic Book Society. The full name of this body was the Catholic Book Society for the Diffusion of Useful Knowledge throughout Ireland; it had published its first report in 1828, showing it to be very active in the publication of such works as the *Grounds of the catholic doctrine*, of which it had printed 10,201 copies.[36] Then follow a number of works, ranging in price from 4*d.* to 1*s.* The advertisement concludes with a paragraph throwing light on a particu-

[34] S. J. Connolly, *Priests and people in pre-famine Ireland 1780–1845* (Dublin, 1982), p. 110.

[35] J. B. Bossuet, *The catholic's manual* (Belfast, 1831), p. 90.

[36] *First report of the Catholic Book Society* (Dublin, 1828), p. 19.

lar aspect of book distribution in early nineteenth-century Ulster: priests are reminded that carmen came to Belfast weekly from almost every town and village of the province, enabling them to be supplied with suitable works. So by this time the catholics of Ulster were being supplied with catholic books by their own efforts; but even after emancipation they also continued to be supplied with a number of books by both Smyth and Simms & M'Intyre.

Returning to the list of Simms & M'Intyre, of the traditional tales we have Aesop, *Valentine and Orson*, the *Seven champions*, and *Dorastus and Fawnia*, all represented on the Smyth list. Simms & M'Intyre, however, have one work in this genre not carried by Smyth, *Reynard the fox*. Of the literature of voyages and shipwrecks, there are seven examples. Of these, all except two are represented on both the lists of Smyth and the Kildare Place Society. These two are *Authentic narratives of the most calamitous shipwrecks and disasters at sea, part first*, which Simms & M'Intyre printed and published themselves, and a volume entitled *Wonders of the world*, which must surely be half of the Kildare Place Society volume *Adventures of Mungo the traveller*. All the 'useful knowledge' books are on the Smyth list as well, and all but one on the Kildare Place Society list. This was the *Accomplished gentleman*, of which Simms & M'Intyre published an edition in 1836. This section of their list is rather heavily moral and didactic. There are no jest books and no works treating of the mysteries of legerdemain – which was no bad thing, as following the advice of Henry Dean could lead to nasty burns if not worse. Of natural history there is only the *Pictures of the seasons*, a Kildare Place publication; of history there is not a single example, and only one biography, the *Life of Frederick Baron Trenck*, unique to the Simms & M'Intyre list. Trenck was a romantic eighteenth-century Prussian soldier.

Turning to literature, we find that drama and song are totally absent, but there is one item representing the field of poetry, and that is, surprisingly, totally absent from Smyth's list. Indeed it only occurs in Simms & M'Intyre's list in one advertisement, thought it may occur in untraced copies in original condition with the advertisements untouched. This oddly rare volume is Burns's *Poems*. Considering the generally received wisdom that the poems of Burns were, next to the Bible, the most popular reading material of the Ulster commonality, it seems indeed astonishing that it is scarcely mentioned in this context, and it is tempting to conclude that Burns was only popular with a small coterie of poetasting weavers who rather enjoyed the feeling of belonging to a wider community, and totally passed by the mass reading public. However, the fact that Burns was protected by copyright provides one explanation.

In the field of novels, Simms & M'Intyre had struck out on independent lines, an attitude that would pay off later. Of fifteen titles that can be so classified, no less than eight are not represented in Smyth's lists. Of this total the oldest is *Don Quixote,* and another is an old friend whose absence from the Smyth list is again perhaps surprising – *Amoranda: or, the reformed coquet* by Mrs Mary Davys, the same novel that so affected the young Carleton. Of the other novels, we have gothic romances such as Clara Reeves's *The old English baron: a gothic romance* and Horace Walpole's *Castle of Otranto.* The more juvenile examples are not omitted among the material not peculiar to Simms & M'Intyre, such as Raspe's *Surprising travels and adventures of Baron Munchausen,* of which they actually printed an edition themselves.

Of the juvenile material peculiar to Simms & M'Intyre, two works by Maria Edgeworth deserve notice, and not only because they were by an Irish author. Maria Edgeworth, in fact, is one of the heroines of Harvey Darton's *Children's books in England.*[37] Of her he said:

She is one of the most natural story-tellers who ever wrote English. She is also one of the most observant and the most easily eclectic. . . . Her . . . father . . . made her use children as the vehicle of progress. They were to grow in the delightful prairie of nature – though with monitors conveniently placed to see that nature was properly appreciated. . . . It is astonishing that with prepossessions and ideals so strongly and sincerely held Maria Edgeworth ever wrote anything that children could read save under duress or mental starvation (there was, at the time, a chance of that alternative). But she did, and her tales can still be accepted by simple hearts with unaffected pleasure. . . . [She] wanted her children to be natural; and if her conception of nature was Irish, full of exceptions and even failures, so much the better. Her characters never became abstractions: they had to work out their own salvation as human beings, not in a groove.[38]

The two books by Edgeworth in the list, *The little merchants* and *History of Simple Susan,* are indeed very readable.

In the field of the short story and the miscellany, we find the *Entertaining medley* and the *Scrapbook* representing the Kildare Place Society, and the *Juvenile budget,* printed and published by Simms & M'Intyre themselves (moral and didactic stories) comprising the more miscellaneous of the volumes. Irish material is represented

[37] Darton, op. cit., pp 140–44.
[38] Ibid., pp 142–3.

by *Hibernian tales* – almost certainly the *Royal Hibernian tales* – and a volume called *Irish legendary stories,* which contains not legendary stories proper but relatively modern productions such as 'Paddy Mullowney's travels in France'. The *Arabian nights* are there, as in Smyth's list, and a volume called *Amusing fairy tales.* Also there is Madame de Genlis's *Abridgement of the tales of the castle: or, stories of instruction and delight,* of which Simms & M'Intyre published an edition in 1842.

Thus it can be conclusively proved that Simms & M'Intyre were not just simple printers when they got the idea of revolutionising the production of cheap fiction. However, this should not take away from their achievement when they launched No. 1 of the Parlour Library on an unsuspecting world in early 1847, priced at 1*s.* in decorative printed boards or 1*s.*6*d.* bound in cloth. This was at a time when an average new novel came out in three volumes, at 31*s.*6*d.*, and even cheap reprint series like Colburn's were priced at five or six shillings.[39] The Parlour Library had been preceded a year earlier by a series called the 'Parlour Novelist', priced at 2*s.* in wrappers and 2*s.*6*d.* in cloth. This was revolutionary enough, but the Parlour Library took the English-speaking world by storm, and the name became a household word. Both new titles and reprints were published, and translations were specially made. The first work was Carleton's *Black prophet,* and such was its success that Carleton wrote an original work for the series, *The emigrants of Aghadarra.*[40] The Belfast connection ended in October 1853, when Simms & M'Intyre sold the series to their London agent and dropped from sight. The final Simms & M'Intyre imprint was on G. P. R. James's *False heir,* no. 101 in the series.[41] So ended a long and honourable career, spanning two generations of the business.

The two Belfast printer-publishers dealt with here illustrate very neatly a transitional phase in the history of popular literature. The little works they produced or distributed (including material not discussed, such as chapbooks proper and large woodcut wall-pictures, of which many were printed) show not only the continued vigorous life of a fair proportion of the material popular in the eighteenth century (especially, and most interestingly, the chivalric prose fictions) but also the newer influences of the early nineteenth century – a classic case of survival and innovation. By the middle of the century one of these firms had succeeded in

---

[39] Sadleir, op. cit., ii, 146.
[40] 'The Parlour Library' in *Irish Book Lover,* ii (1911), p. 134.
[41] Sadleir, op. cit., 147, 155.

changing the whole structure of the business of cheap literature, and the final removal of most of the 'taxes upon knowledge' had made a cheap newspaper press possible. A new age had begun.

STATIONERY,
Valentines,
COMIC AND SENTIMENTAL.

Christmas Cards,
IN GREAT VARIETY

TOYS, MARBLES, TOPS, BALLS, MASKS

FIREWORKS,

Powder, Shot, Firearms, &c.

The Trade Supplied on Liberal Terms

PRINTING CHEAPLY EXECUTED.

J. NICHOLSON,
CHEAPSIDE, GOODS STORE,
CHURCH LANE, BELFAST.

THE NEW
Christmas Rhyme Book

BELFAST:
PRINTED FOR THE BOOKSELLERS
BY
J. NICHOLSON,
CHEAPSIDE, CHURCH LANE, BELFAST.

6

I have done I ll fight ever a champion
in Christendom.

A Doctor, a doctor, ten pounds for a
doctor! is there never a doctor to be
found, who can cure this man of his
deep and mortal wound?

7

I am a doctor, pure and good, and
with my sword I'll staunch his blood;
if you have a mind this man's life to
save, full fifty guineas I must have.

PLATE IX
The last Ulster chapbook, c. 1900

CHAPTER 9

The Coming of Mass Readership

In 1910 the writer J. J. Marshall observed of Ulster popular reading:

The following, up till forty years ago, formed portion of the pedlar's stock: *The academy of compliments, The Arabian nights, The cottagers of Glenburnie, Hocus Pocus, Irish rogues, James Freney, Robin Hood's garland, Seven champions, Tales of the fairies, The Trojan wars, Valentine and Orson, The seven wise masters and mistresses of Rome,* some of them absolutely harmless.[1]

Marshall went on to note that though works of this nature continued to be printed in Dublin, the 'older' literature had disappeared, and he noted a number of titles that were still available from Dublin. These are nearly all familiar titles from the lists of Warren, Smyth, and Simms & M'Intyre, consisting of literary, biographical and useful items, no doubt being reprinted from old stereotype plates of Warren's.

The suggested date of *c.* 1870 for the last, and probably purely rural, popularity of the older material is borne out by the memoirs of Seamus MacManus, who was born in a poor part of Donegal about 1868. He waxes ecstatic about the joys of wandering about the stalls at the country fairs:

Always the Stannins drew Jaimie's heart and held it [McManus refers to himself as Jaimie]. Along with their thousand fairlies, they tempted (in days a little later) with infinite variety of fascinating literature – at least a dozen tuppeny and thruppeny chap-books, put out by publisher Warren of Dublin Quays. There were the Harp of Erin Song Book (itself worth a guinea if it was worth a penny), Valentine and Orson, The True History of Freney the Robber, Paul and Virginia, Hibernian Night's Entertainments, Irish Rogues and Rapparees, The Seven Champions of Christendom, Old Moore's Almanac, and others equally entrancing . . . He didn't buy the books, couldn't buy them – their possession was for the wealthy who had sold a cow or a pig.[2]

---

[1] J. J. Marshall, 'Irish chap books' in *Irish Book Lover,* i (1910), p. 159.
[2] Seumas MacManus, *The rocky road to Dublin* (New York, 1939), p. 15.

Yet the young Jaimie managed, by persistently parking himself at the left-hand corner of the stand where the books were displayed, to get through the entire stock a little at a time, when the owner was not looking or was feeling indulgent. MacManus was looking back at this part of his life in a rather sentimental way; nevertheless this represents the last guttering of the old tales in Ulster. For new influences were sweeping through popular literature, influences that were to sweep away, once and for all, the substantial older tales and other material.

However, one type of popular printed literature survived the end of the century – the ballad sheet. The 'garlands', small chapbooks containing three or four songs, had fallen by the wayside by the middle of the nineteenth century, though vast quantities had been produced in the first few decades. The ballad sheets proved more resilient. Early in the century, as we have seen, the ballad singers could be a nuisance in the crowded streets, and indeed the ballads themselves sometimes came to the notice of the authorities. For instance, at a fair at Carrickmacross, County Monaghan, in 1830, two ballad singers were arrested for selling a song that contained the following immortal lines.

> Morris was our leader, a man that feared no danger,
> With the fire blazing like lightning he did go;
> He received a ball from luter that they have made of puter,
> Which occasioned our fine hero that day for to lie low.[3]

Towards the end of the century one Belfast printer, following in the footsteps of Alexander Mayne, Joseph Smyth's successor, specialised in the production of sheet ballads printed on flimsy paper, with a number of songs on each sheet. Unlike the earlier 'garlands', which were intended to be folded into a small book, J. Nicholson's sheets were intended to be cut up, and the ballads bear Nicholson's imprint at the foot. He was a good business man, printing both Orange and Green songs, as well as songs of sentiment and humour.[4] Presumably it was up to the singer to choose his or her audience carefully.

About this time Nicholson also produced what was probably the very last chapbook proper to be printed in Ulster: the *New Christmas rhyme book*, containing a traditional mummer's play and

[3] Gréagóir Ó Dúghaill, 'Ballads and the law 1830–1832' in *Ulster Folklife*, xix (1973), p. 38.

[4] Alf MacLochlainn, 'Belfast printed ballad sheets' in *Irish Booklore*, i (1971), pp 21–3.

illustrated with crude and archaic woodcuts, of which there had been earlier editions printed locally. This is not only interesting because of its format. The text has very clear links with the text of the *Seven champions of Christendom*, as the following extract shows:

I'll cut you and slash you, and then send you to Turkey, to make mince pies baked in an oven, and after I have done I'll fight ever a champion in Christendom. . . . Here comes I, St Patrick, in shining armour bright, a famous champion and a worthy knight.[5]

This is not to say that the play is in any sense based on the *Seven champions*, but merely that both were created in a society where such material was part of the common cultural heritage. The play, like the *Seven champions* itself, was an importation from England.[6]

Paralleling the decline in the fortunes of the traditional romance, there was a rise in the fortunes of the provincial newspaper press. As mentioned earlier, this had suffered in the earlier part of the century from excessive taxation, resulting in high prices and, in consequence, extremely low circulation. However, things were to improve; though conservative diehards would hardly have looked at it in this fashion. By 1861 all restrictive duties had been abolished – the advertisement tax in 1853, the stamp duty in 1855, and the paper tax in 1860 – which meant that a cheap press could become a reality, hampered only by market-place economic conditions. The press in Belfast did not alter very much in total numbers of papers published between 1850 and 1900, but in the six counties that now form Northern Ireland (excluding Belfast) there were sixteen papers in 1850, twenty in 1860, twenty-four in 1870, twenty-nine in 1880, thirty-four in 1890 and forty-two in 1900 – a substantial and steady rise.[7] The effect on reading ability of this rising tide of cheap print of local interest must have been immense.

But newspapers were not the only reading material to become cheaper, and not only cheaper but produced in vastly greater quantities. The cheap popular books of Simms & M'Intyre, Smyth, and Warren of Dublin have been examined above; but by the middle years of the century Smyth was dead, Simms & M'Intyre had moved on to greater things, and Warren's list, if we can trust the evidence of J. J. Marshall, had not evolved after this period but merely ceased to reprint the traditional material. This

---

[5] *New Christmas rhyme book* (Belfast, c. 1900) pp 5–6, 10.
[6] Alan Gailey, *Irish folk drama* (Cork, 1969), p. 61.
[7] J. R. R. Adams, *Northern Ireland newspapers: checklist with locations* (Belfast, 1979).

was the direct result of several happenings both locally and nationally. The local happening was the launching of the Simms & M'Intyre Parlour Library, which succeeded in revolutionising the publishing industry and starting the era of cheap quality literature. Somewhat earlier in this century had come determined efforts to ensure a supply of cheap non-fiction. These were based in London or Edinburgh, and one of the pioneers was Charles Knight, born in 1791.[8] In 1828 he undertook to supervise the publications of the Society for the Diffusion of Useful Knowledge, founded some months earlier. The most important results were the *Penny Magazine* (1832–45) and a number of volumes in a shilling series, *Knight's Weekly Volume for all Readers*. There is little evidence of mass working-class readership, as was the case with the Irish examples such as the *Dublin Penny Journal* and the *Irish Penny Journal*.

Another determined effort was made by the Edinburgh brothers William and Robert Chambers.[9] In 1832 they started *Chambers' Edinburgh Journal* at a price of 1½d. The Chambers's tendency was to be a little less earnest than Knight, and their journal included a proportion of fiction and lighter material. Produced in vast quantities were the little volumes of Chambers' *Miscellany of useful and entertaining tracts*. Not everyone entirely approved of this. Thackeray, while on his Irish tour, was moved by his purchase of some traditional material to comment disparagingly about penny magazines and books with titles like *The little geologist*, commenting that the world would be a dull place when science had finally banished fancy.[10]

Simms & M'Intyre's Parlour Library was not lacking in almost immediate imitators. Routledge's Railway Library was launched in 1849, and proved even more enduring than the Parlour Library. These were all reprinted, unlike the Parlour Library, but both series were successful, and around the middle of the century the vast majority of cheap novels appeared in one or other of these series.[11] The Railway Library, priced at 1s., was the final surrender of the publishers to the challenge of Simms & M'Intyre. After trying for two years to maintain the old price of about 6s. for reprint novels, the price fell first to 3s.6d., then to 2s.6d., then to the Railway Library's 1s., in direct imitation of the Parlour Library.[12]

[8] V. E. Neuburg, *Popular literature: a history and guide* (Harmondsworth, 1977), pp 195–200.
[9] Ibid., pp 202–5.
[10] W. M. Thackeray, *The Irish sketch book* (London, 1903), pp 178–9.
[11] Margaret Dalziel, *Popular fiction 100 years ago* (London, 1957).
[12] R. D. Altick, *The English common reader* (Chicago, 1957), p. 299.

Not all novels read were standard English Victorian novels, with standard Victorian values. Rev. W. M. O'Hanlon, in his *Walks among the poor of Belfast*, published in 1853, mentions the reading material of the Ulster urban proletariat, though he would, of course, be singling out the worst to highlight.

> The supply of a wholesome, light, cheap literature for the masses, instead of the polluting, licentious productions now circulated (many of them translations of the most infamous French novels) is loudly demanded, too, in proportion as the power of reading becomes diffused.[13]

At the middle of the century cheap translations of French novels were indeed popular among the masses and were regarded with horror by the right-thinking people of Britain. Many of them dealt with vice among those in society and the deeds of criminals, and the most popular of all were the effusions of Paul de Kock.[14]

However, in the latter part of the nineteenth century good cheap literature for the masses became a reality. Simms & M'Intyre and their later imitators deserve every credit for the physical production of this material, but, as Altick observes, none of this could have occurred without the three requisites of a mass reading public: increased literacy, leisure, and a little pocket money.[15] These all became a reality during the latter part of the century, and in addition there were technical improvements in both printing and papermaking which made these processes inherently cheaper.[16]

Cheap series proliferated as the century progressed. One of the great names in late nineteenth-century publishing, that of Cassell, is prominent. The founder of the firm, John Cassell, issued his *Popular Educator* in 1852 at 1*d.* a number. But the most influential and significant of the firm's productions was Cassell's National Library, started in 1886, the volumes of which sold at 3*d.* in paper covers and 6*d.* in cloth. The crowning refinement came in 1896 with Newnes' Penny Library of Famous Books.[17]

To judge from surviving copies, the two most popular Victorian series were the London-based Cassell's National Library and Milner's Cottage Library. The founder of the latter series died in

[13] W. M. O'Hanlon, *Walks among the poor of Belfast* (Belfast, 1853), p. 96.
[14] Louis, James, *Fiction for the working man* (London, 1963), p. 142.
[15] Altick, op. cit., p. 306.
[16] S. H. Steinberg, *Five hundred years of printing* (3rd ed., Harmondsworth, 1974), pp 277–91.
[17] Altick, op. cit., p. 315.

1850,[18] but during the last half of the century the series was omnipresent, and the format – small, dumpy, and cloth-bound – was imitated by others. The Cottage Library itself had several manifestations, such as the Novelist's Library, priced at 1s.6d.; a Miscellaneous Series at various prices; the Wide, Wide, World Library at 1s.3d.; the Cottage Library proper at 1s.; and a Juvenile Library at 6d., as well as several other series.[19] A look at a catalogue of about 1860 shows how little of the older literature remained in print in the British Isles as a whole.[20] From the period of 'traditional literacy' the only classical works remaining are Aesop and Ovid, and of the religious works popular in eighteenth-century Ulster all that remain are the inevitable *Pilgrim's progress* and three others – Matthew Mead's *Almost Christian discovered,* William Dyer's *Christ's famous titles,* and Isaac Ambrose's *Looking unto Jesus.* None of these religious books, though popular in eighteenth-century Ulster, was published in either Smyth's or Simms & M'Intyre's popular series, and their survival in a national list must mean that the market in the English-speaking world would justify publication in a series such as the Cottage Library, but not promotion in any part of that world. In other words, there would always be a market for old-fashioned religious works, if only the area covered was wide enough to render the minority who bought them economically important. The same argument must apply to the only neo-chivalric title to appear. This is the *Seven champions of Christendom,* which was available in several versions: with eight steel plates and gilt back and edges at 3s.6d., with plain edges at 2s.9d., and in the Cottage Library 'Instructive and Entertaining Series' at 1s.

Writers were not slow in exploiting the huge market created by mass literacy. Of all the Victorian writers for a mass readership one of the most prolific was G. W. M. Reynolds, the 'penny dreadful' author. The *Bookseller* stated in 1868 that he had written more and sold in greater numbers than Dickens, and after his death in 1879 the same organ stated that he was 'the most popular writer of our time'.[21] He was not only popular, he was also prolific: it has been estimated that his novel *Mysteries of the court of London* contains just under 4,500,000 words.[22]

---

[18] Neuburg, op. cit., p. 178.
[19] J. L. Stephens, *Incidents of travel in Egypt* . . . (London, c. 1860), advertisement section.
[20] Ibid.
[21] Dalziel, op. cit., p. 36.
[22] James, op. cit., p. 41.

Table II: National schools and population in Ireland and Ulster, 1841–1901.

W. E. Vaughan and A. J. Fitzpatrick (ed.), *Irish historical statistics: population, 1821–1971* (Dublin, 1978), pp 3, 16; *Reports of the commissioners of national education in Ireland: eighth report,* p. 14 [398], H.C. 1842, xxiii, 352; *eighteenth report,* p. xviii [1582], H.C. 1852–3, xlii, 18; *twenty-eighth report,* p. 8 [3026], H.C. 1862, xx, 256; *thirty-eighth report,* p. 10 [C. 599], H.C. 1872, xxiii, 262; *forty-eighth report,* p. 6 [C. 3243], H.C. 1882, xxiv, 82; *fifty-eighth report,* p. 10 [C. 6788], H.C. 1892, xxx, 10; *sixty-eighth report,* p. 38 [Cd. 1198], H.C. 1902, xxx, 440.

	national schools			population		
	Ireland	Ulster	Ulster as percentage of Ireland	Ireland	Ulster	Ulster as percentage of Ireland
1841	2,337	1,005	43	8,175,124	2,386,373	29
1851	4,704	1,878	40	6,552,385	2,011,880	31
1861	5,830	2,153	37	5,798,967	1,914,236	33
1871	6,914	2,561	37	5,412,377	1,833,228	34
1881	7,648	2,890	38	5,174,836	1,743,075	34
1891	8,346	3,125	37	4,704,750	1,619,814	34
1901	8,692	3,256	37	4,458,775	1,582,826	35

The mass readership implied by all this could only be made possible by mass education, which in Ireland was achieved by the national system of education. The system did not suddenly spread throughout the whole country in the 1830s, however. The number of schools in connexion with the system continued to rise throughout the century. Table II shows clearly the rise in both Ireland generally and in Ulster, despite a falling population after the famine. While the system was by no means perfect, it did, by the end of the nineteenth century, create what was to all intents and purposes mass literacy. If we examine the census figures for 1901[23] we find that in the county of Antrim, for instance, about 8 per cent of those over five years of age were totally illiterate, and in the county of Donegal the figure is 26 per cent. The figure for Ulster is about 12½ per cent. These figures, while they are open to varying interpretations, nevertheless show that by the end of the century there was a mass potential readership.

By this time, therefore, there was a cheap literature in many forms. One element was missing in Ulster, however: widespread free public provision. As seen earlier, such institutions as mechanics' institutes and reading societies had by the middle of the century proved themselves either inherently unstable or past their

[23] *Census of Ireland, 1901. Part 1 . . . Vol. III. Province of Ulster: summary tables,* p. 32 (Cd. 1123–IX], H.C. 1902, cxxvii, 796.

prime. Ulster had by the latter part of the nineteenth century reached the position of a society ready for mass library provision. It would be impossible to detail all the various types of library and newsroom provision provided in the late nineteenth century. However, some strands can be identified. First, we can look at some libraries established by mill-owners and landlords. About 1864 the Annsborough Library and Reading Society commenced, under the patronage of Messrs Murland, mainly for the employees of the firm.[24] Similarly in 1888 the Hillsborough Linen Company provided a reading and recreation room for its employees, managed by a committee of the workers – though presumably under the sharp eye of the management.[25]

Landlords still occasionally provided libraries for their tenantry. One such existed on the estate of Lord Bangor at Castle Ward around 1880. In 1878 a notice was inserted in the parish magazine 'to inform those of Lord Bangor's tenantry who have been in the habit of receiving books from this library' that

it is still (notwithstanding absence from home) conducted on the same principle as hitherto. . . . It is to be hoped that the young people who frequently come on those days will not now cease doing so, nor lose the advantages offered to them. We should be glad, on our return, to find by our library list that the same names are therein often recorded. It is most satisfactory to observe that useful and instructive books have been during the past year really appreciated; a preference shown for such, and a welcome granted to them in many of the homes of our parish.[26]

Another phenomenon of the later nineteenth century was the working-man's reading room. One of the first, though it was not actually called by that name, was at Bangor. In 1853 a number of the inhabitants formed themselves into a committee, to take into consideration the best means for getting up a reading and news-room 'for the improvement of the working classes in the town and neighbourhood'. Upwards of 160 people subscribed, and the clergy of the different demoninations, with one unnamed exception, supported the idea. The Bangor Newsroom opened on 22 December 1853.[27] The main spate of these institutions came in the 1880s and 1890s. Most towns in Ulster had one. They seem to have never amounted to much, and that at Annahilt was probably typical. It opened in January 1895, and after a year had 45

[24] *Downpatrick Recorder*, 15 Oct. 1864.
[25] G. H. Bassett, *County Down guide and directory* (Dublin, 1886).
[26] *Home Words for Heart and Hearth* (Mar. 1878), p. 2.
[27] *Northern Whig*, 15 Dec., 29 Dec. 1853.

members.[28] By 1897 the name had changed to the Annahilt Reading and Recreation Room, and the main attraction seems to have been the airgun.[29] By 1898 the name had changed again to the Annahilt Men's Reading and Recreation Room.[30] Such rooms were probably provided as alternatives to the public houses. Holywood went one further, with the provision of a Working Man's Library. This began in 1860, when the Holywood Loan Fund gave a grant of £7.10*s*. to the Holywood Working Classes Improvement Society, the parent body.[31] By 1863 it contained several hundred volumes, and members of the working classes had the use of the library for an annual subscription of 1*s*.; others paid 2*s*.6*d*.[32]

Belfast had the largest institutions of this type. By 1880, for instance, as successors to the Mechanics' Institute there were the Working Men's Institute and Temperance Hall, with a newsroom and a library of nearly 3,000 volumes, and the People's Literary Institute, with a newsroom and a library of about 4,000 volumes.[33] Most towns would have had Young Men's Christian Associations as well, with similar facilities.

The rate-supported public library movement hardly affected Ulster at all during the nineteenth century, though the beginnings of the movement locally will be dealt with shortly. In the absence of public libraries, institutions like those mentioned above and a host of other types of library, such as parochial libraries, provided literature and especially newspapers for the masses. One type of institution stands out, however, as a sort of proto-public library. This was the newsroom and library, existing on its own and not attached to another institution such as a Y.M.C.A. Virtually every town in the north possessed a newsroom and library (or library and newsroom) in the latter part of the century. That in Downpatrick is typical. In existence by 1875,[34] it had an annual subscription of 4*s*., with ladies, boys, and apprentices paying 2*s*. The reading room was supplied with London, Dublin, Belfast, and Downpatrick papers, and the library was furnished with 'a large collection of popular works by the first authors of the day '.[35]

[28] *Lisburn Standard*, 11 Jan. 1896.

[29] Ibid., 9 Jan. 1897.

[30] Ibid., 8 Jan. 1898.

[31] *Belfast News-letter*, 30 Jan. 1860.

[32] Ibid., 11 May 1863.

[33] *Belfast and Province of Ulster directory* (Belfast, 1880), pp 62, 64.

[34] Alexander Knox, *History of the county of Down* (Dublin, 1875), p. 413; see above, p. 150.

[35] *Down Recorder household almanac* (Downpatrick, 1878), pp. 14, 43.

This library and newsroom must have fallen by the wayside, as in May 1886 the Downpatrick Newsroom and Library was set up.[36] In January 1891 it received a useful addition to its funds. When the local savings bank had been wound up in 1848, there was a residuum of £100, deposited by one James Quail to be used towards the building of a new library and news-room to replace that occupied by the old Downpatrick Literary Society.[37] This building had collapsed in 1839,[38] and the society itself came to a formal end in 1849.[39] A surviving trustee of the money, Rev. S. C. Nelson, handed the money over to the Newsroom and Library in 1891, shortly before his death. By this time it amounted to £145.[40] In 1899 the periodical list was revised to include twenty-nine titles,[41] and in 1900 the Library issued a catalogue, containing almost 900 titles.[42] A large number of books seem to have been presented by Rev. J. H. Bibby of Ballee, whose bookplate survives on many of the volumes now held by the South-Eastern Eucation and Library Board.

These newsroom and libraries could only offer a limited service, and their stock would have consisted of novels and such volumes as were presented to them – many of the books presented to Downpatrick by J. H. Bibby were in the Cassell's National Library series, for instance. But these, together with other types of library and of course commercial circulating libraries, were what was available in the absence of rate-supported public libraries, which were slow in coming to Ireland and indeed to Ulster. The first library act to deal with Ireland was the Public Libraries Act, 1853 (16 & 17 Vict., c. 101), which extended the Public Libraries Act of 1850 (13 & 14 Vict., c. 65) to Ireland and Scotland and enabled municipal boroughs with populations exceeding 10,000 to establish libraries; but the main library act for Ireland was the Public Libraries (Ireland) Act, 1855 (18 & 19 Vict., c. 40). This empowered towns with populations exceeding 5,000 to establish libraries, supported by a rate not exceeding 1*d.* in the pound. Ireland was slow to apply the acts, and the first Ulster town to do so was Belfast, in 1888. The first annual report is illuminating.[43] A selection of 14,000 volumes was made, and a newsroom opened.

[36] Bassett, op. cit., p. 199.
[37] *Down Recorder*, 31 Jan. 1891.
[38] Ibid., 21 Dec. 1839.
[39] Ibid., 28 Feb. 1849.
[40] Ibid., 7 Feb. 1891.
[41] Ibid., 4 Nov. 1899.
[42] Ibid., 27 Oct. 1900.
[43] *First annual report of the Committee of the Free Public Library, Belfast* (Belfast, 1889).

Statistics were kept – the total issue for the year was 185,147 volumes. The trades and professions of the users were carefully recorded, and the following groups were able to muster more than a hundred representatives: apprentices (378); clerks, book-keepers, and apprentices (1,539); drapers, hosiers, mercers, and apprentices (169); engineers, fitters, drillers, and apprentices (133); grocers and provision merchants (138); linen business (229); merchants (114); printers, compositors, and apprentices (112); salesmen (124); schoolboys (275); students (263); teachers and monitors (186); and warehousemen (112). Of the 6,572 users, 2,691, were aged between 14 and 20, and 2,014 between 21 and 30 – an overwhelmingly young user group, therefore. Of the types of books borrowed, prose fiction was by far the most popular. The least popular subjects were law, politics, sociology, and commerce. Notable books in each class with their issues are also detailed. Only four books were issued more than three hundred times – Dickens' *David Copperfield* and *Pickwick Papers*, and Marryat's *Midshipman Easy* and *The pirate and the three cutters*. The only novels to score between two and three hundred issues were Lever's *Tom Burke*, Mrs Henry Wood's *East Lynne* and *The Channings*, and Rider Haggard's *King Solomon's mines*.

The act that actually heralded the setting up of public libraries outside Belfast was the Public Libraries (Ireland) Act, 1894 (57 & 58 Vict., c. 38). This empowered all urban districts to form libraries. The local authority could adopt the acts by resolution, and if the resolution was not carried twenty ratepayers could compel a public ballot. Progress was patchy by the turn of the century. Coleraine had adopted the Acts as early as 1881, but had not opened a library; Banbridge had adopted them in 1890, but had likewise not yet opened; Lurgan had adopted them in 1891 and opened in 1895; Newry had adopted them in 1895 and opened in 1897, Newtownards had adopted them in 1896 and opened in 1897; Larne had adopted them in 1897 and had not opened and Londonderry had adopted them in 1898 and likewise not opened.[44]

As an examination of the steps leading up to the provision of public libraries in County Down will show, it was not always easy to get the system going. In Banbridge, for instance, the town commissioners were informed in 1890 that an anonymous lady and gentleman were prepared to donate a free library to Banbridge, at a total cost of £7,000, covering both buildings and books. There were four conditions. Banbridge would adopt the

---

[44] Thomas Greenwood, *British library yearbook* (London, 1900), pp 174–5.

library acts, the library was to be held for the public use, no literature of a controversial or anti-Christian character was to be added or circulated, and it was to be open to all within a radius of seven miles at a charge of not more than 1*s*. a year.[45] The acts were adopted, but things started to go wrong. There were delays in finding a site, and when a site was found there were squabbles over the price. Before the matter was regularised, the intending donor died and the matter went no further.[46] Banbridge had to wait until 1900 for the advent of a second benefactor, this time the ubiquitous Andrew Carnegie, who offered £1,000.[47] The library was finally opened in 1902.[48]

In Newry the town commissioners had considered adopting the acts in 1893, but no action was taken.[49] Shortly after the 1894 act became law, there was a steady stream of approving letters in the local press. One calculated that a 1*d*. rate would provide an 'ample' income of £128 a year.[50] At about the same time the local committee of the Gilchrist lectures announced that the proceeds of the lectures were to go towards the proposed public library.[51] (The Gilchrist Trust had been set up under the terms of the will of the eccentric Scottish orientalist John Borthwick Gilchrist (1759–1841), and was dedicated to furthering education and learning throughout the world.)[52] The acts were formally adopted in July 1895,[53] and when the building was opened in September 1897 it contained some 5,000 volumes.[54] In its first year of operation nearly 40,000 volumes were issued.[55]

The only other public library to be established in nineteenth-century Ulster was in Newtownards. In 1895 the town commissioners received a deputation asking for a library, and resolutions in favour were also received from the Ards Shorthand Association, the Good Templars, and the Working Men's Reading Room.[56] A public meeting was called for 18 February, and at this a wide variety of opinions was expressed. One gentleman 'was not going

[45] *Down Recorder*, 7 June 1890.
[46] Thomas Greenwood, *Public libraries: a history of the movement* (London, 1894), pp 282–3.
[47] *Down Recorder*, 8 Sept. 1900.
[48] W. G. S. Adams, *A report on library provision* (Edinburgh, 1915), p. 64.
[49] *Library*, v (1893), p. 197.
[50] *Newry Commercial Telegraph*, 1 Sept. 1894.
[51] Ibid., 8 Sept. 1894.
[52] Ibid., 11 Sept. 1894.
[53] *Library*, vii (1895), p. 287.
[54] F. C. Crossle, *Notes on the literary history of Newry* (Newry, 1897).
[55] *Library Association Record*, i (1899), p. 180.
[56] *Newtownards Chronicle*, 9 Feb. 1895.

to throw cold water on a library, but what the working men wanted was a reading room, a smoke room, and a recreation room'. Another person apparently believed that the Bible contained all the information it was necessary to know.[57] Discussion went on and on, to such an extent that a writer in the local paper observed:

> Dear *Chronicle*, it seems to me,
> As to the public library
> Enough already has been said,
> Much more, and we shall *talk it dead*.[58]

The remainder of 1895 was spent in setting up a library committee, and indeed it was not until October 1896 that this committee obtained the promise of suitable premises.[59] One body none too pleased with the procrastination was the Working Men's Reading Room, which had been struggling hard for some time to keep its doors open pending the arrival of a functioning public library.[60] About this time the Newtownards Newsroom agreed to hand over its assets to the public library, and in November the newsroom part was opened, with the library due to open in January 1897.[61] By February it was still not open, though news had been received that Andrew Carnegie was prepared to donate £100 – the first Carnegie grant in Ireland. Moreover, the first order for books had gone out.[62] The library finally opened in May 1897.[63]

Other towns attempted to get public libraries going during the later nineteenth century. As seen earlier, one of these was Banbridge, and another was Downpatrick. As early as 1890 a speaker at a meeting of the Newsroom and Library called for a public library,[64] but a more practical gesture came in 1896, when Elizabeth Saul left all the residue of her estate 'in trust to apply the same for the advancement of education and the establishment of a public free library in the town of Downpatrick.' She died in 1902, and the income from her estate was about £69 a year. Help was forthcoming from Andrew Carnegie,[65] and the library was finally

---

[57] Ibid., 23 Feb. 1895.
[58] Ibid., 2 Mar. 1895.
[59] Ibid., 17 Oct. 1896.
[60] Ibid., 26 Sept. 1896.
[61] Ibid., 7 Nov. 1896.
[62] Ibid., 20 Feb. 1897.
[63] Ibid., 5 June 1897.
[64] *Down Recorder*, 18 Jan. 1890.
[65] Ibid., 20 June 1908.

opened in 1909. The figure of £69 a year shows that Downpatrick was fairly lucky – in Newtownards the 1*d*. rate was calculated to produce £51,[66] and Downpatrick would have had the produce of a 1*d*. rate as well as the Saul money.

So in the nineteenth century we have the first stirrings of a universal free public library service for the people, which became a reality in the next century. Books were cheap to buy and becoming free to borrow, there was widespread literacy, there was a little money and leisure. A society whose reading habits had been relatively fixed and traditional had become a society with a mass readership stretching from the songsheet to cheap books and even cheaper newspapers. And of the earlier popular unsophisticated works, what survived this transition, at least to the end of the nineteenth century? Excluding religious works such as those by Bunyan, which in any case were not the exclusive preserve of popular culture, we are left with two. One is that last echo of the *Seven champions* in print, the chapbook mummers' play printed by Nicholson; and the other? E. M. Forster wrote in 1919:

The bookshops of Belfast are instructive. They are not only small, but are incredibly provincial, and breathe Samuel Smiles when they are being responsible and 'Aristotle' when they are not, 'Aristotle' being in these parts the compiler of a pornographic manual who is bound in red and gold and usually tied up with string.[67]

These two contrasting works, the rumbustious play and the under-the-counter popular sexological book, form a rather sad remnant washed up on the beach of the twentieth century.

---

[66] *Newtownards Chronicle*, 23 Mar. 1895.
[67] E. M. Forster, *Abinger harvest* (Harmondsworth, 1967), p. 90.

Conclusion

One popular view of the lower orders in Ireland often held today assumes that they existed in an almost entirely oral culture, albeit an immensely rich one. In those cases where they did come into contact with print, this view runs, it was with material of a radical political outlook (a state of affairs exemplified by the well-known painting by Henry MacManus, 'Reading the *Nation*') and with ballads. This state of affairs represents a heavily romantic image of the past, tinged with wishful thinking about the thought processes of oppressed workers and peasantry.

But the present study shows that the world of printed matter open to the ordinary persons of eighteenth-century Ireland was an infinitely richer one than is commonly supposed. Material of all kinds was sold and eagerly read, not just polemical papers, pamphlets, and slip ballads. This material, which came together in the chapman's pack of the eighteenth century or the small shop of the nineteenth, came from many epochs and countries, sometimes coming from far down the centuries and sometimes from the pens of contemporary hacks, yet because it was read in Ulster it provided as valid an intellectual stimulus as a ballad about a local murder or a piece of Dublin journalism. In the 1980s, which is more eagerly consumed by the masses – 'Dallas' or political manifestoes? *Valentine and Orson* occupied the same mental world as *Billy Bluff*, and the works of Dickens existed alongside the *Nation*. Only the heavily committed, then as now, restricted their reading to a narrow band.

Also, the world of print and the world of oral culture are not too far apart. This is at its most obvious in the matter of ballads, but once books and other printed material penetrated a region one cannot talk of a pure oral tradition. Once something had been read in an area, for better or worse the influence would be felt, as both fiction and fact would be retailed to others, either by word of mouth or by reading aloud. In most parts of Ulster in the eighteenth and nineteenth centuries the literate were not a tiny minority anyway, thanks to the influence of the hedge schools and later of the national board.

Popular readership has several times been studied at the

national level in Britain, but though this presents a broad picture that is useful as a background, a study that picks examples from London, Glasgow, and Liverpool to demonstate a national trend must perforce form a picture that is not necessarily true of any one of these regions. The interactions between people's lives and their reading matter are complicated, and these interactions cannot readily be perceived at a national level. For instance, a study of the vogue for chivalric romances will rightly take in such perennial favourites as *Valentine and Orson*, the *Seven champions of Christendom*, and *Guy of Warwick*, but not a single reference to *Guy of Warwick* (or a number of other examples) could be found in Ulster, and one must conclude that in this area, at least, the romance was not widely read. Similarly there are the items peculiar to Ireland, such as the extremely popular *Battle of Aughrim*. Studies based firmly on regions give a truer picture of actual reading habits, both because they reflect in a much more refined way these habits in a real community, with all the local variations that this entails, and also because a much deeper level of research can be undertaken in a wide variety of sources. A local study can concentrate, not on the production, but on the very much more important matter of distribution, resulting in a more accurate picture of what was happening on the ground.

The account given in these pages shows a very rich tapestry, consisting of materials with very wide origins in space, time, and indeed writing ability. Most (with the exception of ballads) was not only not Irish in origin – it was avidly consumed by both of what tend to be called the two traditions of Ulster. As far as printed matter of a non-political nature was concerned there was, depending on one's point of view, either only one tradition or a multiplicity of individual traditions. The differences were not between protestants and catholics, but between persons of differing tastes in Ulster, and between Ulster and such places as south-east England. These tastes are as important to social and literary history as those of their more elevated countrymen, and, now that they have been charted, the ordinary people of Ulster (and Ireland) in the eighteenth and nineteenth centuries can no longer be seen as either totally immersed in a colourful and backward-looking oral tradition, or deeply versed in classical or biblical lore. In fact this society possessed a wide-ranging printed literature which gave it entrance to worlds far beyond the parish boundary.

APPENDIX I

Ulster Publications, 1699–1800

The items in the following chronological list either are editions of works referred to in the text or contain advertisements for such works. They are numbered consecutively. When these numbers are cited in the list of references, it can quickly be established which local editions of a particular work are extant and the period over which it was advertised, as well as the other works in which it was advertised. The printer's name is given where known.

1. *The Bible the best New Year's gift*. Belfast: P. Neill, 1699.
2. Guthrie, William. *The Christian's great interest*. Belfast: P. Neill, 1699.
3. Bible. Psalms. *The psalms of David in meeter*. Belfast: P. Neill, 1700.
4. Fox, James. *Time and the end of time*. Belfast: P. Neill, 1700.
5. Keach, Benjamin. *War with the devil*. Belfast: P. Neill, 1700.
6. Mead, Matthew. *The almost Christian discovered*. Belfast: P. Neill, 1700.
7. Montgomerie, Alexander. *The cherrie and the slae*. Belfast: P. Neill, 1700.
8. Pearse, Edward. *The great concern*. Belfast: P. Neill, 1700.
9. Craghead, Robert. *Advice for assurance of salvation*. Belfast: P. Neill, 1702.
10. Campbell, Daniel. *Sacramental meditations*. Belfast: J. Blow, 1714.
11. Lyndsay, Sir David. *The works*. Belfast: J. Blow, 1714.
12. *Doctrine of the Bible*. Belfast: J. Blow, 1715.
13. *Testament of the twelve patriarchs*. Belfast: J. Blow, 1720.
14. Henry the Minstrel. *Life and acts of . . . Sir William Wallace*. Belfast: J. Blow, 1728.
15. *Confession of faith*. Belfast: J. Blow, 1729.
16. Sherman, Thomas. *Divine breathings*. Belfast: J. Blow, 1729.
17. Mead, Matthew. *The almost Christian discovered*. Belfast: J. Blow, 1731.
18. Shower, John. *Serious reflections*. Belfast: S. Wilson, J. Magee & J. Potts, 1738.
19. Watts, Isaac. *A guide to prayer*. Belfast: J. Blow, 1739.

Appendix I

20. Bible. Psalms. *The psalms of David in meeter.* Belfast: J. Blow, 1739.
21. Baxter, Richard. *A call to the unconverted.* Belfast: S. Wilson & J. Magee, 1740.
22. Scougall, Henry. *Life of God in the soul of man.* Belfast: S. Wilson & J. Magee, 1740.
23. Colvil, Samuel. *The Whigg's supplication.* Belfast: S. Wilson & J. Magee, 1741.
24. Fowler, Edward. *The design of Christianity.* Belfast: S. Wilson & J. Magee, 1741.
25. Bossuet, J. B. *An introduction to . . . universal history.* Belfast: S. Wilson & J. Magee, 1743.
26. Flavel, John. *A saint indeed.* Belfast: S. Wilson & J. Magee, 1743.
27. Ramsay, Allan. *The gentle shepherd.* Belfast: S. Wilson & J. Magee, 1743.
28. Michelburne, John. *Ireland preserv'd.* Belfast: S. Wilson & J. Magee, 1744.
29. Willison, John. *The afflicted man's companion.* Belfast: J. Magee, 1744.
30. Ramsay, Allan. *The gentle shepherd.* Belfast: J. Magee, 1748.
31. *Foundation of the church.* Belfast: H. & R. Joy, 1750.
32. Henry, Matthew. *A method for prayer.* Belfast: J. Magee, 1750.
33. Michelburne, John. *Ireland preserv'd.* Belfast: J. Magee, 1750.
34. Russell, Robert. *Seven sermons.* Belfast: J. Magee, 1750.
35. Erskine, Ralph. *Christ the peoples' covenant.* Belfast: J. Magee, 1751.
36. *Genuine trial at large of Mary Blandy.* Belfast: J. Magee, 1752.
37. Keach, Benjamin. *Travels of True Godliness.* Belfast: J. Magee, 1752.
38. *Play book for children, to allure them to read.* Belfast: H. & R. Joy, 1752.
39. *Royal primer.* Belfast: H. & R. Joy, 1752.
40. Blair, Samuel. *Doctrine of predestination.* Belfast: for R. Johnston, 1753.
41. Brown, John. *A vindication of fellowship meetings.* Belfast: for W. Murdock, 1753.
42. Caley, Abraham. *A glimpse of eternity.* Belfast: J. Blow, 1753.
43. Russell, Robert. *Seven sermons.* Belfast: J. Magee, 1753.
44. Smith, Walter. *A directory: or, rules and directions for fellowship meetings.* Belfast: for W. Murdoch, 1753.
45. Fisher, George. *Arithmetic.* Belfast: H. & R. Joy, 1754.
46. Fisher, George. *The instructor.* Belfast: H. &. R. Joy, 1754.
47. *The young clerk's vade mecum.* Belfast: H. & R. Joy, 1754.

48. Ramsay, Allan. *The gentle shepherd.* Belfast: J. Magee, 1755.
49. Willison, John. *An example of plain catechising.* Belfast: J. Magee, 1755.
50. Cocker, Edward. *Arithmetic.* Belfast: H. & R. Joy, 1756.
51. Hervey, James. *Meditations and contemplations.* Belfast: for R. Johnston, 1757.
52. *Brief essay upon religion.* Belfast: J. Blow, 1758.
53. Grove, Henry. *A discourse concerning . . . Lord's Supper.* Belfast: J. Blow, 1758.
54. Henry the Minstrel. *Life and acts of Sir William Wallace.* [Modernised]. Belfast: n.p., 1758.
55. TAOALTTBOB. *Diana great at Ephesus.* Belfast: n.p., 1758.
56. *Youth's instructor in prose and verse.* Belfast: J. Blow, 1758.
57. Michelburne, John. *Ireland preserv'd.* Belfast: J. Magee, 1759.
58. Dilworth, W. H. *The protestant hero.* Belfast: for the booksellers, 1760.
59. *Authentic particulars of the life of the late John Macnaghten.* Belfast: J. Magee, 1762.
60. Fisher, George. *Arithmetic.* Belfast: J. Magee, 1762.
61. Hervey, James. *Meditations and contemplations.* Belfast: D. Blow, 1762.
62. Manson, David. *A new pocket dictionary.* Belfast: D. Blow, 1762.
63. Ambrose, Isaac. *Looking unto Jesus.* Belfast: J. Magee, 1763.
64. *Compendious history of all the monarchs of England.* Belfast: for the booksellers, c. 1763.
65. *The most pleasing and delightful history of Reynard the fox and Reynardine his son.* Belfast: D. Blow, 1763.
66. *Young clerk's vade mecum.* Belfast: H. & R. Joy, 1763.
67. Addison, Joseph. *Cato: a tragedy.* Belfast: J. Magee, 1764.
68. Dyer, William. *Christ's famous titles.* Belfast: D. Blow, 1764.
69. Keach, Benjamin. *Travels of True Godliness.* Belfast: J. Magee, 1764.
70. Ramsay, Allan. *The gentle shepherd.* Newry: D. Carpenter, 1764.
71. Russell, Robert. *Seven sermons.* Belfast: D. Blow, 1764.
72. *History of the travels, persecutions and cruel martyrdom of . . . Jesus Christ.* Belfast: n.p., 1765.
73. Lowth, Dr. *A short introduction to English grammar.* Belfast: J. Hay & H. & R. Joy, 1765.
74. Scougall, Henry. *Life of God in the soul of man.* Belfast: J. Magee, 1765.
75. Culpeper, Nicholas. *A directory for midwives.* Belfast: J. Magee, 1766.
76. Ward, Henry. *The vintner trick'd.* Belfast: J. Magee, 1766.

77. Ashton, Robert. *The battle of Aughrim.* Belfast: J. Magee, 1767.
78. Fox, John. *Time and the end of time.* Belfast: J. Magee, 1767.
79. *New academy of compliments.* Belfast: J. Magee, 1767.
80. Ramsay, Allan. *The gentle shepherd.* Belfast: J. Magee, 1768.
81. Gesner, Salomon. *The death of Abel.* Newry: G. Stevenson, 1770.
82. *Letter to the protestant dissenters in the parish of Ballykelly.* Belfast: J. Magee, 1770.
83. Forde, Brownlow. *The miraculous cure.* Newry: G. Stevenson, 1771.
84. Montgomerie, Alexander. *The cherrie and the slae.* Belfast: J. Magee, 1771.
85. *Young clerk's vade mecum.* Belfast: H. & R. Joy, 1771.
86. Hoole, C. *Terminations.* Belfast: n.p., 1772.
87. *Whole duty of man.* Belfast: D. Blow, 1772.
88. *Dealer's companion and trader's assistant improved.* Belfast: J. Magee, 1773.
89. Manson, David. *Pronouncing and spelling dictionary.* Belfast: H. & R. Joy, 1774.
90. Michelburne, John. *Ireland preserv'd.* Newry: D. Carpenter, 1774.
91. Palmer, Samuel. *The protestant dissenter's catechism.* Belfast: J. Magee, 1774.
92. Aubin, Penelope. *The noble slaves.* Belfast: by the booksellers, 1775.
93. Fisher, George. *Arithmetic.* Belfast: J. Magee, 1775.
94. Hervey, James. *Meditations and contemplations.* Belfast: D. Blow, 1775.
95. *Lilliputian magazine.* Belfast: J. Magee, 1775.
96. Cosgrave, John. *Genuine history of the lives and actions of the most notorious Irish highwaymen.* Belfast: for the booksellers, 1776.
97. Ramsay, Allan. *The gentle shepherd.* Newry: D. Carpenter, 1776.
98. Ovid. *Ars amandi: or, Ovid's art of love.* Belfast: J. Magee, 1777.
99. Alleine, Joseph. *An alarm to unconverted sinners.* Belfast: J. Magee, 1778.
100. Erskine, Ebenezer. *The plant of renown.* Belfast: J. Magee, 1778.
101. Erskine, Ebenezer. *A lamp ordained for God's anointed.* Belfast: J. Magee, 1779.
102. Erskine, Ralph. *The best security for the best life.* Belfast: J. Magee, 1779.
103. Fielding, Sarah. *The governess.* Belfast: n.p., 1779.

104. Erskine, Ebenezer. *The rainbow of the covenant.* Belfast: J. Magee, 1780.
105. Flavel, John. *A token for mourners.* Belfast: J. Magee, 1780.
106. *January and May.* Belfast: J. Magee, *c.* 1780.
107. Marshall, Walter. *The gospel mystery of sanctification opened.* Belfast: J. Magee, 1780.
108. Ashton, Robert. *The battle of Aughrim.* Newry: R. Stevenson, 1781.
109. Erskine, Ralph. *The lamb in the midst of the throne.* Belfast: J. Magee, 1781.
110. Willison, John. *Balm from Gilead.* Belfast: J. Magee, 1781.
111. Dyer, William. *Christ's famous titles.* Belfast: J. Magee, 1782.
112. *The history of Valentine and Orson.* Belfast: J. Magee, 1782.
113. Gesner, Salomon. *The death of Abel.* Newry: R. Stevenson, 1783.
114. *Larger catechism.* Belfast: J. Magee, 1784.
115. *The English archer: or, Robert Earl of Huntington, vulgarly called, Robin Hood.* Newry: D. Carpenter, 1784.
116. Willison, John. *An example of plain catechising.* Belfast: J. Magee, 1784.
117. Willison, John. *Sacramental meditations and advices.* Belfast: J. Magee, 1784.
118. Ashton, Robert. *The battle of Aughrim.* Strabane: J. Bellew, 1785.
119. *Easter gift: or, the way to be very good.* Newry: D. Carpenter, *c.* 1785.
120. Lowth, Dr. *Short introduction to English grammer.* Belfast: J. Hay & H. Joy Sen. & Jun., 1785.
121. *Whitsuntide gift: or, the way to be very happy.* Newry: D. Carpenter, *c.* 1785.
122. *Youth's instructor in prose and verse.* Belfast: D. Blow, 1785.
123. Dodsley, Robert. *The preceptor.* Belfast: H. Joy Sen. & Jun., 1786.
124. Erksine, Ebenezer. *The stone rejected by the builders.* Newry: D. Carpenter, 1786.
125. Erskine, Ralph. *Christ the people's covenent.* Newry: D. Carpenter, 1786.
126. Burns, Robert. *Poems.* Belfast: J. Magee, 1787.
127. Day, Thomas. *Sandford and Merton.* Belfast: D. Blow, 1787.
128. Macgowan, John. *The life of Joseph the son of Israel.* Belfast: J. Magee, 1787.
129. Michelburne, John. *Ireland preserv'd.* Strabane: J. Bellew, 1787.
130. *Reasons from prophecy why the second coming . . . is immediately to be expected.* Newry: D. Carpenter, 1787.

131. West, Elizabeth. *Memoirs or spiritual exercises.* Newry: D. Carpenter, 1787.
132. Willison, John. *The afflicted man's companion.* Belfast: J. Magee, 1787.
133. Erskine, Ebenezer. *The plant of renown.* Newry: D. Carpenter, 1788.
134. Gough, John. *Practical arithmetic.* Belfast: n.p., 1788.
135. Moore, Hamilton. *The young gentleman's and ladies monitor.* Belfast: J. Magee, 1788.
136. Burns, Robert. *Poems.* Belfast: J. Magee, 1789.
137. Ramsay, Allan. *The gentle shepherd.* Strabane: J. Bellew, 1789.
138. Day, Thomas. *Sandford and Merton.* Belfast: W. Magee, 1791.
139. Palmer, Samuel. *The protestant dissenter's catechism.* Monaghan: P. J. Brown, 1781.
140. Ramsay, Allan. *The gentle shepherd.* Belfast: W. Magee, 1792.
141. *Young clerk's vade mecum.* Belfast: H. Joy & Co., 1792.
142. Burns, Robert. *Poems.* Belfast: W. Magee, 1793.
143. Gough, John. *Practical arithmetic.* Belfast: W. Magee, 1793.
144. Ramsay, Allan. *The gentle shepherd.* Newry: R. Moffet, 1793.
145. Paine, Thomas. *The age of reason.* Belfast: n.p., 1794.
146. Moore, Hamilton. *The young gentleman's and ladies monitor.* Belfast: W. Magee, 1794.
147. Telfair, Robert. *Key to Gough.* Belfast: T. Storey, 1794.
148. *Youth's instructor in prose and verse.* Belfast: D. Blow, 1794.
149. Brothers, Richard. *Extracts from the prophecies.* Belfast: n.p., 1795.
150. Enfield, William. *The speaker.* Belfast: W. Magee, 1795.
151. *Examination of the scripture prophecies . . . in which . . . the late revolution in France is shewn to be plainly foretold.* Belfast: n.p., 1795.
152. Lowth, Dr. *Short introduction to English grammar.* Belfast: W. Magee, 1795.
153. Porter, James. *Paddy's resource.* Belfast: N. Star, 1795.
154. *Prophetical extracts particularly such as relate to the revolution in France.* Strabane: n.p., 1795.
155. Willison, John. *Sacramental meditations and advices.* Belfast: W. Magee, 1795.
156. Moore, Hamilton. *The young gentleman's and ladies monitor.* Belfast: W. Magee, 1796.
157. Porter, James. *Billy Bluff and Squire Firebrand.* Belfast: N. Star, 1796.
158. Porter, James. *Paddy's resource.* Belfast: N. Star, 1796.
159. *The famous English archer: or, Robert Earl of Huntington, commonly called Robin Hood.* Monaghan: J. Brown, 1796.

160. Day, Thomas. *Sandford and Merton.* Belfast: J. Magee, 1797.
161. Gough, John. *Practical arithmetic.* Belfast: J. Magee, 1797.
162. Orr, William. *The dying declaration of William Orr.* Belfast: n.p., 1797.
163. Porter, James. *Billy Bluff and Squire Firebrand.* Belfast: N. Star, 1797.
164. Ashton, Robert. *The battle of Aughrim.* Belfast: J. Smyth, 1800.
165. Burns, Robert. *Poems.* Belfast: W. Magee, 1800.
166. *Dealer's companion and trader's assistant improved.* Belfast: W. Magee, 1800.
167. Enfield, William. *The speaker.* Belfast: W. Magee, 1800.

APPENDIX II

A Catalogue of Chapmens' Books, 1750

This list is taken from Robert Russell, *Seven sermons* (Belfast, printed by and for James Magee, 1750), p. 176 (copy in Linen Hall Library, Belfast). I have added, in brackets, suggested identifications.

Allein's Alarm
    (Alleine, Joseph. *An alarm to unconverted sinners*)
    —————— Catechism
    (Alleine, Joseph. *A most familiar explanation of the Assembly's catechism*)
Almost Christian
    (Mead, Matthew. *The almost Christian discovered*)
Argalus and Parthenia
    (Quarles, Francis. *Argalus and Parthenia*)
Brown's Spelling Book
    (Unidentified)
Bruce's Wars
    (Barbour, John. *Acts and life of . . . Robert Bruce*)
Boston's Fourfold State of Man
    (Boston, Thomas. *Human nature in its fourfold state*)
Brown's Hope of Glory
    (Brown, John. *Christ in believers the hope of glory*)
Bunyan's Come and Welcome
    (Bunyan, John. *Come and welcome*)
    —————— Grace Abounding
    (Bunyan, John. *Grace abounding*)
    —————— Sighs from Hell
    (Bunyan, John. *Sighs from hell*)
    —————— Holy War
    (Bunyan, John. *Holy war*)
    —————— Pilgrim's Progress, 3 Parts
    (Bunyan, John. *Pilgrim's progress*)
Book of Knowledge
    (Erra Pater. *Book of knowledge, treating of the wisdom of the ages*)
Confession of faith
    (*Confession of faith*)

Ditto with the Scriptures at Large
(*Confession of faith*, bound with Bible)
Campbell's Sacramental meditations
(Campbell, Daniel. *Sacramental meditations on . . . the death of Christ*)
Cocker's Arithmetic
(Cocker, Edward. *Arithmetic*)
Dyer's Christ's Famous Titles
(Dyer, William. *Christ's famous titles*)
Doctrine of the Bible
(*Doctrine of the Bible: or, rules of discipline*)
Divine breathings
(Sherman, Thomas. *Divine breathings*)
Doolittle on the Sacram
(Doolittle, Thomas. *A treatise concerning the Lord's Supper*)
Dyche's Spelling Book
(Dyche, Thomas. *Spelling dictionary*)
Aesop's Fables
(Aesop. *Fables*)
English Empire in Amer.
(Crouch, Nathaniel. *The English empire in America*)
Flavel upon the Heart
(Flavel, John. *A saint indeed,* (often advertised as *Flavel upon the heart, or a saint indeed*))
Fox upon Time
(Fox, John. *Time and the end of time*)
Guthery's Tryal of a saving Interest
(*Guthrie, William. The Christian's great interest: or, a short treatise of I. The trial of a saving interest in Christ . . .*)
History of the Pirates
(Defoe, Daniel. *History and lives of all the most notorious pirates*)
History of England's Monarchs
(Crouch, Nathaniel. *England's monarchs*)
H. of the Nine Worthies
(Crouch, Nathaniel. *History of the nine worthies*)
Jews Wars
(Josephus, Flavius. *History of the Jewish wars*)
Life of Christ
(Unidentified, several such issued)
Life of God in the Soul of Man
(Scougall, Henry. *Life of God in the soul of man*)
Laugh and be Fat
(*Laugh and be fat*)

London Jests
  (*London jests: or, a collection of the choicest jokes and repartees*)
Mute Christian
  (Brooks, Thomas. *The mute Christian under the smarting rod*)
Practice of Piety
  (Bayly, Lewis. *The practice of piety*)
Pearse on Death
  (Pearse, Edward. *The great concern: or, a serious warning to a timely and thorow preparation for death*)
Rutherford's Letters
  (Rutherford, Samuel. *Letters*)
Reynard the Fox
  (*History of Reynard the fox*)
Surprizing Miracles
  (Crouch, Nathaniel. *Surprising miracles of nature and art*)
Sincere Convert
  (Shepard, Thomas. *The sincere convert, discovering the small number of true believers*)
Secretary's Guide
  (Hill, John. *The young secretary's guide*)
Token for Children
  (Janeway, James. *A token for children*)
Vincent on Judgment
  (Vincent, Thomas. *Christ's certain and sudden appearance to judgment*)
———— On the Catechism
  (Vincent, Thomas. *An explication of the Assembly's shorter catechism*)
Valentine and Orson
  (*The history of Valentine and Orson*)
Winter Evening Entertainments
  (Crouch, Nathaniel. *Winter evening entertainments*)
Welwood's Glimpse of Glory
  (Wellwood, Andrew. *Meditations: representing a glimpse of glory*)

ALSO
Bibles, testaments, and Common-Prayer-Books, of several Vols. Psalm-Books, Psalters, Primers, Child's-Guides, Horn-Books, etc.

APPENDIX III

A Catalogue of Chapmen's Books, 1777.

This list is taken from Ovid, *Ars amandi: or, Ovid's art of love* (Belfast, printed by James Magee, 1777), pp 179–180 (copy in Linen Hall Library, Belfast). I have added, in brackets, suggested identifications.

Fisher's Arithmetic. To this Edition is added, an Appendix, containing the Construction and Uses of Tables, for calculating questions in Compound Interest, and Annuities, or leases in Possession or Reversion
(Fisher, George. *Arithmetic in the plainest and most concise method*)
Manson's Spelling Book
(Manson, David. *Spelling book*)
The Reform'd Coquet, or Memoirs of Amoranda, A surprizing Novel. By Mrs Davys.
(Davys, Mary. *The reform'd coquet*)
The complete history of Valentine and Orson
(*History of Valentine and Orson*)
A new Academy of Compliments, or the Lover's Secretary, being Wit and Mirth improved
(*New academy of compliments*)
A Pocket Companion for Free Masons
(*Pocket companion for Freemasons*)
A Collection of Songs to be sung by Free Masons, with Prologues, Epilogues, etc. To which is added, Solomon's Temple, an Oratorio, as it as perform'd at the Philharmonic-Room in Fishamble-street, Dublin
(*A collection of songs . . .*)
The Life of JOSEPH the Son of ISRAEL. In Eight Books. Chiefly design'd for the Use of Youth. By the Rev. John Macgowan.
(Macgowan, John. *The Life of Joseph*)
The DEATH of ABEL. In Five Books. Attempted from the German of Mr GESSNER
(Gessner, Salomon. *The death of Abel*)
Solomon in all his Glory: or, the Master-Mason. Being a True Guide to the minutest Recesses of Masonry, both ancient and

modern, etc. Illustrated with Copper-Plates, most elegantly engraved, etc.

(*Solomon in all his glory*)

GOUGH'S ARITHMETICK, FOR THE USE OF SCHOOLS. To this Edition is added, an Appendix of Algebra, by W. ATKINSON, Teacher of the Mathematicks in BELFAST (Gough, John. *Practical arithmetic*)

Manson's Pronouncing and Spelling Dictionary, Being an excellent Pocket Companion for Young People, Tradesmen, and others, who desire Improvement in Reading, Spelling, and the Knowledge of Words, etc. etc.

(Manson, David. *Pronouncing and spelling dictionary*)

Forty-two Stories, Fables and Allegories, such as were thought most proper to please, and form the Minds of Youth. Collected from the Spectator, Guardian, Adventurer, Rambler, etc.

(*Forty-two stories*)

Wit's Cabinet. Containing, a Select Collection of the best English, Scotch, and Irish Songs, in the true Spirit and Taste of the Three Different Nations. The Art of Complimenting – curious Letters and Answers – Titles of Honour, and Directions for Letters – Interpretations of Dreams – Palmestry – The mystery and Art of Canting, etc.

(*Wit's cabinet*)

Solomon's Temple Spiritualiz'd. By J. Bunyan

(Bunyan, John. *Solomon's temple spiritualised*)

Arabian Tales

(*Arabian nights' entertainment*)

Winter Evening Tales

(Crouch, Nathaniel. *Winter evening entertainments*)

Seven Champions

(Johnston, Richard. *The seven champions of Christendom*)

Parismus and Parismenus

(Forde, Emmanuel. *The history of Parismus*)

Lilliputian Magazine

(*Lilliputian magazine*)

Seven Wise Masters

(*Famous history of the seven wise masters of Rome*)

Charles the 12th

(Defoe, Daniel. *The wars of Charles XII*)

Hocus Pocus

(Dean, Henry. *Hocus pocus: or, the whole art of legerdemain*)

Aristotle

(Aristotle, pseud. *Masterpiece*)

Book of Knowledge
  (Erra Pater. *The book of knowledge*)
Secretary's Guide
  (Hill, John. *The young secretary's guide*)
Anson's Voyages
  (Walter, Richard. *A voyage round the world . . . by George Anson*)
Reynard the Fox
  (*History of Reynard the fox*)
Moll Flanders
  (Defoe, Daniel. *Moll Flanders*)
Twelve delightful novels
  (unidentified)
Irish Rogues
  (Cosgrave, John. *Genuine history . . . highwaymen*)
Life of St. Patrick
  (Unidentified)
Laugh and be Fat
  (*Laugh and be fat*)
Noble slaves
  (Aubin, Penelope. *The noble slaves*)
History of Ireland
  (Crouch, Nathaniel. *History of the kingdom of Ireland*)
Esop's Fables
  (Aesop. *Fables*)
Boyle's Voyages
  (Chetwood, W. R. *The voyages and adventures of Capt. Robert Boyle*)
Gulliver's Travels
  (Swift, Jonathan. *Gulliver's travels*)
Watt's Spelling Book
  (Watts, Isaac. *Compleat spelling book*)
Dilworth's ditto
  (Dilworth, Thomas. *New Guide to the English tongue*)
Dyche's ditto
  (Dyche, Thomas. *Spelling dictionary*)
Fenning's Universal ditto
  (Fenning, Daniel. *Universal spelling book*)
Drake's Voyages
  (Crouch, Nathaniel. *The English hero: or, Sir Francis Drake revived*)
Garden of Love, or, Flower of Fidelity
  (Reynolds, John. *The garden of love, and royal flower of fidelity*)

With Variety of Plays, Farces, School-Books, Histories, Novels, etc.

APPENDIX IV

A Catalogue of Chapmen's Books, 1780

This list is taken from John Flavel, *A token for mourners* (Belfast, printed by James Magee, 1780), p. 180 (copy in Linen Hall Library, Belfast). I have added, in brackets, suggested identifications.

Allein's Alarm
    (Alleine, Joseph. *An alarm to unconverted sinners*)
Almost Christian
    (Mead, Matthew. *The almost Christian discovered*)
Ambrose looking to Jesus
    (Ambrose, Isaac. *Looking onto Jesus*)
Brown's Spelling-Book
    (Unidentified)
Boston's Fourfold State of Man
    (Boston, Thomas. *Human nature in its fourfold state*)
Bunyan's Holy War
    (Bunyan, John. *Holy war*)
———— Grace Abounding
    (Bunyan, John. *Grace abounding*)
———— Sighs from Hell
    (Bunyan, John. *Sighs from Hell*)
———— Pilgrim's Progress
    (Bunyan, John. *Pilgrim's progress*)
Culpeper's Midwifery
    (Culpeper, Nicholas. *A directory for midwives*)
Confession of Faith
    (*Confession of faith*)
Ditto with the Scriptures at Large
    (*Confession of faith, bound with Bible*)
Campbell's Sacramental Meditations
    (Campbell, Daniel. *Sacramental meditations on the . . . death of Christ*)
Dickson's Psalms
    (*Psalms, together with the annotations of David Dickson*)
Dyer's Christ's Famous Titles
    (*Dyer, William. Christ's famous titles*)

Divine breathings
    (Sherman, Thomas. *Divine breathings*)
Doolittle on the Sacrament
    (Doolittle, Thomas. *A treatise concerning the Lord's Supper*)
Dealer's Companion
    (*Dealer's companion, and trader's assistant improved*)
Elizabeth West
    (West, Elizabeth. *Memoirs or spiritual exercises*)
Fisher's Arithmetick
    (Fisher, George. *Arithmetic in the plainest and most concise method*)
Flavel on the Heart
    (Flavel, John. *A saint indeed*)
Fox on Time
    (Fox, John. *Time and the end of time*)
Guthery's Trial of a saving Interest
    (Guthrie, William. *The Christian's great interest*)
Grove on the Sacrament
    (Grove, Henry. *A discourse concerning the nature and design of the Lord's Supper*)
Henry on the Sacrament
    (Henry, Matthew. *The communicant's companion*)
Life of Joseph the Son of Israel
    (Macgowan, John. *Life of Joseph the son of Israel*)
Manson's Spelling Book
    (Manson, David. *Spelling book*)
Pearse on Death.
    (Pearse, Edward. *The great concern*)
The Death of Abel. In Five Books. Attempted from the German of GESSNER
    (Gesner, Solomon. *the death of Abel*)
Protestant Dissenters Catechism
    (Palmer, Samuel. *Protestant dissenter's catechism*)
Seven Champions
    (Johnston, Richard. *The seven champions of Christendom*)
Valentine and Orson
    (*The history of Valentine and Orson*)
Vincent on Judgment
    (Vincent, Thomas. *Christ's certain and sudden appearance to judgment*)
———— On the Catechism
    (Vincent, Thomas. *Explication of the Assembly's shorter catechism*)
Welwood's Glimpse of Glory
    (Wellwood, Andrew. *Meditations, representing a glimpse of glory*)

War with the Devil
   (Keach, Benjamin. *War with the devil*)
Webster's Communion Sermons
   (Webster, William. *Communion sermons*)
Willison's Sacramental Meditations
   (Willison, John. *The afflicted man's companion*)
————Balm from Gilead
   (Willison, John. *Balm from Gilead*)
————On the Sabbath
   (Willison, John. *A treatise concerning the sanctifying the Lord's Day*)

ALSO
Bibles, Testaments, and Common-Prayer-Books, of several sizes,
Psalm-Books, Psalters, Primers, Child's Guide, etc. etc.

APPENDIX V

Publications of the Kildare Place Society

Sources: H. K. Moore, *An unwritten chapter in the history of education* (Dublin, 1904), pp 248–51; *First report of the Commissioners on education in Ireland* (London, 1825), Appendix, pp 559–61.

RELIGIOUS, MORAL, AND ILLUSTRATIVE OF SCRIPTURE
Scripture zoology
Manners and customs of the Israelites
Selection from the Psalms, Proverbs, and Book of Ecclesiasticus
Sturm's Reflections on the wisdom, power and goodness of God
Views of the creation
The bee, a collection of poems
Scripture geography
Destruction of Jerusalem
History of Joseph, and of the Creation
Nature displayed
Moral essays
The wreath, a collection of poems

INSTRUCTIVE IN ARTS OR ECONOMY
Treatise on practical mechanics
The cabinet of arts
The cottage fireside
The farmer's lad
James Talbot
The widow Reilly
Hints to farmers
Useful arts and manufactures
The school mistress
Tom Higgins, the cottage visitor
The pedlars

NATURAL HISTORY
Natural history of remarkable beasts
Natural history of domestic animals
Natural history of animals
Natural history of trees

Natural history of fishes
Natural history of birds
Natural history of insects
Natural history of reptiles
Animal sagacity, exemplified by facts
Picture of the seasons

VOYAGES, TRAVELS, ETC.

Commodore Anson's voyage around the world
Voyage in the Arctic regions, 1818–19, & 20
Byron's narrative of the loss of the Wager sloop of war
Discovery of America by Columbus
Wonderful escapes
History of Prince Lee Boo
Voyages and travels in the islands of the Pacific Ocean
Voyages in the northern Pacific Ocean
Voyages in the Arctic regions, 1821–1825
Bligh's dangerous voyage in an open boat
Life of Captain Cook
Shipwrecks of the Alceste and Medusa frigates, with reflections
History of Mungo Park
Travels in the Arctic regions
Travels in North America
Travels in South America
Travels in England and Wales
Travels in Sweden, Denmark and Norway
Travels in Spain and Portugal
Travels in Northern Italy
Travels in Southern Italy
Travels in European Turkey
Travels in Switzerland
Travels in Africa
Travels in South Asia (prior to 1825 this volume was enlarged, and
divided into two – *South Eastern Asia* and *South Western Asia*.)
Travels in Northern Asia
Travels in European Russia
Travels in Germany
Travels in Northern France
Travels in Southern France
Travels in Greece

MISCELLANEOUS
Elizabeth, or the exiles of Siberia
Entertaining medley, with true and curious anecdotes

Robinson Crusoe
History of the Robins
Adventures of Mungo the traveller, and the seven wonders of the world
Keeper's travels
Select story teller
Amusing stories
Gleanings (poems)
History of little Jack, a foundling: together with the history of William, an orphan (This was also issued as two smaller books.)
Fables of Aesop
Miscellany, or evening entertainment
Campe's New Robinson Crusoe
Scrap book
History of Isaac Jenkins, and a friendly gift for servants
The brothers, and an account of savings banks etc.
Selection of poems

APPENDIX VI

The Popular Books of Joseph Smyth

This list is derived from the books themselves. Those that survive with their original paper covers intact bear on the rear cover details of the works currently on his list. Those that have been rebound without retaining the paper covers at least reveal publication details in the imprint.

The author's name (if any) is followed by the title, then the date of publication (or, if no date is given, the symbol N.D. to indicate an edition printed by him), then, in brackets, the earliest and latest dates for which an advertisement has been traced on the paper covers of the other volumes in the series. Since many volumes have been rebound this cannot be a reflection of the length of time a book was current on his list, but it is a valuable indication. Finally, on a separate line are symbols to indicate whether the book also appears in the Kildare Place Society series (*KPS), the Simms & M'Intyre series (*SM), or the series of C. M. Warren of Dublin (*W). The last is not exhaustive.

Note that those entries that bear neither a date of publication nor an N.D. note might represent titles distributed but not printed by Smyth (e.g. Kildare Place Society volumes or C. M. Warren volumes) or alternatively titles not now to be traced.

Accomplished gentleman: or, principles of politeness, and of knowing the world . . . to which is added, the economy of human life. 1827. (1835–1850)
  *SM; *W
Aesop's fables, accompanied by many hundred proverbs and moral maxims. 1840. (1826–1850)
  *KPS; *SM; *W
Animal sagacity exemplified by facts. (1826–1835)
  *KPS
Anson, George. *Commodore Anson's voyage round the world.* (1826–1835)
  *KPS; *SM
Arabian nights entertainment. (1826–1850)
  *SM; *W

Ashton, John, and Michelburne, John. *Two historical plays. The battle of Aughrim. Ireland preserved.* 1826, 1830. (1841–1850)
*W

Aubin, Penelope. *[Life of] Lady Lucy.* (1826–1850)
Banquet of wit. (1835–1850)
The bee (1826–1833)
*KPS

Bligh, William. *Dangerous voyage . . . with a part of the crew of his majesty's ship Bounty, in an open boat.* (1826–1835)
*KPS; *SM

Byron's narrative containing an account of the great distress suffered by himself and his companions off the coast of Patagonia. 1844. (1826–1835)
*KPS; *SM; *W

Cabinet of useful arts and manufactures. (1826–1850)
*KPS; *SM; *W

Campe, Joachim Heinrich. *New Robinson Crusoe.* (1826–1850)
*KPS

[Cosgrave, John] *Irish rogues and raparees [Genuine history . . . highwaymen].* (1835–1850)
*W

Cottin, Marie. *Elizabeth: or, the exiles of Siberia.* 1834. (1826r–1850)
*KPS; *SM; *W

Cattle keeper's guide: or, complete directory for the choice and management of cattle. N.D. (1835–1850)
*W

Challoner, Richard. *Think well on't.* 1823. (1826–1850)
*SM

Cottage fireside. (1826–1835)
*KPS; *SM

Davis, John. *The post captain: or, the wooden walls well manned.* (1841–1850)
*W

Dean, Henry. *The whole art of legerdemain: or, hocus pocus in perfection.* 1844. (1835–1850)
Discovery of America by Christopher Columbus. (1831–1835)
*KPS; *SM

Elegant poems. 1835. (1841–1850)
Entertaining medley, with true and curious anecdotes. (1826–1833)
*KPS; *SM

Farmer's daughter. (1835)
Farmer's lad. (1826–1833)
*KPS; *SM

Gesner, Salomon. *The death of Abel.* 1827. (1835–1850)
Goethe, Johann Wolfgang. *Sorrows of Werter: a German story.* 1844.
  (1835–1850)
Goldsmith, Oliver. *The vicar of Wakefield.* (1835–1850)
  *SM; *W
Griffiths, Ralph. *Ascanius: or, the young adventurer.* 1841. (1843–1850)
Hamilton, Elizabeth, *Cottagers of Glenburnie, a tale for the inglenook.*
  N.D. (1841–1850)
  *SM; *W
History of Joseph and of the creation. (1826–1833)
  *KPS; *SM
History of Mungo Park. (1826–1835)
  *KPS
History of Prince Lee Boo, a native of the Pelew Islands. (1826–1833)
  *KPS
History of Sir William Wallace, the Scottish patriot. 1841. (1843–1850)
History of the tales of the fairies. (1835–1850)
  *W
Honour of chivalry: or, the famous history of Don Belianis of Greece. 1831.
  (1835)
Irish humourist. N.D. (1826–1835)
Johnson, Richard. *The most illustrious and renowned history of the seven
  champions of Christendom.* 1832. (1835–1850)
  *SM; *W
Josephus etc. *The history of the siege and destruction of Jerusalem.*
  (1826–1850)
  *KPS; *SM; *W
Life of Captain James Cook. N.D. (1826–1850)
  *KPS; *W
Life of General Jackson. (1841–1850)
  *W
*Life and adventures of James Freney, together with an account of the actions
  of several other noted highwaymen.* 1835. (1841–1850)
  *W
Life and actions of Robert Emmet, leader of the insurrection of 1803. 1842.
  (1841–1850)
  *W
Life on board a man of war. (1843–1850)
Mariner's compass: a selection of favourite naval songs. 1828.
Miscellany: or, evening's entertainment. (1826–1833)
  *KPS
Modern Irish tales and stories, anecdotes etc. Vol. I. 1837. (1841–1850)
  *W

Modern polite letter writer. (1826–1850)

Moral essays. (1826–1833)
*KPS

Mungo: or, the little traveller, to which is annexed, the seven wonders of the world. (1826–1850)
*KPS; *W

Narrative of the Irish rebellion. (1841–1850)
*W

New academy of compliments. 1833. (1826–1850)
*W

New history of the Trojan wars, and Troy's destruction. (1835–1850)
*W

New Lilliputian magazine. 1819. (1826–1833)
(Note: Printed by Smyth before precise 'house style' developed, but obviously absorbed into series until edition exhausted)

Ovid. *Art of love; remedy of love, art of beauty and amours.* 1821, 1828. (1825–1850)

Patriotic sailor: or, adventures of a naval life. (1835–1850)
*W

Picture of the seasons. (1826–1835)
*KPS; *SM

Porter, James. *Billy Bluff.* 1840? (1835–1850)

Protestant's trial. N.D. (1835)

Ramsay, Allan. *The gentle shepherd.* 1826, 1835. (1841–1850)

Raspe, Rudolf Erich. *Surprising travels and adventures of Baron Munchausen.* (1835–1850)
*SM

Reynolds, John. *Garden of love and royal flower of fidelity.* (1835–1850)

Richmond, Legh. *Dairyman's daughter.* (1835)

Robin Hood's garland. (1841–1846)
*W

Roche, Regina Maria. *Children of the abbey: a tale.* 3 vols. 1835–6. (1835–1850)

Royal Hibernian tales. (1835–1850) (Advertised as *Hibernian tales*)
*SM; *W

Russell, Robert. *Seven sermons.* (1835–1850)

St Pierre, Bernardine. *Paul and Virginia.* 1831. (1835–1850)
*SM; *W

St Pierre, Bernardine. *The Indian cottage.* (1835)
*W

Scott, J. G. *Life of Napoleon Bonaparte.* 1835. (1835–1850)
*W

Scrapbook: or, a selection of interesting and authentic anecdotes. (1826–
1833)
  *KPS; *SM
Selection of poems. (1826–1835)
  *KPS
Seven wise masters and mistresses. (1835–1850)
  *W
Sherwood, Mary Martha. *History of Lucy Clare.* 1838. (1826–1850)
Sherwood, Mary Martha. *History of Susan Gray.* (1826–1850)
  *W
Shipwreck of the Alceste . . . also, the shipwreck of the Medusa. 1846.
  (1826–1833)
  *KPS; *SM
Stanhope, Hugh. *Dorastus and Fawnia and Hero and Leander.* (1835–
  1850)
  *SM
Stavely, Mrs. *Housewives guide: or, a complete system of modern cookery.*
  1831, 1839. (1826–1850)
Sturm, Christophe. *Reflections.* (1826–1833)
  *KPS
Swift, Jonathan. *Travels of Lemuel Gulliver.* 1828. (1835–1850)
Tom Higgins: or, the cottage visitor. (1826–1833)
  *KPS; *SM
Travels in Africa. (1826–1835)
  *KPS
Travels in England and Wales. (1826–1835)
  *KPS
Travels in Northern Asia. (1826–1833)
  *KPS
Travels in North America. (1826–1835)
  *KPS
Travels in South America. (1826–1833)
  *KPS
Travels in South Eastern Asia. (1826–1835)
  *KPS
Travels in South Western Asia. (1826–1833)
  *KPS
Trimmer, Sarah. *History of the Robins.* (1826–1835)
  *KPS
*Unfortunate concubines: or, the history of fair Rosamond . . . and Jane
  Shore.* 1832
Valentine and Orson. 1831. (1826–1835)
  *SM; *W

Views of the creation. (1826–1835)
  *KPS

Voyage among the islands of the Pacific Ocean. (1826–1833)
  *KPS

Voyage in the Northern Pacific Ocean (1826–1833)
  *KPS

Voyages and adventures of Sir Francis Drake. 1843. (1841–1850)
  *W

Ward, Edward. *Female policy detected.* (1835–1850)

Willison, John. *The young communicant's catechism.* 1831.

Wonderful escapes. (1826–1835)
  *KPS

APPENDIX VII

The Popular Books of Simms & M'Intyre

This list is compiled from the advertisements on the rear paper covers of those copies that have survived in original condition, and from title-page information.

The author's name, if any, is followed by the title, the date of a surviving Simms & M'Intyre edition (or N.D. if that edition is undated), and on a separate line an indication of the title's appearance in another series: *KPS = Kildare Place Society, *S = Joseph Smyth and *W = C. M. Warren of Dublin. As so many of the books are undated, no indication of the spread of years over which the title was advertised is given, as this would be misleading.

The lack of either a date or the symbol N.D. may mean either that Simms & M'Intyre were distributing a work produced by another publisher, such as the Kildare Place Society or C. M. Warren of Dublin, or that a work produced by them is no longer traceable.

Abridgement of the Christian doctrine.
Accomplished gentlemen. 1836.
   *S; *W
Aesop. *Fables.* 1841.
   *KPS; *S; *W
Amusing fairy tales.
Anson, George. *Commodore Anson's voyage round the world.*
   *S; *W
Arabian night's entertainment.
   *S; *W
Authentic narratives of the most calamitous shipwrecks and disasters at sea.
   Part first. 1842.
Bible stores, adapted for young persons.
Bligh, William. *Dangerous voyage.*
   *KPS; *S
Burns, Robert. *Poems.*
Byron's narrative containing an account of the great distresses suffered by
   himself and his companions on the coasts of Patagonia.
   *KPS; *S; *W

Cabinet of useful arts and manufactures.
*KPS; *S; *W
Cottin, Marie. *Elizabeth: or, the exiles of Siberia.*
*KPS; *S; *W
Cerevantes, Saavedra, Miguel de. *Exploits of Don Quixote.*
Challoner, Richard. *Think well on't.*
*S
Constant lover; or, William and Jeanette.
Cooke, Dr. *Larger catechism.*
Cottage fireside.
*KPS; *S
Davys, Mary. *Amoranda: or, the reformed coquet.*
Defoe, Daniel. *Robinson Crusoe.*
*KPS
Discovery of America by Columbus.
*KPS; *S
Edgeworth, Maria. *The little merchants.* N.D.
Edgeworth, Maria. *Susan Price: or, Simple Susan.*
Entertaining medley, with true and curious anecdotes.
*KPS; *S
Genlis, Madame de. *Abridgement of tales of the castle.* 1842.
Goldsmith, Oliver. *The vicar of Wakefield.* N.D.
*S; *W
Grounds of Catholic doctrine.
Hamilton, Elizabeth. *The cottagers of Glenburnie.*
*S; *W
History of Joseph. 1837.
*KPS; *S
History of Richard Macready, the farmer's lad. (Sometimes referred to
in other lists simply as 'Farmer's lad'.)
*KPS; *S
Irish legendary stories.
*W
Johnson, Richard. *The most illustrious and renowned history of the seven
champions of Christendom.*
*S; *W
Josephus etc. *History of the siege and destruction of Jerusalem.*
*KPS; *S; *W
Juvenile budget: or, evenings at home. N.D.
Life of Frederick Baron Trenck.
Mackenzie, Henry. *The man of feeling.*
Picture of the seasons.
*KPS; *S

Raspe, Rudolf Erich. *Surprizing travels and adventures of Baron Munchausen.* N.D.
   *S

Reeves, Clara. *The old English baron, a gothic story.* N.D.
Reynard the fox.
Royal Hibernian tales. (Advertised as 'Hibernian tales'.)
   *S; *W

St Pierre, Bernardine. *Paul and Virginia.* 1818. (Probably earlier than the series, but in similar format.)
   *S; *W

Scrapbook: or, selection of interesting and authentic anecdotes.
   *KPS; *S

Shipwreck of the Alceste . . . also, the shipwreck of the Medusa.
   *KPS; *S

Stanhope, Hugh. *Dorastus and Fawnia, and Hero and Leander.*
   *S

Tom Higgins: or, the cottage visitor.
   *KPS; *S

Valentine and Orson.
   *S; *W

Walpole, Hugh. *The castle of Otranto.*
Winter evening tales.
Wonders of the world. (Probably a part of 'Mungo'.)
   *KPS

APPENDIX VIII

Catholic Books Sold by Simms & M'Intyre, 1832

The following list is shown as it appears in P. Baker, *The devout communicant* (Belfast, 1832), p. 205

Abridgement of the Christian doctrine, 8*d.*
Bona mors, 32mo, 1*s.*
Catechism (Butler's), 1*d.* – large, 4*d.*
      (Reilly's), 3*d.*
Catholic piety, single, 18mo, 1*s.*6*d.*
      doub. 2*s.* – fine, 2*s.*6*d.* – roan gilt, 3*s.*6*d.*
Daily companion, 32mo. 1*s.*
Devout communicant, 18mo. 2*s.*
Douay Testament, Belfast edition, 2*s*6*d.* – Dublin edition, 3*s.* – with
   Notes, 3*s.*6*d.*
Following of Christ, 32mo. 1*s.*3*d.*
Garden of the soul, 18mo, 2*s.*
Grounds of the catholic doctrine, 8*d.*
Hell opened, 18mo. 8*d.*
[Prince] *Hohenlohe's prayer book,* 18mo, 1*s*6*d.*
Hymns for children, 18mo, 3*d.*
Key of heaven, 18mo, 2*s.*
Key of paradise, 18mo, 2*s.*6*d.*
Path to paradise, 32mo, in various bindings, from 6*d.* to 2*s.* – doub.
   8*d.* to 2*s.*6*d.* – miniature, 2*s.* to 3*s*6*d.*
Missal for the use of the laity, containing the masses for Sundays and festivals
   throughout the year, 32mo. very neat edition, stereotyped, accom-
   panied with beautiful engravings, and in various bindings, from
   3*s.*6*d.* to 8*s.*6*d.*
Poor man's manual, 18mo, 1*s.* – double, in various bindings, from
   1*s.*6*d.* to 4*s.*
Roman missal. 18mo, 7*s.*
St Mary of Egypt, 18mo, 8*d.*
Saint Winifride, 18mo, 8*d.*
Soul united to Jesus, 32mo, 1*s.*
Spiritual combat, 32mo, 2*s.*
Stations of the Cross, with fine wood engravings, 6*d.*
Stations of the Passions, 32mo, 1*s.*

Think well on't, 18mo, 8*d*. – 32mo, 1*s*.
True piety, 18mo, 1s.6*d*. – fine, 2*s*. 6*d*.
Vespers, or the evening offering of the church, in Latin and English, according to the Roman breviary, 18mo, 4*s*.

BIBLIOGRAPHY

1 GENERAL

Birn, Raymond. Livre et societe after ten years: formation of a discipline. In *Studies on Voltaire and the eighteenth century*, cliv (1976), pp 287–312.

Burke, Peter. *Popular culture in early modern Europe*. London, 1978.

———. Popular culture: between history and ethnology. In *Ethnologia Europaea*, xiv (1984), pp 5–13.

Carpenter, Kenneth E. (ed.). *Books and society in history*. New York, 1983.

Davis, Natalie Z. *Society and culture in early modern France*. London, 1975.

Eisenstein, Elizabeth L. *The printing press as an instrument of change*. 2 vols. Cambridge, 1979.

Feather, John. Cross channel currents: historical bibliography and l'histoire du livre. In *Library*, 6th ser., ii (1980), pp 1–15.

Febvre, Lucien, and Martin, H.-J. *The coming of the book: the impact of printing, 1450–1800*. London, 1976.

Herrick, C. A. The early New Englanders: what did they read? In *Library*, 3rd ser., ix (1918), pp 1–17.

Hirsch, Rudolf. *The printed word: its impact and diffusion*. London, 1978.

Hunter, Michael. The impact of print. In *The Book Collector*, xxviii (1979), pp 335–52.

Joyce, William L., and Hall, David D. (ed.). *Printing and society in early America*. Worcester, 1983.

Kaplan, Stephen L. (ed.). *Understanding popular culture*. Berlin, 1984.

Leavis, Q. D. *Fiction and the reading public*. London, 1932.

Small, Christopher. *The printed word: an instrument of popularity*. Aberdeen, 1982.

Tanselle, G. T. From bibliography to histoire totale: the history of books as a field of study. In *Times Literary Supplement*, no. 4,079 (5 June 1981), pp 647–9.

Williams, Raymond. *Culture and society*. Harmondsworth, 1963.

2 PRINTING AND PUBLISHING

(a) *General works*

Aldis, H. G. Book production and distribution, 1625–1800. In *Cambridge history of English literature* (14 vols, Cambridge, 1922), xi, 311–42.

Clair, Colin. *A history of printing in Britain*. London, 1965.

Esdaile, Arundell. *Manual of bibliography*. London, 1967.

Feather, John. *The provincial book trade in eighteenth-century England*. Cambridge, 1985.

Glaister, Geoffrey A. *Glossary of the book*. London, 1960.

Lehmann-Haupt, Hellmut. *The book in America*. New York, 1952.

M'Murtie, Douglas C. *The book: the story of printing and bookbinding*. 3rd ed. London, 1962.

Mumby, F. A., and Norrie, Ian. *Publishing and bookselling . . . from the earliest times to . . . 1970*. 5th ed. London, 1974.

Plant, Marjorie. *The English book trade: an economic history of the making and sale of books*. 2nd ed. London, 1965.

Steinberg, S. H. *Five hundred years of printing*. 3rd ed. Harmondsworth, 1974.

Tebbel, John. *A history of book publishing in the United States*. 3 vols. New York, 1972–8.

(b) *Ireland*

Catalogue of the Bradshaw collection of Irish books in the University Library, Cambridge. 3 vols. Cambridge, 1916.

Cole, Richard Cargill. *Irish booksellers and English writers 1740–1800.* London, 1986.

O'Casaide, Seamus. *Typographical gazetteer of Ireland: or, the beginnings of printing in Irish towns.* Dublin, 1923.

Phillips, James W. A bibliographical enquiry into printing and bookselling in Dublin from 1670 to 1800. (Ph.D. thesis, University of Dublin, 1952.)

Wheeler, W. G. The spread of provincial printing in Ireland up to 1850. In *Irish Booklore,* iv (1978), pp 7–18.

(c) *Belfast*

Anderson, John. *Catalogue of early Belfast printed books, 1694 to 1830, with lists of early Belfast printers.* New ed. Belfast, 1890; Supplements, Belfast, 1894, 1902.

Benn, George. *A history of the town of Belfast.* Belfast, 1877.

Bigger, F. J. *The Magees of Belfast and Dublin, printers.* Belfast, 1916.

Dix, E. R. McC. The earliest Belfast printing. In *Irish Book Lover,* vi (1914–15), pp 157–8.

———. Early Belfast printing: the Bible printed by Patrick Neill, 1699. *Ulster Journal of Archaeology,* 2nd. ser., xii (1906), pp 44–5.

———. List of books and tracts printed in Belfast in the seventeenth century. In *Proceedings of the Royal Irish Academy,* sect. C, xxxiii (1916–17), pp 73–80.

Greeves, J. R. H. Two Irish printing families (Blow of Belfast and Grierson of Dublin). In *Proceedings and Reports of the Belfast Natural History and Philosophical Society,* 2nd ser., iv (1955), pp 38–44.

Kernohan, J. W. Blow's books and Bibles. In *Irish Book Lover,* vi (1914–15) pp 197–8.

Marshall, John J. Notes on old Belfast printers. In *Belfast Municipal Museum and Art Gallery Quarterly Notes,* lii (1937), pp 15, 18.

Moore, F. F. Belfast booksellers. In *Irish Book Lover,* vi (1914–15), pp 6–7.

(d) *Antrim*

Bigger, F. J. Printing in Ballyclare. In *Irish Book Lover,* vii (1915–16), pp 33–4.

Crone, J. S. Ulster bibliography: Antrim. In *Ulster Journal of Archaeology,* 2nd ser., xi (1905), pp 108–112, 163–7.

Dix, E. R. McC. Irish provincial printing (Lisburn). In *Irish Book Lover,* vii (1915–16), pp 90–91.

(e) *Armagh*

Crone, J. S. Ulster bibliography: Armagh. In *Ulster Journal of Archaeology,* 2nd ser., xiv (1908), pp 120–26.

Dix, E. R. McC. The first printing presses in Armagh and Newry. In *Ulster Journal of Archaeology,* 2nd ser., xvi (1910), p. 46.

———. *List of books and pamphlets printed at Armagh in the eighteenth century* 2nd ed. Dundrum, 1910.

———. Printing in Armagh, 1801–24. In *Irish Book Lover,* iv (1912–13), pp 93–4.

———. Printing in Armagh since 1825. In *Irish Book Lover,* xiv (1924), pp 7–10, 55–6.

———. Printing in Lurgan in the nineteenth century. In *Irish Book Lover,* xiii (1921–2), pp 54–6.

———. Printing in Portadown (1851–1900). In *Irish Book Lover,* vii (1915–16), pp 123–4, 164–5.

———. Ulster bibliography: Armagh. In *Ulster Journal of Archaeology,* 2nd ser., vi (1900), pp 245–6; vii (1901), pp 53–7.

McClelland, Aiken. Provincial printing: Tanderagee. In *Irish Book*, i (1962), pp 98–100.

(f) *Cavan*

Dix, E. R. McC. Early printing in Cavan. In *Breifne Antiquarian Society Journal*, i (1922), pp 279–86.

———. Printing in the town of Cavan. In *Irish Book Lover*, i (1909–10), pp 83–4.

———. Printing in Cavan, 1801–27. In *Irish Book Lover*, iv (1912–13), pp 165–7.

———. Printing in Cavan, 1828–1900. In *Irish Book Lover*, xi (1919–20), pp 6–7, 22–3, 40–41.

(g) *Donegal*

Dix, E. R. McC. Printing in Ballyshannon to 1900. In *Irish Book Lover*, xvii (1929), pp 101–2.

———. Printing in Letterkenny. In *Irish Book Lover*, xii (1920–21), p. 31.

(h) *Down*

Crone, J. S. Ulster bibliography: Co. Down. In *Ulster Journal of Archaeology*, 2nd ser., xii (1906), pp 35–9, 57–62; xiii (1907), pp 105–8.

Crossle, F. C. *Notes on the literary history of Newry*. Newry, 1897.

Crossle, Philip. The printers of Newry. In *Newry Reporter*, 30 Mar.–7 Oct. 1911.

Dix, E. R. McC. List of books, pamphlets, newspapers, etc. printed at Newry from 1764 to 1810. In *Ulster Journal of Archaeology*, 2nd ser., xiii (1907) pp 116–19, 170–73; xiv (1908), pp 95–6; xv (1909), pp 184–5.

———. Printing in Banbridge to 1900. In *Irish Book Lover*, xvii (1929), pp 7–8.

———. Printing in Newtownards in the nineteenth century. In *Irish Book Lover*, xii (1920–21), pp 101–2.

———. Ulster bibliography: Downpatrick, Dungannon and Hillsborough. In *Ulster Journal of Archaeology*, 2nd ser., vii (1901), pp 172–4; ix (1903), pp 42–3.

———. Ulster bibliography: Newry printing. In *Ulster Journal of Archaeology*, 2nd ser., ix (1903), pp 69–71.

Latimer, W. T. Newry printing. In *Ulster Journal of Archaeology*, 2nd ser., vii (1901), pp 175–6.

Maffett, R. S. Printing in Newry. In *Irish Book Lover*, vi (1914–15), pp 17–18.

(i) *Fermanagh*

Dix, E. R. McC. Printing in Enniskillen 1798–1825. In *Irish Book Lover*, ii (1910–11), pp 185–6; v (1913–14), p. 147.

———. Printing in Enniskillen (1826–1900). In *Irish Book Lover*, vii (1915–16). pp 3–5, 32, 47, 92.

(j) *Londonderry*

Crone, J. S. Ulster bibliography: Derry. In *Ulster Journal of Archaeology*. 2nd ser., x (1904), pp 151–6; xi (1905), pp 27–32.

Dix, E. R. McC. *List of books, pamphlets, newspapers etc. printed in Londonderry prior to 1901*. Dundalk, 1911.

———. Printing in Limavady. In *Irish Book Lover*, xii (1920–21), pp 78–9.

———. Ulster bibliography: Coleraine. In *Ulster Journal of Archaeology*, 2nd ser. (1907), pp 22–3.

———. Ulster bibliography: Derry printing. In *Ulster Journal of Archaeology*, 2nd ser., vii (1901), pp 132–6, 174; viii (1902), p. 24; ix (1903), p. 71.

(k) *Monaghan*

Dix, E. R. McC. *List of books, pamphlets and newspapers printed in Monaghan in the eighteenth century.* 2nd ed. Dundalk, 1911.
————. Printing in Monaghan, 1801–25. In *Irish Book Lover,* iv (1912–13). pp 200–02; v (1913–14), pp 26–7.
————. Printing in Monaghan, 1825–30. In *Irish Book Lover,* x (1918–19), pp 34–5, 55–6.

(l) *Tyrone*

Campbell, A. A. *Notes on the literary history of Strabane.* Omagh, 1902.
————. Omagh printing. In *Irish Book Lover,* vii (1915–16), p. 7.
Crone, J. S. Ulster bibliography: Tyrone. In *Ulster Journal of Archaeology,* 2nd ser., xv (1909) pp 95–102.
Dix, E. R. McC. *List of books and pamphlets printed in Strabane in the eighteenth century.* 2nd ed. Dundrum, 1908.
————. Printing in Dungannon 1801–27. In *Irish Book Lover,* iv (1912–13), pp 188–9.
————. Printing in Dungannon 1827–1900. In *Irish Book Lover,* viii (1916–17), pp 75–6.
————. Printing in Strabane 1801–1825. In *Irish Book Lover,* iv (1912–13), pp 114–116, 134–5.
————. Printing in Strabane, 1825–1900. In *Irish Book Lover,* vii (1915–16), pp 68–9, 91; ix (1917–18), p. 60.
Marshall, J. J. *History of Dungannon . . . and bibliography of Dungannon printing.* Dungannon, 1929.

3 NEWSPAPERS, ALMANACS ETC.

Adams, J. R. R. *Northern Ireland newspapers: checklist with locations.* Belfast, 1979.
————. *Northern Ireland newspapers on microfilm: checklist with locations.* Belfast, 1983.
————. The use of newspapers as an historical source. In *Ulster Local Studies,* vii (1983), pp 10–14.
Bowen, B. P. Old Moore's almanack. In *Dublin Historical Record,* iii (1940–41), pp 26–37.
Boyce, George, Curran, James and Wingate, Pauline (eds). *Newspaper history from the seventeenth century to the present day.* London, 1978.
Campbell, A. A. *Belfast newspapers past and present.* Belfast, 1921.
————. Early Strabane newspapers and magazines. In *Ulster Journal of Archaeology,* 2nd ser., vii (1901), pp 176–7.
Evans, Edward. *Historical and bibliographical account of almanacs . . . in Ireland.* Dublin, 1897.
Inglis, Brian. *The freedom of the press in Ireland, 1784–1841.* London, 1954.
McClelland, Aiken. The Ulster press in the eighteenth and nineteenth centuries. In *Ulster Folklife,* xx. (1974), pp 89–99.
————. An unknown Fermanagh newspaper (*Newtownbutler Herald*). In *Irish Booklore,* ii (1972), p. 162.
Madden, R. R. *History of Irish periodical literature.* London, 1867.
Munter, R. L. *The history of the Irish newspaper, 1685–1760.* Cambridge, 1967.
O'Neill, Charles Patrick. *Newspaper stamps of Ireland.* Enniskillen, 1978.
Oram, Hugh. *The newspaper book: a history of newspapers in Ireland, 1649–1983.* Dublin, 1983.
Shearman, Hugh. *News Letter 250 years 1737–1987.* Belfast, 1987.

4 EDUCATION

Akenson, Donald H. *The Irish education experiment: the national system of education in the nineteenth century.* London, 1970.

Atkinson, Norman. *Irish education: a history of educational institutions.* Dublin, 1969.

Barkley, J. M. *The Sabbath School Society for Ireland, 1862–1962.* Belfast, 1961.

Corcoran, Timothy. *Education systems in Ireland from the close of the middle ages: selected texts.* Dublin, 1928.

Dobbs, A. E. *Education and social movements, 1700–1850.* London, 1919.

Dowling, Patrick John. *The hedge schools of Ireland.* Dublin, 1935.

———. *A history of Irish education: a study in conflicting loyalties.* Cork, 1971.

First report of the Commissioners on Education in Ireland. H.C. 1825 (400), xii.

Goldstrom, J. M. *The social content of education, 1808–1870: a study of the working class school reader in England and Ireland.* Shannon, 1972.

Goody, Jack (ed.). *Literacy in traditional societies.* Cambridge, 1968.

Hudson, J. W. *The history of adult education.* London, 1851.

Incorporated Society in Dublin, for Promoting English Protestant Schools in Ireland. *Abstract of the proceedings, from . . . 1733 to . . . 1737.* Dublin, 1737.

Leslie, T. E. C. *An enquiry into the progress and present condition of mechanic's institutes.* Dublin, 1852.

McClelland, Aiken. The early history of Brown Street Primary School. In *Ulster Folklife,* xvii (1971), pp 52–60.

McIvor, John. *Popular education in the Irish Presbyterian Church.* Dublin, 1969.

Marshall, J. J. David Manson, schoolmaster in Belfast. In *Ulster Journal of Archaeology,* 2nd ser., xiv (1908), pp 59–72.

Moore, H. Kingsmill. *An unwritten chapter in the history of Irish education: being the history of the Society for the Education of the Poor of Ireland, generally known as the Kildare Place Society, 1811–1831.* London, 1904.

Morton, R. G. Mechanics' institutes and the attempted diffusion of useful knowledge in Ireland. In *Irish Booklore,* ii (1972), pp 59–74.

Neuburg, V. E. *Popular education in eighteenth-century England.* London, 1971.

Smith, W. S. *Doagh and the 'first' Sunday school in Ireland.* Belfast, 1890.

Sunday School Society for Ireland. *Hints for conducting Sunday schools.* 7th ed. Dublin, 1836.

———. *Monthly extracts,* xxvi (1822) – xlvi (1823).

Tynan, Michael. *Catholic instruction in Ireland 1720–1950.* Dublin, 1985.

5 LIBRARIES

Adams, J. R. R. Books and libraries in Bangor and Holywood. In *Linen Hall Review,* ii, no. 1 (spring 1985), pp 14–15.

———. A history of libraries in County Down from the earliest period to the year 1900. (F.L.A. thesis, Library Association, 1977.)

———. Library provision for children in County Down prior to 1850. In *Irish Booklore,* iv (1978), pp 19–23.

———. The old circulating libraries of Newry. In *Linen Hall Review,* i, no. 2 (summer 1984), pp 11–12.

———. Reading societies in Ulster. In *Ulster Folklife,* xxvi (1980), pp 55–64.

Adams, W. G. S. *A report on library provision . . . to the Carnegie United Kingdom Trust.* Edinburgh, 1915.

Anderson, John. *History of the Belfast Library and Society for Promoting Knowledge, commonly known as the Linen Hall Library.* Belfast, 1888.

Barnes, M. Repeal reading rooms. In *An Leabharlann,* xxiii (1965), pp 53–7.

Bigger, F. J. Rural libraries in Antrim. In *Irish Book Lover,* xiii (1921–2), pp 47–52.

Casteleyn, Mary. *A history of literacy and libraries in Ireland.* Aldershot, 1984.

Catalogue of the library of the Unitarian Presbyterian Congregation, Needham Place, Newry. Newry, 1856.

Catalogue of the Newtownlimavady Library. Belfast, 1815.
Cole, R. C. Community lending libraries in eighteenth-century Ireland. In *Library Quarterly*, xciv (1974), pp 231–47.
Downpatrick Literary Society. Catalogue with the laws. Downpatrick, 1801.
First annual report of the Committee of the Free Public Library, Belfast. Belfast, 1889.
Greenwood, Thomas. *British library year book, 1900–1901.* London, 1900.
———. *Public libraries: a history of the movement.* 4th ed. London, 1894.
Rules and catalogue of the Gilnahirk Religious Reading Society. Belfast [*c.* 1833].
Rules of the Belfast Society for Promoting Knowledge, with a catalogue. Belfast, 1808.
Rules of the Comber Society for Acquiring Knowledge. Belfast, 1828.
Shillito, Charles. *The country book-club: a poem.* Dublin, 1790.
Wheeler, W. G. Libraries in Ireland before 1855: a bibliographical essay (thesis, submitted in part requirement for the University of London Diploma in Librarianship, 1957).

6 POPULAR LITERATURE

(a) *Chapbooks etc.*

Ashton, John. *Chapbooks of the eighteenth century.* London, 1882.
Collison, Robert. *The story of street literature.* London, 1973.
Cunningham, R. H. *Amusing prose chapbooks, chiefly of the last century.* Hamilton, 1889.
Dix, E. R. McC. Irish chap books, song books and ballads. In *Irish Book Lover,* ii (1910–11), pp 33–5.
Fraser, John. *The humorous chap books of Scotland.* 2 vols. New York, 1873–4.
Gailey, Alan. Grinding old people young. In *Ulster Folklife,* xvii (1971), pp 95–7.
Harvey, William. *Scottish chapbook literature.* Paisley, 1903.
Hindley, Charles. *Curiosities of street literature.* Facsimile ed. 2 vols. London, 1966.
———. *The old book collector's miscellany.* 3 vols. London, 1871–3.
John Cheap the chapman's library: the Scottish chap literature of the last century classified. 3 vols. Glasgow, 1877–8.
Lane, W. C. (ed.). *Catalogue of English and American chapbooks and broadside ballads in Harvard College Library.* Cambridge, Mass., 1905.
McClelland, Aiken. Irish Chapbooks. In *Ulster Folk & Transport Museum Yearbook, 1971–2,* pp 24–5.
Marshall, J. J. Irish chap books. In *Irish Book Lover,* i (1910), pp 157–9.
Neuburg, Victor E. *Chapbooks: a guide to reference material on English, Scottish and American chapbook literature of the eighteenth and nineteenth centuries.* 2nd ed. London, 1972.
———. *Companion to popular literature.* London, 1982.
———. *The penny histories.* London, 1968.
———. *Popular literature: a history and guide.* Harmondsworth, 1977.
Shephard, Leslie. *The history of street literature.* Newton Abbot, 1973.
Spufford, Margaret. *The great reclothing of rural England: petty chapmen and their wares in the seventeenth century.* London, 1984.
———. *Small books and pleasant histories.* London, 1981.
Thompson, Alistair R. Chapbook printers. In *The Bibliothek,* vi (1971), pp 76–83.
Thompson, Roger. *Samuel Pepys' 'Penny merriments'.* London, 1976.
Weiss, Harry B. *A book about chapbooks.* Hatboro, 1969.

(b) *Material originating before the eighteenth century*

Ashton, John. *Romances of chivalry.* London, 1887.
Baker, Ernest A. *The history of the English novel: the age of romance, from the beginnings to the renaissance.* London, 1924.

Bibliography

Beall, Otho T. Aristotle's Master Piece in America: a landmark in the folklore of medicine. In *William & Mary Quarterly*, 3rd ser., xx (1963), pp 207–22.

Bigger, F. J. Alexander Peden the 'prophet'. In *Ulster Journal of Archaeology*, 2nd ser., ix (1903), pp 116–27.

Brunner, Karl. *The seven sages of Rome.* London, 1933.

Campbell, Killis. *The seven sages of Rome.* Boston, 1907.

Clouston, W. A. *Popular tales and fictions: their migrations and transformations.* Edinburgh, 1887.

Dickson, Arthur (ed.). *Valentine and Orson.* London, 1937.

Dobson, R. B., and Taylor, J. *Rymes of Robyn Hood: an introduction to the English outlaw.* London, 1976.

Ellis, George. *Specimens of early English metrical romances.* London, 1848.

Elmen, Paul. Richard Allestree and the *Whole duty of man.* In *Library*, 5th ser., vi (1951), pp 19–27.

Esdaile, Arundell. *A list of English tales and prose romances printed before 1740.* London, 1912.

Ferguson, John. Books of secrets. In *Transactions of the Bibliographical Society*, xii (1914), pp 145–76.

Halliwell, J. O. *Descriptive notices of popular English histories.* London, 1848.

Hazlitt, W. C. *Studies in jocular literature.* London, 1890.

Henderson, T. F. *Scottish vernacular literature: a succinct history.* Edinburgh, 1910.

Loomis, Laura H. *Medieval romance in England.* New York, 1960.

Morley, Henry. *Early prose romances.* London, 1889.

Murray, J. A. H. (ed.). *The romance and prophecies of Thomas of Erceldoune.* London, 1875.

Roscoe, S. Early English, Scottish and Irish thumb bibles. In *The Book Collector*, xxii (1973), pp 189–207.

Scanlon, Paul A. A checklist of prose romances in English 1474–1603. In *Library*, 5th ser., xxxiii (1978), pp 143–52.

Schlauch, Margaret. *Antecedents of the English novel, 1400–1600.* London, 1963.

Swan, Charles (trans.). *Gesta Romanorum.* London, 1924.

Van Duzee, Mabel. *A medieval romance of friendship: Eger and Grime.* New York, 1963.

Wasserman, Earl R. *Elizabethan poetry in the eighteenth century.* Urbana, 1947. Includes prose.

Wright, Louis B. *Middle-class culture in Elizabethan England.* Chapel Hill, 1935.

(c) *Material relating to the eighteenth and nineteenth centuries*

Altick, Richard, D. *The English common reader: a social history of the mass reading public, 1800–1900.* Chicago, 1957.

Bigger, F. J. Catholic books printed in Belfast. In *Irish Book Lover*, vi (1914–15), pp 207–8.

Craig, David. *Scottish literature and the Scottish people, 1680–1830.* London, 1961.

Dalziel, Margaret. *Popular fiction 100 years ago.* London, 1957.

Donnelly, J. S. Propagating the cause of the United Irishmen. In *Studies*, lxix (1980), pp 15–23.

Feeney, Mary I. Print for the people: the growth in popular writings and reading facilites in Ireland, 1820–1850. (M.Litt. thesis, University of Dublin, 1982.)

Fergus, Jan. Eighteenth century readers in provincial England: the customers of Samuel Clay's circulating library and bookshop in Warwick, 1770–72. *Papers of the Bibliographical Society of America*, lxxviii (1984), pp 155–218.

James, Louis. *Fiction for the working masn, 1830–1850.* London, 1963.

———. *Print and the people, 1819–51.* London, 1976.

McBurney, W. H. *A check list of English prose fiction, 1700-1739.* Cambridge, Mass., 1860.
———. *Four before Richardson.* Lincoln, Neb., 1978.
Marshall, J. J. *Irish tories, raparees and robbers.* Dungannon, 1927.
Montgomery, H. R. *Essay towards investigating the causes that have retarded the progress of literature in Ireland.* Belfast, 1840.
Ó Duilearga, Séamus. The Royal Hibernian Tales. In *Béaloideas*, x (1940), pp 148-203.
O'Hanlon, Terence. *The highwayman in Irish history.* Dublin, 1932.
Richetti, John J. *Popular fiction before Richardson.* Oxford, 1969.
Rivers, Isabel (ed.). *Books and their readers in eighteenth-century England.* Leicester, 1982.
Rogers, Pat. *Literature and popular culture in eighteenth-century England.* Brighton, 1985.
Sadleir, Michael. *XIX century fiction: a bibliographical record.* 2 vols. Cambridge, 1951.
Tompkins, J. M. S. *The popular novel in England, 1770-1800.* London, 1932.
Walbank, Alan. Railway reading. In *The Book Collector*, ix (1960), pp 285-91.
Wall, Thomas. *The sign of Dr Hay's Head: being some account of the hazards and fortunes of catholic printers and publishers in Dublin from penal times to the present day.* Dublin, 1959.
Webb, R. K. *The British working-class reader, 1790-1846.* London, 1955.
Wittig, Kurt. *The Scottish tradition in literature.* Westport, Conn., 1972.

(d) *Material relating to individual publishers of popular material*

Chambers, William. *A memoir of William Chambers.* 2nd ed. Edinburgh, 1872.
Clowes, Alice A. *Charles Knight: a sketch.* London, 1892.
Gettmann, R. A. *A Victorian publisher: a study of the Bentley papers.* Cambridge, 1960.
Knight, Charles. *Passages of a working life.* 3 vols. London, 1864-5.
McClelland, Aiken. The Parlour Library. In *Ulster Folk & Transport Museum Yearbook 1968-9*, pp 16-17.
Mumby, F. A. *The house of Routledge, 1834-1934.* London, 1934.
Nowell-Smith, Simon. *The house of Cassell, 1848-1958.* London, 1958.
The Parlour Library. In *Irish Book Lover*, ii (1911), pp 133-5.
Sadleir, Michael. *Bentley's Standard Novel Series.* New York, 1932.
Smiles, Samuel. *A publisher and his friends: memoir and correspondence of John Murray.* 2 vols. London, 1891.
Smith, Harold. *The Society for the Diffusion of Useful Knowledge, 1826-1846.* Halifax, Nova Scotia, 1974.
Sutherland, John. Henry Colburn, publisher. In *Publishing History*, xix (1986), pp 59-84.

(e) *Religious tracts*

Allen, W. O. B. and McClure, Edmund. *Two hundred years: the history of the Society for Promoting Christian Knowledge, 1698-1898.* London, 1898.
Clarke, William K. L. *A history of the S.P.C.K.* London, 1959.
Grimshawe, T. S. *A memoir of the Reverend Legh Richmond.* 10th ed. London, 1840.
Hopkins, Mary Alden. *Hannah More and her friends.* New York, 1947.
Jones, Mary Gwladys. *Hannah More.* Cambridge, 1952.
Jones, William. *The jubilee memorial of the Religious Tract Society.* London, 1850.
Magee, William. *A sermon preached before the Association for Discountenancing Vice.* Dublin, 1796.
Spinney, G. H. Cheap Repository Tracts: Hazard and Marshall editions. In *Library*, 4th ser., xx (1940), pp 295-340.
The story of the Religious Tract Society. London, 1898.
Weiss, Harry B. The deathless dairyman's daughter. In *American Collector*, v (1928), pp 250-52.

(f) *Children's literature*

Avery, Gillian. *Nineteenth century children: heroes and heroines in English children's stories, 1780–1900.* London, 1965.

Cutt, Margaret N. *Mrs Sherwood and her books for children.* London, 1974.

Darton, F. J. Harvey. *Children's books in England: five centuries of social life.* Cambridge, 1970.

Grey, J. E. The Lilliputian Magazine: a pioneering periodical. In *Journal of Librarianship,* ii (1970), pp 107–115.

Muir, Percy. *English children's books, 1600 to 1900.* London, 1954.

Roscoe, Sydney. *John Newbery and his successors, 1740–1814: a bibliography.* Wormley, 1973.

Turner, E. S. *Boys will be boys.* 3rd ed. Harmondsworth, 1976.

(g) *Folk drama*

Gailey, Alan. The Christmas rhime. In *Ulster Folklife,* xxi (1975), pp 75–84.

———. *Irish folk drama.* Cork, 1969.

———. A missing Belfast chapbook. In *Irish Booklore,* ii (1972), pp 54–8.

Helm, Alex. *The chapbook mummer's plays.* Ibstock, 1969.

Smith, Georgina. Chapbooks and traditional plays: communication and performance. In *Folklore,* xcii (1981), pp 208–18.

(h) *Songs and ballads*

Ashton, John. *Modern street ballads.* London, 1888.

The ballad minstrelsy of Scotland, romantic and historical. London, 1871.

Harding, Walter N. H. British song books and kindred subjects. In *The Book Collector,* xi (1962), pp 448–59.

Henderson, W. (ed.). *Victorian street ballads.* London, 1937.

Lyle, E. B. Song chapbooks with Irish imprints in the Lauriston Castle Collection, National Library of Scotland. In *Irish Folk Music Studies,* ii (1974–5), pp 15–30.

McCance, Stoupe. Some old Ulster song books. In *Irish Book Lover,* vii (1915–16), pp 108–9.

MacLochlainn, Alf. Belfast printed ballad sheets. In *Irish Booklore,* i (1971), pp 21–3.

Murphy, Maura. The ballad singer, and the role of the seditious ballad in nineteenth-century Ireland: Dublin Castle's view. In *Ulster Folklife,* xxv (1979), 79–102.

O Dúghaill, Gréagóir. Ballads and the law 1830–1832. In *Ulster Folklife,* xix (1973), pp 38–40.

Shields, Hugh. Some 'Songs and ballads in use in the province of Ulster . . . 1845'. In *Ulster Folklife,* xvii (1971), pp 3–24; xviii (1972), pp 34–65.

Shepard, Leslie. *John Pitts: ballad printer of Seven Dials, London, 1765–1844.* London, 1969.

———. *The broadside ballad: a study in origins and meanings.* Hatboro, 1978.

Williams, W. H. A. The broadside ballad and vernacular culture. In *Irish Folk Music Studies,* iii (1976–81), pp 45–60.

Zimmerman, Georges-Denis. *Irish political street ballads and rebel songs, 1780—1900.* Geneva, 1966.

———. What is an Irish ballad? In *Irish Folk Music Studies,* iii (1976–81), pp 5–17.

7 SOCIAL BACKGROUND

This section is necessarily very selective.

Akenson, D. H. *Between two revolutions: Islandmagee, County Antrim, 1798–1920.* Port Credit, Ontario, 1979.

———, and Crawford, W. H. *James Orr, bard of Ballycarry.* Belfast, 1977.

Beckett, J. C. *The making of modern Ireland 1603–1923*. London, 1969.

Bowen, Desmond. *The protestant crusade in Ireland, 1800–70*. Dublin, 1978.

Brooke, Peter (ed.). *Problems of a growing city: Belfast 1780–1870*. Belfast, 1973.

Burdy, Samuel. *Life of Philip Skelton*. Oxford, 1914.

Carleton, William. *The life of William Carleton*. 2 vols. London, 1896.

———. *Traits and stories of the Irish peasantry*. 4th ed. 5 vols. Dublin, 1836.

Chart, D. A. (ed.). *The Drennan letters*. Belfast, 1931.

Clarkson, L. A. and Crawford, E. M. *Ways to wealth: the Cust family of eighteenth-century Armagh*. Belfast, 1985.

Connolly, S. J. *Priests and people in pre-famine Ireland 1780–1845*. Dublin, 1982.

Crawford, W. H., and Trainor, Brian (ed.). *Aspects of Irish social history 1750–1800*. Belfast, 1969.

Cunningham, Patrick. *The life of Patrick Cunningham*. Belfast, 1806.

Dickson, R. J. *Ulster emigration to colonial America, 1718–1775*. Belfast, 1966.

Doyle, Lynn. *An Ulster childhood*. Dublin, 1921.

Elliott, Samuel. *The world as I found it*. Belfast, 1887.

Evans, E. E. *Irish folk ways*. London, 1957.

———. *Mourne country: landscape and life in south Down*. Dundalk, 1951.

Evidence taken before her majesty's commissioners of inquiry into the state of the law and practice in respect to the occupation of land in Ireland [Devon commission] H.C. 1845, xix–xxii.

Gaffikin, Thomas. *Belfast fifty years ago, now (1894) seventy years ago*. 3rd ed. Belfast, 1894.

[Gallagher, Patrick.] *My story, by Paddy the Cope*. London, 1939.

Gamble, John. *Sketches of history, politics and manners in Dublin and the north of Ireland 1810*. London, 1826.

———. *A view of society and manners in the north of Ireland in the summer and autumn of 1812*. London, 1813.

Goldstrom, J. M. and Clarkson, L. A. (ed.). *Irish population, economy and society: essays in honour of the late K. H. Connell*. Oxford, 1981.

Gwynn, Stephen. *Highways and byways in Donegal and Antrim*. London, 1899.

Hall, Mr & Mrs S. C. *Ireland: its scenery, character etc.* 3 vols. London, 1841.

Hewitt, John (ed.). *Rhyming weavers and other country poets of Antrim and Down*. Belfast, 1974.

Latimer, W. T. *History of the Irish presbyterians*. Belfast, 1893.

Lepper, J. H., Crossle, P., and Parkinson, R. E. *History of the Grand Lodge of Free and Accepted Masons of Ireland*. 2 vols. Dublin, 1925–57.

Life of William Scott, alias Tantra Barbus. Belfast, 1833.

M'Alester, C. *A sketch of the life and literary labours of the late Robert Sullivan*. Belfast, 1870.

McCarron, Edward. *Life in Donegal 1850–1900*. Dublin, 1981.

McDowell, Florence M. *Other days around me*. Dublin, 1966.

MacManus, Seamus. *The rocky road to Dublin*. New York, 1938.

M'Skimin, Samuel. *Annals of Ulster*. Belfast, 1849.

Martin, R. M. *Ireland before and after the union with Great Britain*. 2nd ed. 2 vols. London, 1848.

Mason, William Shaw (ed.). *A statistical account: or, parochial survey of Ireland*. 3 vols. Dublin, 1814–19.

Moody, T. W., and Beckett, J. C. (ed.). *Ulster since 1800, second series: a social survey*. London, 1957.

O' Hanlon, W. M. *Walks among the poor of Belfast*. Belfast, 1853.

O'Neill, Kevin. *Family and farm in pre-famine Ireland: the parish of Killashandra*. Madison, Wis., 1984.

Porter, Hugh. *Poetical attempts*. Belfast, 1813.

Records of the General Synod of Ulster, 1691–1820. 3 vols. Belfast, 1890–98.

Reid, J. S. *History of the presbyterian church in Ireland*. 3 vols. Belfast, 1834–53.

Stevenson, John. *Two centuries of life in Down*. Belfast, 1920.
Thackeray, W. M. *The Irish sketch book*. 2 vols. London, 1843. Many subsequent editions.
Tynan, Hugh. *Poems*. Belfast, 1803.
Walker, Brian M. *Sentry Hill: an Ulster farm and family*. Belfast, 1981.
Walsh, John E. *Sketches of Ireland sixty years ago*. Dublin, 1847.
Wright, William. *The Brontes in Ireland*. 3rd ed. London, 1894.
Young, Arthur. *A tour in Ireland*. 2nd ed. 2 vols. London, 1780.
Young, R. M. (ed.). *Town book of the corporation of Belfast, 1613–1816*. Belfast, 1892.

INDEX

Note: For reasons of space, authors and titles of works mentioned in the text are not included in the index.

Index